The Trouble with Tea

D1712971

STUDIES IN EARLY
AMERICAN ECONOMY AND SOCIETY
FROM THE LIBRARY COMPANY
OF PHILADELPHIA

Cathy Matson, *Series Editor*

THE TROUBLE WITH TEA

The Politics of Consumption in the Eighteenth-Century Global Economy

JANE T. MERRITT

OLD DOMINION UNIVERSITY
Norfolk, Virginia

Johns Hopkins University Press
Baltimore

Johns Hopkins University Press
2715 North Charles Street
Baltimore, Maryland 21218-4363
www.press.jhu.edu

Library of Congress Cataloging-in-Publication Data

Names: Merritt, Jane T., author.
Title: The trouble with tea : the politics of consumption in the
eighteenth-century global economy / Jane T. Merritt.
Description: Baltimore : Johns Hopkins University Press, 2017. | Series:
Studies in early American economy and society from the Library Company of
Philadelphia | Includes bibliographical references and index.
Identifiers: LCCN 2016012792| ISBN 9781421421520 (hardcover : alk. paper) |
ISBN 9781421421537 (pbk. : alk. paper) | ISBN 9781421421544 (electronic) |
ISBN 1421421526 (hardcover : alk. paper) | ISBN 1421421534 (pbk. : alk.
paper) | ISBN 1421421542 (electronic)
Subjects: LCSH: Tea trade—Political aspects—History—18th century | Great
Britain—Commerce—History. | United States—Commerce—History. | United
States—Foreign economic relations. | Great Britain—Foreign economic
relations. | United States—Economic conditions—To 1865.
Classification: LCC HD9198.A2 M47 2017 | DDC 339.4/8663940941—dc23
LC record available at https://lccn.loc.gov/2016012792

A catalog record for this book is available from the British Library.

*Special discounts are available for bulk purchases of this book. For more
information, please contact Special Sales at 410-516-6936 or
specialsales@press.jhu.edu.*

Johns Hopkins University Press uses environmentally friendly book
materials, including recycled text paper that is composed of at least
30 percent post-consumer waste, whenever possible.

CONTENTS

This addition to the series Studies in Early American Economy and Society, a collaborative effort between Johns Hopkins University Press and the Library Company of Philadelphia's Program in Early American Economy and Society (PEAES), takes readers on a journey of new discoveries about the political economy of one of the world's most widely used commodities: tea. Jane Merritt's compelling study places tea not only in the homes of myriad North Americans but also traces tea's role at the center of global events encompassing Atlantic revolutions and imperial contests during the eighteenth century's closing years. As her story unfolds, readers see through the lens of a commodity—its growth, processing, trade, and consumption—how continents of early modern peoples were interconnected by trade for this highly desirable item.

Many readers are undoubtedly accustomed to placing tea within the narrative of the North American Revolution's approaching declaration of independence from British taxation and political might. In addition to the dramatic tea parties of 1773, waves of colonial nonimportation boycotts of tea and other articles of "necessity" in the colonial economy sparked deepening tests that challenged the rights of Britain to control the North American colonial economies. The cries of "no taxation without representation" seemed to be a firm, definitive renunciation of British efforts to undermine hard-won economic opportunities and political rights. Merritt agrees with many scholars of nonimportation movements that tea was one of the powerful instruments of symbolic and political economic protest in the final colonial years. But she takes our understanding much further back in time, and more deeply into global commercial relationships, than interpretations about the immediate imperial crisis permit. She insists on a wider narrative that includes India and Asia as equally important centers of the British Empire's trade, as well as transnational economic imperialism and local resistance. And for decades before the 1760s, she argues, tea was key to the expansion of imperial trade networks and the introduction of new goods and ideas that few colonists or imperial policy makers understood in those years.

The ubiquity of tea consumption by the 1760s had a long and troubled rise. Widespread doubts about spending on the commodity and consuming it across class lines only slowly transformed into acceptance, then eagerness. Tea became one of many new commodities that filled the coffers of trading merchants, seemed to cultivate refined taste among consumers, and called forth the need to use new kinds of bookkeeping, credit instruments, navigation equipment, and shipping strategies. The English East India Company became a behemoth, largely in the context of expanding tea trading. And, as Merritt argues, tea was one of the important exotic goods that "stirred the English commercial imagination."

But although tea spurred more extensive commerce in relatively unknown parts of the world, which in turn deepened Britain's (including its colonies) claims of dominion in far-flung places, tea also inflamed tensions between traders, middlemen, and policy makers in different cultures. It was no minor task to navigate the shoals of global markets, where culture and language differences provided constant obstacles to open trading. Pushing our perspective beyond the popular Atlantic world paradigm, Merritt demonstrates that the political economy of settled British imperial cities and frontiers—including the colonies of the Western Hemisphere—was in fact deeply dependent on the connections, credit, and silver economies within the orbit of India and Asia. The demand for tea in the Western Hemisphere and Europe, however, was not evenly and happily welcomed by China's premier tea traders. Regulations about who could enter China's trading arenas and restrictions about how, and whether, European merchants could trade at Canton sustained a level of commercial anxiety that was only intermittently relieved with Chinese people's own demands for externally produced goods and the ever-necessary silver specie Europeans brought in their ships.

In addition, Merritt's study moves readers beyond a familiar story in which consumers in Europe and North America seemed to have a "natural" propensity for drinking tea, that somehow the growing market for that commodity did not need much of a jump start before an unstoppable desire for tea unfolded. She shows that like other imperially integrated commodities markets, tea's success was never assured. It always had a complex history of commercial risks, technological changes, adaptations of labor regimes and slave trading, merchant network building, and much more. Any of the links from agricultural cultivation to teatime consumption could snap, and for decades many of them did. It was never a foregone conclusion that tea, among other new goods entering daily lives by the mid-eighteenth century, would propel forward the consumer revolution that increased the circulation of goods, give myriad people new choices, and become recognizable to everyone before the American Revolution.

CATHY MATSON
Professor of History, University of Delaware
Director, Program in Early American Economy and Society,
Library Company of Philadelphia

ACKNOWLEDGMENTS

Many individuals and organizations made this book possible. The Program in Early American Economy and Society (PEAES) at the Library Company of Philadelphia (LCP), was willing to take a chance on a vague idea with a clever title back in 2002. Many thanks to PEAES director Cathy Matson and the Historical Society of Pennsylvania for providing a home during the initial year of research. LCP staff, especially Connie King and Jim Green, gave guidance, tracked down obscure sources, and referred me to a good chiropractor. Cathy Matson (who should be thanked twice) and fellow fellows at both PEAES and the McNeil Center for Early American Studies provided invaluable comments and camaraderie. Thanks to Michelle Craig McDonald, Stephen Mihm, Carl Robert Keyes, Kathleen Duval, and all who attended the joint PEAES/MCEAS seminar in Spring 2003. I will never forget Michelle's cookies, cakes, and Cassatt House hospitality. Sean X. Goudie's invitation to participate in the Circum-Atlantic Studies Group at Vanderbilt University in April 2003, with helpful feedback from participants Jane Landers and Daniel Usner, paved the way for publication of an initial article.

Only now can I appreciate how appropriate it was to receive what may have been the last Boston Marine Society Fellowship from the Massachusetts Historical Society in 2005–2006. As the "oldest association of sea captains in the world," the Boston Marine Society has been around since 1754, and many of its early members had connections to the post-Revolution China trade. Thanks to Conrad E. Wright, Kate Viens, and the helpful staff at MHS for making my time in Boston productive. Similarly, in 2008–2009 the Kate B. and Hall J. Peterson Fellowship administered by Paul J. Erickson, Director of Academic Programs at the American Antiquarian Society, helped uncover sources from the revolutionary period.

More recently, colleagues and participants at the PEAES conference in

October 2014, Economic History's Many Muses, took me back to larger questions of consumer culture and economies in meaningful ways. Thanks to Seth Rockman, Ellen Hartigan-O'Connor, Danielle Skeehan, Dael Norwood, and others who are named above. The graphics department at Old Dominion University provided assistance for the maps, and colleagues in the Department of History cheered me on and cheered me up. Thanks to our Associates Reading Group, including Maura Hametz, Erin Jordan, Michael Carhart, Austin Jersild, Kathy Pearson, Martha Daas, and Heidi Schlipphacke.

Finally, a heartfelt shout out to Dr. Claire Carman, Dr. Michael Danso, Dr. Mark Shaves, and Team Tina for attentive care; they made the final revisions possible, if not always painless. And to Bob, who made me smile, laugh, and live through it all.

Consumer Revolutions

At first glance, the 1778 image *The Tea-Tax Tempest, or the Anglo-American Revolution*, attributed to Carl Guttenberg of Nuremberg, appears to be a straightforward depiction of the origins of the American Revolution. The focal point, a teapot that has reached its boiling point, figuratively depicts the colonial reaction to unwanted taxes on tea. In the midst of the roiling steam, the British army, partially yoked on the left, flees a group of united and organized colonials who, with serpant-emblazoned flag raised, demand their economic and political freedoms. Projecting this scene on the wall is Father Time with four female figures—metaphoric personifications of America, Africa, Europe, and Asia—who gaze in amazement (perhaps approval, perhaps reproach), at the unfolding revolution, which is quite literally set off by a tempest in a teapot.

On further examination, however, the image yields much more than a simple tale of American resistance to British taxation. Instead it places tea at the center of a global saga of revolution and empire during the late eighteenth century. It depicts the world's continents interconnected by networks of trade; "America," a feathered native with bow in hand, sits to the left on bales of goods, perhaps homegrown tobacco to be exchanged for foreign commodities, while Father Time leans haphazardly on a globe. The image also underscores the rising importance of colonial peoples to imperial economies; although a native American woman on the right leads the colonial opposition to the British, turbaned Sepoy soldiers, like those hired by and loyal to the English East India Company in South Asia, have joined the Americans to rise up against colonial masters. By the mid-eighteenth century, India and Asia had become important centers of trade for European nations, but they were also places of economic imperialism and local resistance. The image foreshadows the decline of Old Europe and the rise of new revolutions of liberation and colonial independence beyond North America. On the left of the steaming fracas, three animals (a lion, lioness, and bear cub representing Spain, Portugal, and Holland) fight among themselves while the British lion sleeps by the fire, even as the native woman reaches for a liberty cap on a pole springing from the teapot. An alternative version of the image includes a rooster pumping bellows

The Tea-Tax Tempest; or, The Anglo-American Revolution, 1778. Engraving attributed to Carl Guttenberg of Nuremberg, who worked in Paris. Courtesy Library of Congress.

to fan the flames underneath the pot, suggesting that the French, too, might be drawn into, even incite, this "Anglo-American" rebellion.[1]

Like Guttenberg, Americans imagine tea as central to their revolution. From 1767 to 1773 it provoked widespread colonial boycotts, and when the Sons of Liberty finally dumped tea in Boston harbor, it kindled the fire of independence. To reject tea as a consumer item was to reject Great Britain as master of the American economy and government. If tea is viewed through the limited lens of prerevolutionary nonimportation protests and the rhetoric of "taxation without representation," it might seem that the momentary de-nunciation of tea signified a far-reaching economic and political expression of the masses, as some recent historians have claimed.[2] Certainly, boycotts that curtailed importation and restrained consumption were powerful tools Americans used at various times in the 1760s and 1770s to pressure English merchants and Parliament to change colonial commercial policies. Still, as Guttenberg's engraving also implies, tea had a longer and more complicated role in American economic history than the events in Boston suggest. Indeed, the expansion of imperial trade networks and the introduction of new goods and ideas opened up a world of consumption and political possibilities not foreseen by Great Britain or its colonies. This book explores tea as a component of eighteenth-century global trade and its connections to the politics of consumption. Tea caused trouble over the course of the eighteenth century in several ways. As a commodity of exchange, it stimulated commercial expansion that provided Great Britain long-term and far-ranging imperial claims. However, tea proved problematic for the companies and merchants who traded it. As an increasingly available luxury consumer product, tea made people both contented and uncomfortable. Tea drinking eventually became a widespread pleasurable habit, but it also incited debates about the influence of consumption on social morality. As an item of American colonial consumption, tea was taxed and thus it resonated with negative political symbolism, yet it also helped a newly independent United States to extend its commercial power to Asia and to shape a workable domestic political economy.

Decades before British commercial policies provoked American colonists to toss some tea into Boston harbor, the innocuous leaf complicated the relationship between global trading companies, merchant middlemen, and the consuming public. By the turn of the eighteenth century, English political economists were extolling the virtues of foreign trade that exchanged home products for exotic and desirable goods. Tea was among a long list of new commodities that changed European and American consumer tastes, merchant habits, and national commercial policies. Long-distance trade in and consumption of foreign goods were made possible by technological changes in ship-making and navigation, as well as in bookkeeping, instruments of credit, trade charters, and calendar standardization.[3] But individual desire and demand for luxury goods further stimulated trade, granting merchant investors of many countries abundant opportunities to accumulate great wealth and rise as a consuming class. In turn, investment in large European mercantile companies, such as the English East India Company (EIC), pushed commercial networks farther into South Asia, Indonesia, and China. Tea and other luxury commodities thus became the building blocks for the imperial expansion of Europe and a window into the eighteenth-century British commercial empire and America's place in an increasingly global consumer economy.[4]

By the eighteenth century, Great Britain was intently focused on the Atlantic world and exploiting the products of its American and Caribbean colonies; however, the transnational links between Atlantic participants and Asian trade played an important role in nurturing the economic imperialism of Great Britain.[5] Whereas the American continent provided key resources and a place for colonization, the East Indies stirred the English commercial imagination with new and exotic commodities: spices such as pepper, cinnamon, nutmeg, and mace, which offered tasteful ways to preserve meats and other perishable foods; sugar from India; coffee from Arabia and Indonesia; and tea from China eventually seeped in from the margins of empire. Tracing the distribution of commodities through an expanding maze of global markets requires a broader lens than one trained on British colonial activities alone. Scholars of the Atlantic world note the economic interconnections across national boundaries. Peoples of Europe, Africa, and the Americas participated in an Atlantic economy where manufactured goods circulated in exchange for colonial resources such as furs, timber, sugar, rice, indigo, and human laborers. And within the Atlantic network, imperial restrictions rarely kept Spanish, French, Dutch, Portuguese, and English colonials from trading privately among themselves or with each other. Smuggling, for instance, became an important mechanism for circulating tea within and among colonial economies. An Atlantic world paradigm has limitations, however. Eighteenth-century Atlantic trade networks grew more dependent on links to credit, services, and goods from India, Asia, and the Pacific beyond. Spanish American silver, for instance, made the tea trade possible; it connected the Americas to European merchants who required hard currency to purchase commodities in the East Indies. Silver's purchasing power was far greater in India and China than in Europe. And of course, American demand brought these Asian commodities full circle, making tea one of the fastest growing consumer products in the colonies by the mid-eighteenth century.[6]

Although this story is told from an Anglo-American perspective, the present volume recognizes, like many recent studies of early modern economies, that European demands and consumption alone did not drive the engine of global markets. Rather than dominating the rest of the world economically, by the seventeenth and eighteenth centuries European merchants had to negotiate for inclusion in the vibrant commercial life of Central, South, and East Asia.[7] Indeed, the international ports of call in these regions offered a wealth of goods and, according to Kenneth Pomeranz, "came closer to resembling the neoclassical ideal of a market economy than did western Europe."[8] Even eighteenth-century political economists recognized the preeminent wealth of Asia; Adam Smith, noting the lower cost of living and labor, admitted that "China is a much richer country than any part of Europe, and the difference between the price of subsistence in China and in Europe is very great."[9] Leaders in Asia carefully restricted access to merchandise and markets to keep the balance of trade and repercussions of cultural contact in their favor. In turn, European nations sometimes armed merchants who forced access to these markets. They hoped that commercial aggression would make up for the hegemony they lacked.

Still, Asian merchants accommodated foreign trade, making European economic expansion possible and spurring competition that created a supply of goods that sometimes preceded European consumer demand. For example, England challenged the economic and political ascendency of the Portuguese and Dutch by granting a monopoly corporate charter to the EIC, allowing it great powers to establish trading posts in Asia by the seventeenth century. China, in turn, limited commercial interactions with outsiders to its port cities, where the global tea trade came to life. Canton was central to the production, sale, and distribution of tea. In the 1720s and 1730s European merchants, and the EIC in particular, attempted to corner the market in tea as a political strategy to thwart commercial competition and to influence Chinese trade policy. As a result, the EIC collected surplus tea in its warehouses and struggled to stimulate consumer demand for the relatively novel commodity. Not until the 1740s did American colonists lap up the surplus, helping to initiate a so-called consumer revolution that characterized the long eighteenth century.[10]

Tea, like many commodities, once unleashed in the circulating global marketplace, easily moved from producers to merchants to consumers across permeable imperial boundaries in ways that neither China nor Great Britain could always predict or control. Indeed, recent commodity studies demonstrate the complex life cycles of everything from cod to salt, sugar, mahogany, and coffee. Anthropologist Sidney Mintz's classic study, *Sweetness and Power*, for example, crosses the world and many centuries to explore how sugar drove Europeans to exploit slave labor and dominate New World economies. Eager consumers quickly added sugar to their diets, helping to perpetuate cycles of enslavement. The availability of sugar, of course, was integral to the increased consumption of tea and other caffeinated beverages, and it helped generate the related commercial networks connecting the Americas, Europe, and the East Indies.[11] Although tea was never produced by bound labor, as a "consumption bundle" in the seventeenth and eighteenth centuries, sugar and the tea it sweetened undoubtedly fueled the Atlantic slave trade. Even merchants involved in American intercolonial commerce probably shipped tea and slaves together, if not exchanging one commodity for the other.[12] However, I am more interested here in the unpredictable path that tea took from production to the consumer's table and how its political meaning shaped the culture and economy of the Anglo-American world before, during, and after the Revolution. In that context, Americans evoked "enslavement" only as a metaphor when describing their relationship to the EIC and the tax duties Great Britain imposed on tea, despite its tangential relationship to human trafficking.

Expanding trade beyond the Atlantic and the availability of new luxury commodities changed how people ate and lived, laying the groundwork for what has been called a consumer revolution. The transformation of consumption was not new to the turn of the eighteenth century. Historians have traced the appearance of "Worldly Goods" in Europe to the fifteenth and sixteenth centuries, when maritime and commercial technologies made exploration and foreign commerce not only possible but increasingly common. Wealthy families, not just those with title or political power, sponsored mercantile enterprises and collected rarities and consumable luxuries that gave them elevated cachet and status.[13] Only in the late seventeenth and early eighteenth centuries, however, did Europe and British North America experience what Jan de Vries has called an "industrious revolution," which helped more households "increase *both* the supply of market-oriented, money-earning activities *and* the demand for goods offered in the marketplace."[14] In other words, families were making conscious decisions about reallocating their time and wages in order to maximize the purchase of ready-made goods. Increased productivity gave rise to an ability to consume and the ensuing demand increased the circulation of goods and choices for the rising middling and new moneyed classes. Aided by competition between and among European merchants, global trade grew commonplace, and luxury goods (especially groceries) became more readily available and cheaper.[15]

In this manner, tea came to be ubiquitous throughout the Anglo-speaking world and pushed consumers to think differently about the things they bought. Indeed, as I argue in this book, the "revolution" in consumer activity took place not on account of a simple proliferation of goods but because the meaning of these goods changed. From the 1720s, tea began to grace the tables of

American colonial homes. Although exotic (evocative of its Chinese origin), tea became increasingly common to men and women of all classes and ranks. Scholars, however, debate whether consumer demand preceded supply or vice versa. Cary Carson famously asked "why demand?" in his examination of consumption in colonial British America, contending that consumer desires prompted merchants to increase the amount and type of goods they carried.[16] However, prior to the 1740s, the supply of tea provided by the EIC outpaced demand, challenging merchants and retailers to find new ways of connecting to their customers. Advertising, marketing, and improved distribution helped circulate luxuries, such as tea, across ranks; together, merchants and consumers shared the pursuit of commercial interests that expanded choice and penetration of goods.[17] Availability habituated consumers to the use of new merchandise, and since sumptuary laws no longer artificially restricted the purchase of certain items, laboring classes could emulate the refined style they saw among their betters. In other words, men and women sought aspirational consumption, or a respectability that added social, moral, and political meaning to their purchases.[18] Still, aspiring to genteel living did not necessarily lead to an exact emulation of the elite. Consumers of tea and sugar were not passive or simply imitative; rather, they were enthusiastic participants in Atlantic trade and markets. Expanded choices brought new items and new comforts to more households where the nonelite helped to redefine the meaning of luxury. By the 1750s, British subjects at home and in America increasingly purchased and consumed tea as an everyday item; once thought of as a luxury, tea had become a necessity.[19]

The increased use of new goods in England and its colonies, enabled by the reallocation of resources or a rising standard of living, intensified paradoxical moral questions about what, how much, and why people consumed luxury goods. Economics and ethics have often pitched battle as opposing forces in society. Some social commentators at the turn of the eighteenth century complained that the spread of luxuries ruined individual virtue and social well-being; they criticized the habits of working poor and women consumers in particular. Gendered images of weak women prone to licentious and luxurious living associated women with scandal and gossip at the tea table.[20] By mid-century, however, economic theorists (no doubt with the help of merchants and their customers) were in the process of redefining economic behavior, separating morality from merchandising, secularizing market activities, and even promoting the accumulation of goods as beneficial to the nation. They especially wanted to distinguish the new luxuries arriving from the East Indies or grown in New World colonies as an impetus for national prosperity rather than as a prelude to sin and lost salvation. To David Hume, for instance, luxury represented a positive good to society; selfishness that stimulated individual prosperity might raise all boats. Adam Smith in the late eighteenth century went even farther. In *The Theory of Moral Sentiments,* he argued that, far from being selfish, the pursuit of luxury made an individual interested "in the fortunes of others, and render their happiness necessary to him, though he derives nothing from it except the pleasure of seeing it."[21] In other words, a society based on consumption would not necessarily decay, but consumer demand and its attendant industry and prosperity would allow a greater benefit to all in society through philanthropy. Rather than indications of vice and excess, items once labeled luxuries became justifiably indispensable.[22]

The shift in consumer sentiment, however, left behind an enduring ambivalence about consumption and the social behaviors it engendered. Even as the concept of "luxurious vices" faded, anxiety about consumption lingered in the Anglo-American world. The luxury debates of the 1720s and 1730s provided a moral lexicon that Americans readily adopted as they began to question the constitutionality of British economic sovereignty, trade monopolies, and political economy in the mid-eighteenth century. In the debates over nonimportation and tea, in particular, merchants and their customers struggled with the political and moral implications of consuming goods. Drunk by the rich and the poor, tea represented the changing fashion of a self-conscious consumer class, but it was also politicized in a variety of ways that make tea a barometer for understanding the American Revolution. In the 1760s, boycott supporters called for consumer restraint and blamed luxury consumption for threatening American liberties. The nonimportation agreements reflected these moral arguments. Still, economic self-interest shaped the politics of consumption on the part of merchants and consumers. Republican political ideals, which demanded virtuous restraint from luxury, often collided with consumer appetites and inherent problems within the colonial economy. When merchants adhered to nonimportation agreements they did not reject consumer luxuries in favor of the supposed moral ideology of republicanism, as some scholars have contended.[23] Rather, they used boycotts as a way to rebalance colonial economies that were overburdened with an excess of British manufactures. Merchants, juggling the political demands of patriot activists with the scarcity of credit and currency, could adhere to the policies of nonimportation even while disposing of inventory on hand, including a great deal of surplus tea.[24]

American merchant response to nonimportation, driven by economic self-interest, also resonated with the ideals of free trade. When restricted by British economic policies, colonial merchants often established and used intercolonial and transnational Atlantic commercial networks to participate in illicit trade, even as they cultivated familiar avenues of legal trade.[25] Family and friends who shared religious views or social relations built trade ties between and among merchants in Philadelphia, Boston, and New York, the geographic nexus for this study. The sources reveal both cooperation and competition between and among mid-Atlantic merchants, which helps highlight the extent and importance of tea to trade networks that also extended to London, Lisbon, Amsterdam, and the non-British West Indies. Merchants sought profit from commodities that could be purchased as cheaply as possible. During the imperial wars of the 1740s and 1750s, for example, with British trade often expensive, uncertain, or prohibited, American merchants turned to the Dutch Caribbean. They smuggled tea, which was lightweight and easily sold, bringing the popular item through regions that previously had little access to consumer goods but also raising the ire of British imperial customs services. When convenient or useful, the interests of merchant smugglers intersected with the interests of American activists, combining arguments in support of political liberties with those demanding freedom of trade.[26]

Consumers, too, had tasted a new commercial marketplace and sometimes acted in self-interest when asked to change their buying habits in the 1760s and 1770s. The discourse that permeated early American pamphlets and the press during the prerevolutionary period demanded that colonists restrain consumption to maintain their virtue and political freedoms. By using these sources alone, one could assume a far greater political consensus or unity of action among Americans based on their "shared experience as consumers."[27] However, another discourse also runs through the sources. Early American merchant ledgers and customs records that map the flow of goods to the colonies show that consumer restraint and consensus about boycotting products such as tea are less clear and far from unanimous. Kate Haulman, in *The Politics of Fashion in Eighteenth-Century America*, traces the tensions between consumer desire and revolutionary mandates to embrace homespun and a republican style of dress; "the personal politics of fashion persisted," she argues, "especially among women and other feminized figures that became a political problem for Whigs."[28] Women also played an important role as consumers of tea and experienced comparable conflicts of interest. Revolutionary committees called on female shoppers to stop buying goods listed in nonimportation agreements. Often with reluctance, women acknowledged the political necessity to change their shopping habits. However, both women and men continued to purchase forbidden goods for their families at local shops when available.[29] Internal anxiety and doubt instilled by burgeoning economic self-interest, rather than a clear ideological vision of right economic behavior, fueled the revolutionary movement.

Despite more than a half century of enthusiastic participation in consumer markets, Americans managed to generally unite behind the nonimportation of British goods in 1773, after the passage of the Tea Act. The protesters expressed ambivalence about the political consequences of that consumption. As tea became problematic for American colonists, some clung to earlier moral outrage over foreign luxuries. Rather than parochial concerns about the harmful physical and mental effects of tea drinking or the burdens of local taxation, however, activists more often pointed to the broader global dimensions of the tea crisis. British and American critics questioned the policies that regulated companies, such as the EIC, and its abusive actions in commercial markets abroad. By boycotting the commodities that the EIC traded—in particular tea—Americans criticized the company's role in creating and monopolizing a British imperial economy. Indeed, during the early 1770s, the EIC's recent conquest of Bengal, partially paid for by the sale of Chinese tea, became a point of contention for a cross-Atlantic critique of empire. The company's actions in Asia demonstrated the grim possibilities of corporate powers exercised under the name of government. Thus, activists, fearing the potential commercial sovereignty of the EIC in America, planned "tea party" protests and expressed alarm over the prospective corporate takeover of American commercial markets. Americans engaged in a rhetorical battle with the policies that regulated tea's sale and taxation, rebranded tea as symbol of imperial tyranny, and helped generate a call to revolution.[30]

Placing the Boston Tea Party and the crisis of 1773 into their international context helps make sense of why Americans returned so quickly to consuming tea following these events. Americans did not reject luxury goods or consumption. Despite the restrictions put in place by the Continental Articles of Association in 1774 and the widespread public promise to give up tea as a symbol of British oppression, tea continued to be ubiquitous, consumed with relish even at the height of the tea protests. It even became the basis for several American fortunes during the Revolutionary War. American merchants and consumers continued to seek out, trade, and purchase tea where they could and when it was available. During the initial years of war, nonimportation and nonconsumption of tea proved difficult to enforce through local committees of compliance. Between 1774 and the late 1770s, merchants petitioned Congress to allow the sale and use of already stockpiled tea, especially non-EIC tea. In addition, they demanded that a ban on exportation be lifted to allow the trade of provisions with the Dutch and French West Indies. In return, Americans purchased tea. Consumers also pressured merchants and governmental bodies to regulate the price and availability of scarce commodities like tea. Women condemned merchants who hoarded supplies or charged excessive amounts, demanding that state and national legislatures enact price controls to regulate the distribution and sale of tea. Congress reopened markets to foreign trade in the spring of 1776, and by the later years of the war, tea had returned widely to shops in Philadelphia, New York, and Boston. Although economic matters were never the sole motivation for fighting a war of independence, the accessibility of goods and fairness in the marketplace remained vital to Americans' daily lives.[31]

After the Revolution, tea continued to drive discussion and disagreement over an emerging American political economy. Rather than disappearing from merchant shelves, it provided a potential windfall for American merchants and a key source of revenue for government treasuries. In order to finance the war debt, the Continental Congress attempted to renew international trade and credit by extending commercial treaties to potential allies. Traders using connections in the Caribbean, as well as French free ports like Nantes and L'Orient, helped raise money for arms during the war. With the British defeat, American merchants, still advocating the advantages of free trade, began to send ships directly to China rather than purchasing tea and silks through European allies. In turn, individual states and Congress competed for the rights to tax those foreign luxuries to raise revenue. By the 1780s and 1790s self-interested merchants vied with European trade companies to dominate the Asian marketplace, bringing otter skins from the Pacific Northwest and American ginseng in hopes of finding the perfect commodity to exchange for tea. Although many were proponents of free trade, American merchants also demanded commercial policies that gave their maritime enterprises advantages over European rivals. Rather than granting monopoly rights, like Britain had to the EIC, a newly empowered Congress under the federal Constitution conceded to the interests of private traders abroad and vowed to protect new commercial "privileges of independence."[32] American diplomats and statesmen bowed to the realities of commercial regulations as part of foreign policy, enacting restrictions and tariffs, even as consumers, long habituated to tea and no longer worried about its moral implications, had no trouble financing merchants' entanglement with a vibrant global market economy.

CHAPTER ONE

The English Commercial Empire Expands

> To found a great empire for the sole purpose of raising up a
> people of customers may at first sight appear a project fit only for
> a nation of shopkeepers. It is, however, a project altogether unfit
> for a nation of shopkeepers; but extremely fit for a nation that is
> governed by shopkeepers.
>
> —*Adam Smith,* The Wealth of Nations

By the late sixteenth and early seventeenth centuries, the English had turned their gaze to the wider world, hoping to expand their political power and economic empire. In his *Discourse of Western Planting* (1584), Richard Hakluyt articulated a commercial strategy that would "yelde unto us all the commodities of Europe, Affrica, and Asia, as far as wee were wonte to travell, and supply the wantes of all our decayed trades." Besides procuring new resources, exploration and colonization would create markets to "vente" English manufactures and provide "for the manifolde imployment of numbers of idle men."[1] Surely Hakluyt envisioned the mercantilist mind-set that would produce the "nation governed by shopkeepers" and its consuming subjects that Adam Smith later scorned.[2]

Mercantilism generally posited that if a country encouraged foreign commerce but managed to balance or excel in trade with competing nations, it could accumulate and control a greater portion of global wealth. The state, through its laws and banking system, would promote, protect, and regulate merchant traders in order to raise revenue by duties on the commodities they imported and exported. Simultaneously, home manufacturing would be secured from any foreign or colonial competition by tariffs and restrictions. Of course, some merchants, at least those who flourished under the protection of monopoly charters, supported these policies; others bristled at the interference of regulation that kept them from profitable markets.[3] In that regard, mercantilism was never an entirely coherent or consistent ideology, per se. Still, English merchants usually chose to work with policy makers to find a middle ground between overbearing regulation and unrestrained commerce, hoping to benefit from the intersection of self-interest and national need. In the mid-seventeenth century, Thomas Mun, a member of the increasingly influential, though still emerging, English East India Company (EIC), succinctly described this commercial theory: "The ordinary means to increase our wealth and treasure is by *Foreign Trade*, wherein we must ever observe this rule, to sell more to strangers yearly than we consume of theirs in value."[4] In essence, a nation's economic success was predicated on gaining access to foreign goods and maintaining a positive balance of trade. Additionally, foreign trade would stimulate industry at home—providing work for merchant marines, shipbuilders, sailors, and shopkeepers—which would lead to new prosperity. As Hakluyt had hoped, consumer societies and commercial empires put "idle men" to work.[5]

By the eighteenth century this mercantilist model came to fruition for Great Britain when commercial organizations acted as its political arm abroad. Indeed, political economists argued that aggressive commercial expansion, rather than warfare alone, would assure the British Empire's dominance in the global marketplace and enhance its political power. Adam Anderson insisted that "*Conquest* were to ancient *Rome*, what *Commerce* is now to other Nations," an idea that stretched back to the Renaissance.[6] James Steuart, in *An Inquiry into the Principles of Political Oeconomy*, argued, "A nation which remains passive in her commerce, is at the mercy of those who are active."[7] Not only influenced by shopkeepers, Great Britain increasingly turned to merchants and trade companies to negotiate, finance, and maintain permanent imperial infrastructure at the new "oceanic and territorial peripheries" of empire, regions far different from the maturing colonies of North America.[8] British mercantile enclaves of the early modern period included the West African coast (dominated by the Royal African Company), Mocha and Smyrna (where the Muscovy Company and Levant Company operated), and the beginnings of an English presence in South Asia at Bombay, Madras, and Calcutta.[9] English merchants slowly insinuated themselves into already existing transnational networks of trade, even as these new commercial markets provided a locus for competition between nations of Europe. In the seventeenth century, for instance, the Dutch dominated the pepper and spice trade in Indonesia and Japan, but their primacy gave way slowly under English commercial pressure. Even though merchants had great leeway in how they conducted business, commercial enterprises also relied on British naval power to protect and extend trading activities abroad.[10] Still, the merchants who made foreign trade possible in these enclaves were expected to be the political face of empire, as well as a civilizing force, in essence masking the aggressive, calculating nature of commercial expansion. Foreign trade was a "Means of conveying all Benefits to Mankind," Adam Anderson optimistically added to his treatise on the *Origin of Commerce*.[11] Yet the rise of commercial civility, with its central tenets of contractual law and fair negotiation, just as often posed moral dilemmas for British merchants, who justified some very unethical practices under the guise of peaceful national policies.[12]

Although North America provided Great Britain with raw materials, a place for settlement, and a proving ground for imperial supremacy among European nations, the lands that became known as the East Indies stirred the European commercial imagination. It was no exaggeration when the eighteenth century French cleric Abbé Raynal cited the discovery of "the passage to the East-Indies by the Cape of Good Hope" as "one of the most important events in the history of the human species," a sentiment Adam Smith reiterated in his *Wealth of Nations*.[13] Charted by the Portuguese under Vasco da Gama in 1497, the sea route around Africa opened trade between Europe and limited portions of South Asia and countries beyond the Strait of Malacca, including Indonesia, Japan, and China. Well-established port cities such as Goa and Madras in India and Canton in China drew Europeans into vibrant global marketplaces where Persians, Jews, Arabs, Armenians, Indonesians, Japanese, and ethnic Chinese already traded.[14] Rather than exploiting non-European producers for luxury commodities, English merchants had to trade in markets dominated by Asians, who controlled goods and services. Whereas Raynal insisted that trade with Asia would help all nations "consider themselves as one great society, whose members have all an equal right to partake of the conveniencies of the rest," because of local limitations, fierce competition broke out among European nations to gain and control access to the East India trade.[15]

In order to retain its advantage in the East Indies, Great Britain encouraged merchants to invest in maritime adventures but also struggled to harness and regulate the wealth generated by that trade and the manner in which commercial traders acted abroad. Theoretically, at least, open and free trade abroad would encourage consumption at home and promote new industry and competition in the marketplace, thereby bringing profit to merchants, new markets for English goods, and revenues to the nation through duties and taxes on foreign commodities. William Mildmay, for instance, argued, "The Freedom of Sale is the first general principle so often recommended before, and to which we must again recur, and perpetually adhere, in our commerce abroad as well as in our Trade at home."[16] Yet the British government, and even those who advocated free trade, acknowledged that too much commercial liberty could quickly turn into chaos; individual merchants acting on self-interest could import a glut of certain goods, for instance, that might wreck havoc on pricing and profit, in turn damaging credit markets and tax revenue streams. Mildmay, while promoting the "Freedom of Sale," also recognized that state-sanctioned charters or corporate monopolies helped rein in excessive commercial activity and were not necessarily an obstacle to expanding trade. Free trade should not be a license for merchants to act freely.[17] Through careful regulation of foreign imports, manufacturing within the empire, and select national monopolies, Great Britain hoped to create dependence on English markets within the empire and to control peripheral economies, even while expanding its presence in the East Indies.[18] British colonies would supply raw materials and eager consumers for both manufactured goods and foreign reexports. Through regulated domestic and colonial consumption, Britain could maintain its advantageous balance of trade abroad. Still, the incoherence and shifting nature of its so-called mercantilist system created myriad tensions between commercial force and beneficence, between commercial freedoms and restraints, which often triggered unexpected consequences for Great Britain by the eighteenth century.

The English entered commercial competition in the East Indies relatively late. Although individual English trade vessels had plied Asian waters from the early seventeenth century, their efforts were little more than privateering ventures against Portuguese and Dutch ships or trips to purchase goods, such as silks and spices, secondhand from Chinese traders at Bantam (on Java) or from the Portuguese in Surat, on the west coast of India. In the 1640s, however, assisted by a Dutch-Portuguese conflict, the English negotiated a treaty with Portugal to open more formal access to Macao, the gateway to Canton. A "Company of Merchants of London trading to the East Indies," initially sanctioned by Queen Elizabeth in 1600, emerged as the key player in this commercial chess game. In 1644, merchant Edward Knipe speculated that the company could "reap the Advantages of a Trade between China & India," provided that its ships carried goods that interested the Portuguese and avoided Dutch intervention at sea.[19] The group received a new royal charter with expanded powers to build fortifications and raise an army in South Asia, along with territory in Bombay, after Charles II returned to the throne in 1660, clinching its power of governance abroad.[20] Only in 1709, however, when the "Merchants of London" consolidated commercial forces with a competing company, did the "United Company of Merchants of England trading to the East Indies" (soon known simply as the English East India Company) come into being and start its campaign to become the premier shipper of Asian consumer goods to Great Britain and its colonies. In 1713, the EIC secured rights from the Chinese to enter the port of Canton for trade, and by 1717 it mustered regular, annual commercial voyages to China.[21]

With the benefits of a state-sanctioned monopoly, the EIC became the sole British entity to trade legally between Asia and Great Britain. The author of *Some Thoughts Relating to Trade in General, and to the East India Trade in Particular* praised the monopoly granted the EIC, since it imported foreign goods that would otherwise have to be purchased through other European nations, at a loss of tax revenue to England. He worried that "the Trade to the *East Indies* will be entirely lost to this Nation, if it should be laid open."[22] Others worried that a monopoly created economic interdependence between the company and nation, which was potentially disastrous.[23] Financially, the EIC capitalized itself through subscriptions of stock to investors and issuance of short-term bonds, which provided operating cash. But in practical terms, its financial health was intrinsically tied to the British government, customs revenue, and the national debt. Because the EIC directors and shareholders came from London moneyed interests and had considerable influence on politics, they were able to sustain long-term commercial activity in Asia.[24] However, the United Company charter of 1709 came with the expectation that the EIC would also provide a cash-strapped nation funds for its wars. By the 1740s, these accumulated loans to government amounted to £4.2 million, for which Parliament assured the company monopoly privileges in Asia and autonomy of its internal affairs. In exchange, the EIC could draw on governmental funds through the Bank of England for short-term loans and working capital. Trading profits paid for generous dividends (consistently 7 to 10 percent yield) distributed among shareholders.[25] The company was not yet an explicit arm of the British government, as it would become in late-eighteenth-century India, but by midcentury the government and the EIC were mutually dependent on each other to operate and the EIC often acted as the political face of Britain abroad.

The main commodity that fueled co-dependence between company and nation, that became the mechanism through which their relationship functioned, was Chinese tea. Although introduced to European elites sometime in the mid-sixteenth century, tea did not become a viable commercial commodity until after 1660 and the Restoration of the Stuart monarchy. Tradition suggests that Catherine of Braganza, daughter of King Juan IV of Portugal, brought a chest of tea to the English court in the 1660s as part of her dowry, which included the islands of Bombay, when she married Charles II.[26] At the turn of the eighteenth century, the poet Edmund Waller dubbed Catherine "the best of Queens" and the tea she made popular "the best of herbs."[27] Tea not only constituted a new luxury good for English consumption but also provided a livelihood to the king and, later, general revenue to the British government. Charles II relied on the "Tonnage and Poundage" paid on many exotic commodities brought from the West and East Indies, including coffee, tea, and chocolate. His brother and successor, James II, received further duties from tobacco and sugar.[28] By the early eighteenth century, tea and the China trade provided hundreds of thousands of pounds sterling in annual tax revenue for the crown and helped finance the expansion of the British Empire into India and beyond.[29]

Because the EIC had political clout and managed currency and credit, which it extended to the government, Great Britain shaped an increasingly complicated tax structure to favor the company and discourage purchase of luxury items through nonsanctioned merchants or outside nations. The New Duties on Coffee, Tea, and Drugs of 1712, for instance, meant to help pay for Queen Anne's War, gave preference to EIC tea, which was assessed at two shillings per pound, whereas "all kinds of Tea Imported from any other place or places" carried five shillings a pound duty.[30] Great Britain also attempted to control the flow and distribution of EIC commodities in order to track and collect revenues. It presumably collected about £264,534 in revenue on 2,645,337 pounds of tea imported by the EIC during the 1710s (table 1.1). The British government also required company merchants to identify tea that would be consumed in England versus that slated for reexport, for which the EIC received drawbacks (or rebates) on tax duties. Further, the EIC was required to warehouse and certify all tea before sale at auction.[31] Throughout the early eighteenth century, the EIC and Parliament heatedly negotiated the amount of import duties imposed on tea and other East India goods. The EIC worried that too much tax would choke consumer ability to purchase these goods and ultimately hurt its sales and decrease state revenue; even the Commissioners of the Customs, in "their own private opinions," believed that lower tax duties would ultimately "bring more to the Crown."[32] Still, the British government most often won the battle to control taxation and the cost of foreign trade; it took advantage of importation, reexportation, and growing domestic usage of tea to raise revenue.

TABLE 1.1
*English East India Company (EIC) Tea Imported to England
(in lbs.)*

Date	EIC General Ledgers	Board of Customs
1700–1710	877,509	842,326
1711–1720	2,645,337	3,567,836
1721–1730	8,879,862	9,129,049
1731–1740	11,663,998	12,346,005
1741–1750	20,214,498	21,262,490
1751–1760	37,350,002	38,347,381

Source: Data for the EIC General Ledgers figures are compiled from K. N. Chaudhuri, *The Trading World of Asia and the English East India Company, 1660–1760* (Cambridge: Cambridge University Press, 1978), 388, and Earl H. Pritchard, *Anglo-Chinese Relations During the Seventeenth and Eighteenth Centuries* (New York: Octagon Books, 1970), Appendix XIX: "East India Company's Tea Trade," n.p. Data for the Board of Customs are compiled from Great Britain, Board of Customs & Excise, Ledgers of Imports and Exports, 1696–1780, in the Public Records Office, London, reels 3–37.

During the first half of the eighteenth century, the importation and sale of Chinese tea increased dramatically and provided a reliable, taxable commodity. By the 1740s, EIC tea imports to England had risen more than twentyfold, prompting the British government to add distribution and consumption taxes to tea (see table 1.1). In the 1720s, Robert Walpole, chancellor of the exchequer and effective prime minister, reformed the import tax structure, adding an inland duty of four shillings per pound on "all Tea [to] be sold in Great Britain." Walpole's Act of 1724 required that everyone, from the EIC merchant and local wholesaler to "every Druggist, Grocer, Chandler, Coffeehouse-keeper, [and] Chocolate-house keeper," pay a duty and provide certificates for any tea purchased for retail sale or public consumption.[33] After nearly a decade of revenue collection, Walpole lauded the taxes on tea, coffee, and chocolate as paramount to paying down the national debt, which was only possible by *"that alteration . . .* made *in the then method of collecting these revenues."* He defended his revenue bill, arguing "that considerably above a *million of money* has been paid into the *Exchequer* MORE in the last eight years, than in the former."[34] Between 1721 and 1730, with 9,129,049 pounds of tea imported, the Board of Customs could have collected as much as £1.8 million in inland duties alone (see table 1.1). Still, the mercantilist policies that emerged from negotiation between company and nation, although mutually beneficial, left merchants with a series of practical problems to overcome. The EIC had to establish a commercial presence in China, which entailed forcing open notoriously restrictive Chinese markets. It had to ward off English interlopers and smugglers, surpass the European competition, and find viable commodities of exchange. Before the 1740s, these tasks proved far more complicated than expected.

From its base of operations in Madras (Fort St. George), the EIC successfully expanded its commercial empire with the help of nationally sanctioned monopoly powers. Still, the company struggled to find its footing in Asian markets restricted by Chinese trade policies and procedures that stymied the EIC's strategy and influence over the emerging tea trade. The Chinese emperor, through regional Mandarins, controlled all commerce in China. Prior to the seventeenth century, the imperial government discouraged maritime trade by banning foreign travel of Chinese nationals, curtailing supplies to coastal regions, and burning ships. But Chinese merchants, even ordinary people, evaded government edicts to trade a variety of consumer goods at ports throughout South Asia and Indonesia, forcing the government to open Chinese markets to outsiders.[35] In the mid-seventeenth century, acknowledging that "commerce is a way to enrich our nation, and to open foreign trade is a special means of raising income (from taxation)," the recently ascendant Qing emperor granted Portuguese in residence at Macao access to Canton, opening the way for other European traders in 1684.[36] By the turn of the eighteenth century, imperial Mandarins and local Hoppos, who oversaw customs collection and port activities, had created a complicated set of rules for foreign commerce in China. They restricted foreign trade to Canton alone, allowing Europeans temporary residence only during the trade season. In the 1720s, the English had "no settled Factory at *Canton*" and were "only permitted to hire large *Hongs*, or *Houses*, near the water side, conveniently accommodated with ware-houses to receive their goods before they are shipp'd off."[37] When Europeans did come to port, the Hoppos usually boarded their ships in Macao or Whampo, three miles outside of Canton, to oversee the surrender of any arms and "to see that nothing is smuggled out of or into the ship." The Hoppos searched every crate and piece of cargo, complained *The Chinese Traveller*, "and sometimes even our pockets do not escape them."[38] A series of fees and charges had to be paid by foreign traders in silver, including import and export duties on goods brought in and purchased. Besides a measurage charge based on length and tonnage of each vessel, additional presents, some may say bribes, to various officials—the linguist (translator), weigher, Hoppo, security officer, and Mandarin—greased the wheels of commerce.[39]

The cost of doing business in China was high, but the English objected most to the restricted access to the goods and services of local merchants, which

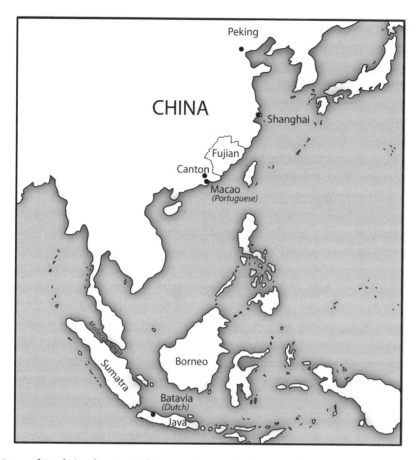

Ports of Trade in The East Indies, 1700–1740. Map by Taya Barnett, Old Dominion University.

hurt the EIC's ability to negotiate direct competitive contracts. Since there was no permanent post in Canton, the EIC sent teams of supercargoes (merchant agents for the company who also had rights to limited private trade) with each ship that entered port. Laden with instructions from the company directors at Fort St. George in Madras, where all orders originated, each ship, captain, and agent recorded his experiences for the China Diary and Consultations so that future ventures could deal more effectively with Chinese trade policies, merchants, and commodity pricing.[40] Throughout the early eighteenth century, EIC agents "demanded a free Trade with all people without restriction" from officials at Canton.[41] In 1704, for instance, the Hoppo at Canton prevented an English merchant named Alexander Hamilton from directly hiring

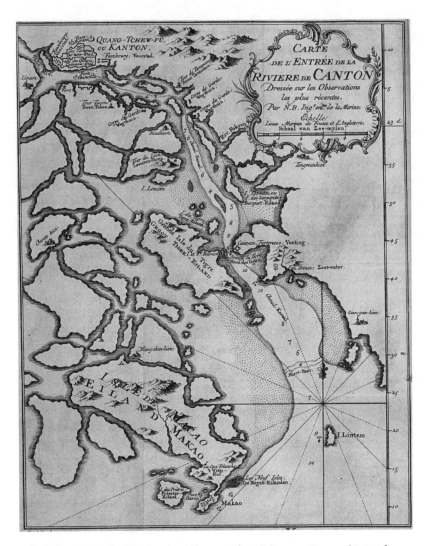

Jacobus van der Schley, *Kaart van't Inkoomen der Riviere van Kanton / Carte de l'Entrée de la Riviere de Canton, Dressée sur les Observations les plus récentes*, 1749. From *Atlas of Mutual Heritage and the Koninklijke Bibliotheek*. Courtesy National Library of the Netherlands. Public Domain under a Creative Commons Public Domain Dedication (CC-ZERO).

river pilots or linguists to take his goods to market. Hamilton found that "no Merchants came near me," making him suspect that local officials and merchants had conspired to engage or threaten every available linguist, forcing him and other European traders to contract with a sanctioned group of dealers who set the price of goods "40 and 50 *per Cent.* higher" than the current, open market.[42] By midcentury, the Hoppos at Canton required that English traders negotiate only with particular Hong merchants who had paid off local authorities for exclusive rights to oversee trade with Europeans. The Hong merchants could set prices, arrange the sale of goods, and rent facilities to foreign merchants, reaping higher fees on their exclusive contracts. However, they also had to put up security against any problems that might arise from European merchant or mariner behavior in Canton.[43] With a few sanctioned merchants in place to service all Europeans, the EIC merchants felt disadvantaged as competition for Chinese commodities increased. In 1719, supercargoes William Fazakerley, Robert Gascoigne, and Whichcott Turner of the *Carnaroon* complained, "Tea was growing excessive dear, from the great demand, and preknowledge the Chinese had of our arrival."[44]

Despite the restrictions placed on access to Chinese markets, English merchants quickly garnered expertise in every aspect of tea production, packaging, and shipment, purchasing more and greater variety with each passing year. Usually cultivated and harvested by tenants on small farms in the hills of nearby Fujian Province, all varieties of tea leaves sold in Canton came from the same plant species, although raised in slightly different soils and picked at different times during the growing season. The drying and curing process was labor intensive and painstaking. Most tea leaves were dried in flat baskets, heated in a caldron over a fire, and turned by hand before packing.[45] Initially, the EIC agents under consultation in Canton purchased mainly Singlo, a delicate variety of green tea "most valued and used in China," according to one observer.[46] Merchants thought green teas, whose qualities were judged by smell and taste, to be the most profitable and easily resold "to all Parts of the World, where they have the Knowledge of it."[47] In 1719, 75 percent of the teas sold at the EIC's London auction were green teas and during the 1720s, Singlo represented more than 50 percent of all Chinese tea imported to England (table 1.2).[48] Within a few decades, however, company agents shifted to a cheaper black tea variety, Bohea, which proved more durable during long sea voyages. By the 1740s, barely 30 percent of the EIC's imports consisted of green tea. The EIC even changed its storage and shipping procedures to accommodate increasing amounts of tea purchased. After local Chinese laborers tramped down the tea by foot into lead-lined chests, English traders inspected "one chest in five of all the Green Tea" to check for damaged product.[49] By standardizing the size and tare of tea chests, the company could maximize storage capacity for outgoing vessels. The *Macclesfield*, which arrived in Can-

TABLE 1.2

Types of Tea Imported to Great Britain by the EIC (in lbs.)

Date	Bohea (black)	Percentage of Total	Singlo (green)	Percentage of Total
1721–30	3,360,497	37.8	4,577,279	52.0
1731–40	5,337,807	45.4	3,642,271	30.9
1741–50	10,130,247	49.6	8,029,616	29.4
1751–60	23,634,760	63.3	11,259,684	30.0

Source: Compiled from K. N. Chaudhuri, *The Trading World of Asia and the English East India Company, 1660–1760* (Cambridge: Cambridge University Press, 1978), 397–98. The higher quality black teas, Pekoe and Souchong, represented less than 2% of the total EIC imports, while lower grades of Congou and Bohea made up 7% and 38%, respectively, in the first four decades of the century. Bohea tea, which was a black tea from Fujian Province, eventually became the most popular in Europe and the Americas during the eighteenth century.

ton late summer 1724, was instructed only to use chests in which "the Wood be first season'd and . . . Take care that no Camphire be Laden with the Tea in this Ship least its Scent spoil it."[50] Supercargoes discovered that chinaware cushioned by rice straw provided the best ballast for their ships and did not emit any smell that might further contaminate the tea.[51] The EIC used every free nook and cranny of a ship to stow tea, including "the after hould" and "the Breadroom," even stashing tea "Between Decks, and abaft the Well in the Hold."[52]

Even though the EIC gained access to the Canton tea market by the 1720s, it struggled with a growing presence of commercial interlopers from England and smugglers from many nations that undermined the company's monopoly charter rights. Paradoxically, supercargoes brought tea home legally as part of their personal compensation package, some of which never reached London port, let alone the EIC warehouse and auction. Company agents, enticed by potential profits, at times certified for "reexport" tea from their "private trade" along with product from the regular cargo manifest. They could then receive a drawback (rebate) on the inland duty, after which they would land the tea elsewhere along the coast of Wales or England to be resold illegally.[53] Still, this "fictitious export trade" was less damaging to the EIC sales than teas smuggled directly into England from across the Channel. Swedish and Danish merchants infiltrated Scotland and northern England, while the Dutch and French plied coastal waters from the south. Smuggling had become commonplace in England after 1721, especially through the Isle of Man and Channel Islands, providing extra work for law enforcement and exciting tales of chase and capture for the media. In December 1734, newspapers across the Atlantic carried stories of local officers in Winchelsea and Pett, who "with three

Dragoons, seized and carried to his Majesty's Warehouse" 2,559 pounds of tea.[54] A parliamentary committee investigating smuggling in 1745 estimated that after 1721, of the estimated 3 million pounds of tea consumed at home per year, 2 million pounds were "openly, and in Defiance of the Laws and the Civil Government, smuggled and run in."[55]

Faced with restrictions on Chinese trade and the commercial threat of European smugglers, the EIC developed a strategy to corner the tea market. Between 1720 and 1740, the Court of Directors instructed supercargoes to systematically "engross," or purchase, as much tea as possible to keep the commodity out of the hands of French, Dutch, Danish, or Swedish competitors who patronized the Canton markets. Of great concern was the Flemish Ostend Company, chartered by the Austrian emperor, which acted as a front for English, Scottish, and Dutch merchants denied legal access to Asian markets by the EIC's monopoly powers. In 1720, EIC agents attempted to purchase "all the Tea procurable that is either very good, or but tolerable, and not damaged," no matter the cost. They hoped to "make these Interlopers sick of their voyages, which can never be done unless they are prevented getting Tea."[56] The attempt to corner the tea market, especially highly desirable green tea, eventually expanded. In 1729, the EIC instructed its agents to quickly buy up all the green tea that Chinese merchants could supply, "sufficient to prevent the Ships coming after us of obtaining any quantity." As a further precaution, the agents agreed to buy future contracts for Bohea tea in case additional European traders arrived unexpectedly.[57] With little concern for the quality, and no clear connection to increased consumer demand, the EIC simply wanted to take as much tea out of the hands of its competitors as needed to secure a market for company tea at home and the European re-export markets.[58]

In 1727, the Ostend Company lost its charter and went out of business under pressure from the Dutch, who quickly became the EIC's chief rival for Chinese tea. Although the Anglo-Dutch wars had ended long before, English and Dutch merchants fought each other ruthlessly in the economic arena. During the seventeenth century, the Dutch aggressively inserted themselves into the political and commercial lives of the Javanese, dominating the spice trade from a base at Batavia.[59] The Dutch bought only certain Chinese commodities indirectly during the first twenty years of the eighteenth century, either through Batavian markets or from other European merchants. Paradoxically, Holland became the most important reexport market for EIC tea. From 1700 to 1710, the Dutch purchased 269,010 pounds of Chinese tea from

English merchants, or one-third of the EIC's total sales. The following decade, they imported 649,462 pounds of tea, one-quarter of all the tea that the EIC sold. During the first three years of the 1720s, Holland bought an astounding 1,196,984 pounds of tea from England.[60] However, Dutch buying habits changed dramatically during the late 1720s, after the Dutch East India Company ruined a group of British traders at Mocha (Yemen). The Dutch company had bid up the price of coffee without eventually buying any, effectively blocking English access to that commodity. The EIC, hoping to prevent a similar disaster to its business in Canton, stepped up efforts to monopolize the Chinese tea market, cut back reexports to Holland, and successfully obstructed Dutch commerce in China.[61] During the 1729–1730 season, company agent William Fazakerley even tried to promote cooperation with Britain's perpetual enemy, the French, in order to marshal their "mutual interest . . . to hinder the Dutch trading to China."[62] But English merchants found that the French also sought to monopolize the tea trade. In December 1730 company agents swore to the directors that they were blameless for failing "to engross the Green Tea," since the French ship *Mars* had arrived before them. Still, EIC agents prevented "the French Gentlemen" from procuring "but little more than one half of what they intended to purchase," promising to send a large quantity of tea home in their vessels.[63]

The EIC's machinations failed to undermine Dutch or French access to tea, however. Instead it helped initiate a frenzy of commercial activity in Asia by a growing number of European traders, allowed competing companies to smuggle cheap tea into England, and produced a glut of tea at home. Although the total sales of EIC goods surpassed the Dutch, by the 1740s Dutch merchants managed to purchase comparable amounts of tea directly from Canton, even as the EIC lost Dutch customers for tea reexports (table 1.3). The Danish and Swedish East India Companies also increased direct trade with China, perhaps allowing other European nations like Germany and Flanders to stop purchasing tea from the EIC altogether by midcentury. Conversely, Dutch, French, Danish, and Swedish merchants were able to smuggle tea back into Great Britain and still sell it for less than the EIC auction price, thus further undermining the company's trade monopoly.[64]

The EIC's decision to purchase increasing amounts of Chinese tea in the early decades of the eighteenth century generated competition among European merchant companies but also placed pressure on tea production and distribution networks within China. Chinese officials tried to control foreign trade and traffic, but their participation in the new global economy made them

TABLE 1.3
English versus non-English Tea Importations (in lbs.)

Date	English	French	Dutch	Danish	Swedish
1719–25	918,777	178,662	—	—	—
1726–33	1,098,506	523,187	397,900	78,265	70,798
1734–40	1,386,499	947,576	863,178	705,316	626,651
1741–48	1,981,684	1,067,440	2,017,683	1,766,356	1,394,232
1749–55	3,064,323	1,928,752	2,809,796	1,706,624	1,787,289

Source: Louis Dermigny, *La Chine et l'Occident: Le commerce à Canton au XVIIIᵉ siècle, 1719–1833* (Paris: École pratique des hautes études, 1964), 2:539. Although some dispute the accuracy of his numbers, Dermigny is one of the few sources that provide comparative figures for several nations.
   Notes: Dermigny's figures, originally in piculs, have been converted to pounds using the formula 1 picul = 133.33 lbs. Em dash indicates data not available.

increasingly dependent on foreign merchants. By the late 1720s, demand for tea by European traders had risen so sharply that Canton producers had trouble supplying the market. The EIC agents on *Prince Augustus* reported to company directors in 1728 that only one merchant, Suqua, could obtain any great quantity of teas since two or three years of heavy taxation by the Mandarins and falling profits had curtailed production of green tea especially.[65] The more tea that the EIC and other European trade companies ordered, the more Chinese merchants exerted power over the supply of the commodity, attempting to keep the price high.[66] In 1729, EIC agents tried to negotiate exclusive contracts with cooperative merchants; Suqua, for instance, helped the EIC monopolize the green tea market in the 1720s and 1730s. However, more Canton merchants, including Suqua, undercut the company's contracts by selling to other European traders and colluding with other Chinese merchants to set prices and control distribution.[67] Soon every small merchant in Canton "who expected any Business with the Europeans" had joined a frenzy of speculative buying from countryside tea growers.[68] High demand led to hasty orders and little quality control; at times Chinese producers and merchants mixed old or cheaper teas with new crops to get product to market quickly. The EIC agents complained in 1730 that the unusual demand for tea from the year before inspired Canton merchants to provide "incredible Quantities of Tea, or rather something like Tea," to fill their current contracts.[69]

   By the mid-1730s, an elite Chinese merchant syndicate called the Co-Hong emerged using their wealth to buy favor from imperial Mandarins and appropriate exclusive trade rights with all foreigners. The Co-Hong's rise to power further delimited the EIC's ability to directly hire or fire local workers, pay duties on goods brought off ship, and control the parameters of commercial contracts. In 1736, supercargo Andrew Reid warned the company directors about the potential power of the Co-Hong cartel over the sale of teas. Calling it a "Secret Combination," Reid and his colleagues pondered how "to prevent if possible, the Teas from falling into their Hands, & our being at their discretion for them."[70] The persistence of the Co-Hong and pressures from the EIC agents in Canton led to growing disagreements over contract provisions, taxes, credit, payments, and the quality of tea. For instance, when the Chinese emperor Qianlong (Ch'ien-Lung) liberalized imperial tax policy in 1736, including the abolition of a supplemental 10 percent tax on foreign silver entered for trade, the company agents and Canton merchants argued over who should benefit most from the reform. Supercargoes Andrew Reid, Charles Rigby, and Frederick Pigou delayed the receipt of their tea purchases, demanding a full rebate of the supplemental tax from merchants with whom they already held contracts. However, the Chinese merchants refused to return the remitted duties on any goods already purchased "on pretence that we did not stipulate it in our Contract."[71] More insulting to the company agents, Tsong-ton, the Hoppo who had announced the tax edict, insisted that all Europeans attend a reading of it and "prostrate themselves, kneeling on both their knees" in honor of the emperor. The Hoppo threatened them with "ill consequences . . . & possibly with an entire Exclusion from Commerce with China" if they refused to comply.[72] English merchants considered "kowtowing" too high a price to pay for doing business in the tightly regulated Chinese market.

The real price to pay for doing business, however, was a growing imbalance of trade with China. Although the EIC managed to establish a place for itself in the Canton system and to surpass other European companies in the purchase of tea, England had few export products that sold well on the Chinese market. When asked in 1734 "what sort of European or British Goods will sell best in China," the EIC agents found that only common lead found a market; English woolens, a staple in the Atlantic trade, fell flat in a country used to fine cottons and silk.[73] Clocks and curios worked well as presents for Mandarins and Hoppos, but the EIC agents had to ship vast amounts of silver bullion and coins to purchase goods in China. Although restricted in the seventeenth century, Charles II loosened English monetary policy after the Restoration, allowing the EIC and other traders to export silver bullion.[74] During the first decade of the eighteenth century, a total of £8,973,875 sterling was shipped to India, China, Japan, and Batavia to purchase goods.[75] Silver bullion made up 80 to 90 percent of all exports that the EIC carried to Canton in the first half of the eighteenth century.[76] This gave rise to a great fear that the nation's wealth would be depleted through foreign trade. Carew Reynell, a Whig economic writer of the late seventeenth century, worried that "to the *East-Indies* we carry nothing but ready Money, and bring in again nothing worth anything but Spices."[77]

Still, rather than draining the empire of wealth, as some political economists feared, silver gave the English commercial leverage in China. First, the EIC had to purchase silver and gold bullion for trade from London bankers, especially the Bank of England, or through European traders. For instance, the company purchased Spanish silver in Amsterdam to settle accounts with Lisbon and Cádiz merchants. Silver also made its way to India directly from Mexico via Manila, or the EIC minted its own silver coins in Bombay and Madras, which the company then exchanged for tea and silks in China.[78] Indeed, from the mid-sixteenth century Spanish silver flowed through Manila to the Portuguese at Macao, then on to the EIC in India, which fueled the expansion of Chinese commercial markets. By the eighteenth century, silver had become the most important commodity for the Chinese market, commanding prices that were 50 percent higher than in European markets, which helped compensate merchants for the cost of shipping goods to Asia.[79] Thus, silver became a necessary incentive to the production and distribution networks for tea. Chinese merchants had to advance cash (sometimes up to 70 or 80 percent of the cost) to growers in the countryside when they ordered tea for the coming trade season. In contracts with the EIC agents, they demanded advance payments or loans to pay off government officials and buy product for sale in Canton. In its efforts to corner the tea markets, the EIC, courting the cooperation of Co-Hong merchants, at times prepaid up to 50 percent of the negotiated contract price.[80] In 1734, for instance, EIC agents agreed to advance Tingua "a Couple of Chests of Treasure which he said at this juncture would be of great service to him in buying up the Hyson Tea in the country." Whereas prepaying a contract provided assurances to tea producers and stabilized the price of tea to some extent, the EIC also used loans and advances to leverage contract concessions from Chinese merchants. The cash advance to Tingua in 1734 was made to "facilitate his Complyance with the Contract."[81] Throughout the 1730s, as it attempted to corner the tea market, the EIC hoped to both placate and frustrate the Co-Hong.

Far from fulfilling the mercantilist aspirations of dominating foreign trade, by the 1740s the EIC struggled with logistical and financial problems. The company's government-sanctioned trade monopoly may have cut down on competition, and using cash to purchase goods may have given it leverage with Canton merchants, but commercial entanglements in China, especially the prolonged attempt to corner the tea market, proved a double-edged sword. Indeed, tea had quickly become the commodity that the EIC relied on for its survival, a commodity that helped fund its expansion into South Asia and China. Easily transported, relatively durable, and one of the most profitable commodities available in the East Indies, tea had risen to between 20 and 40 percent of all the company's Asia trade by midcentury, with millions of pounds imported annually.[82] Yet, the proliferation of tea in the early eighteenth century came at a price. As the EIC alienated competing European merchant companies, faced a rising tide of smuggled goods, and lost reexport markets in Holland and Germany, it found itself burdened with far more tea than it could possibly sell in England alone. Strangely, the company continued to pursue adamantly a monopoly on tea, even as a glut of product filled its warehouses. The directors instructed agents in Canton for the 1732 trade season to keep any discussion of "our Marketts in England being over stock'd with green tea" private, especially from the Chinese, yet suggested that the supercargoes still "make as brisk an enquiry after green tea now as when it was at its highest demand in England."[83] The EIC feared a glut would erode profits, so it attempted to raise the sale price artificially by withholding surplus tea from sale, usually for an average of seventeen months, and setting minimum prices for teas at auction. Perhaps the EIC directors determined that if they created a demand for tea, they could retain their commercial interests in China. With a warehouse full of "engrossed" tea on hand, the company turned to the maturing British colonies across the Atlantic to find Hakluyt's promised new markets to "vente" its goods.

CHAPTER TWO

The Rise of a "Tea-fac'd Generation"

> Many who are crying out against wheat at 6 or 7 s. a bushel, will
> give up a pound of bread, rather than a quarter of an ounce of
> tea, or *afternoon's amusement in drinking* this infatuating drug . . .
> Yet it is amazing how the people are tea-bitten, and become as
> tenacious of drinking this infusion, as a mad dog to avoid
> drinking at all.
> —*Jonas Hanway,* Letters on the Importance of the Rising
>   Generation of the Laboring Part of our Fellow-Subjects

As tea flooded London markets in the 1720s and 1730s, merchants pressured their American correspondents to buy it, releasing thousands of pounds on the American marketplace. But did Americans want to drink this new beverage? Could they afford to buy it? The first half of the eighteenth century proved pivotal for the tea trade, as merchants and their customers began to participate in a nascent consumer revolution. American merchants, encouraged by their London correspondents, embraced tea—sometimes as consumers themselves—but they also saw great opportunity in and potential profit from its sale. American customers, however, were more reticent about tea; they had to get used to it, to learn how to brew it and how to drink it. Only after oversupply forced merchants to lower the price of tea in the late 1730s and early 1740s did reluctant Americans start to love it. The shift from oversupply to demand paralleled an emerging debate over tea's physiological and cultural effects in the early eighteenth century. Contemporary critics like Jonas Hanway, noting a growing usage of the commodity, raised moral questions about how much people should consume, or if they should drink it at all. As part of a growing "luxury debate," the critique of tea and its effects often targeted laborers, the poor, and women—those who, amid more readily available and cheaper goods, could afford small luxuries for the first time. Although framing their criticism as moral concern for the physical and spiritual well-being of others, the elite more likely disdained the aspirational consumption that placed their less fortunate neighbors on equal footing in the marketplace. Paradoxically, American consumers were both a driving force in the British commercial empire and a scapegoat for its critics, who drew on the language of virtue to rein in the supposed excesses of the individual consumer. In this respect, the rise in consumption was less a "revolution" than an evolution; tea drinking, like other consumer spending, required gradual habituation and the right market conditions to become widespread.

By the early eighteenth century, American colonists, along with their English brethren, were beginning to purchase a new world of goods. Despite the myth of self-sufficiency, Americans depended on imports for most durable nonconsumable items, which they could not produce themselves.[1] The economic historian Carole Shammas estimates that during the early decades of the eighteenth century colonists spent as much as 30 percent of their income on imports, most of them consumer commodities, and thus often looked abroad for clues to market trends.[2] New amenities such as kitchen- and tableware, ceramic dishes, and silverware eased food preparation and intake; wool, linen, and cotton textiles enhanced personal appearance; and mahogany furniture, clocks, and books filled ever-larger domestic spaces. And, of course, during the first half of the eighteenth century, commercial expansion and rising colonial prosperity opened an avenue for the proliferation of exotic consumables from various parts of the world.

The spread of consumer goods in America began in urban areas, especially among the merchant class and those with access to commercial markets. Philadelphia, a key colonial entrepôt that received and distributed goods of the British Empire, benefited from trade and became home to a growing number of successful merchants and shopkeepers who not only introduced consumer items to Americans but often took the lead in their use, publicly displaying their new wealth. For example, Peter Baynton, a merchant and sometime ship captain who dealt in coastal transportation of staples like wood, flour, tar, and pitch, ordered six silver teaspoons and a pair of tea tongs for himself in May 1724.[3] During the 1720s, new fabrics, silks from China, "sundry India Goods," "Japans," silver ware, snuffboxes, chocolate, saffron, and, of course, tea and the equipage used to prepare and drink it began to appear in Philadelphia shops and houses.[4] A city of nearly fourteen thousand in midcentury, Philadelphia boasted a vibrant economy and commercial trade; it had a busy and prosperous merchant class who traded furs, timber, and agricultural produce for British goods, either directly or through credit exchange with southern Europe or West Indian purchasers of provisions.[5] Even less wealthy colonists enjoyed access to consumer markets. Urban artisans and tradespeople, perhaps aspiring to imitate the elite, began to purchase small luxuries as goods became more readily available and affordable.[6]

Beyond the city, farmers and rural communities also participated in global market economies.[7] Inventories of southern New England rural households reveal a wealth of amenities appearing during the early decades of the eighteenth century, whether families were rich, middling, or poor. By midcentury nearly 40 percent of the richest households had silverware, but so did 10.3 percent of the poorest households; 72.8 percent of the richest households used imported foods, such as pepper, spices, tea, or chocolate, as did 44.4 percent of the poorest.[8] Country traders, peddlers, and small shopkeepers helped distribute goods into the hinterlands. During the 1720s, inhabitants of small towns throughout New England could buy silk ribbons and threads, lace, fine buttons, handkerchiefs, cottons and calicos from India, and other "smole trifles" that brightened the appearance of once-dour Puritans.[9] Even in the Philadelphia countryside, farmers, who "commonly raise Wheat, Rye, Indian Corn, and Tobacco; and have store of Horses, Cows and Hoggs," had access to an increasing number of consumer goods. William Becket, who lived 150 miles outside Philadelphia, contended that despite the enormous markup on the cost of goods, his neighbors sold their produce "to purchase such European or West India Commodities as they want for their families use."[10]

At the turn of the eighteenth century, new consumer goods started to permeate the southern colonies as well. As Virginia gentry strove to imitate their English counterparts, tea and teaware began to show up in estate inventories, accelerating in the decades after 1710, first in the wealthiest households but then spreading to people of lesser estates.[11] Whether urban or rural, whether middling families or the poor, by the 1730s colonists in the Chesapeake and other regions of the South became owners and consumers of what were once nonessential items.[12] In 1738, Robert Pringle, a Scottish merchant in Charleston, South Carolina, ordered a large quantity of "Single reffin'd Loaf Sugar," several canisters of Bohea tea, pepper, spices, chinaware, and a punch bowl from a London correspondent; he often traded in textiles, gunpowder, paper, and hats. Pringle also resold goods on 5–10 percent commission for friends in Philadelphia and London, thus helping to circulate and recirculate new consumer goods.[13]

Tea, of course, was an important commodity for the growing consumer trade as well as for the political economy; it tied Britain to Asia and provided a medium of exchange across the Atlantic. However, for the first three decades of the eighteenth century the supply of tea greatly outpaced consumer

TABLE 2.1
EIC Tea Reexported to the American Colonies and Ireland,
1700–1750 (in lbs.)

Date	American Colonies (mainland and Caribbean)	Ireland
1700–1705	1,983	1,783
1706–1710	2,236	7,174
1711–1715	9,601	26,772
1716–1720	18,165	51,515
1721–1725	43,301	213,353
1726–1730	106,815	218,243
1731–1735	204,354	383,643
1736–1740	459,779	708,613
1741–1745	763,527	1,103,692
1746–1750	653,163	636,775

Source: Compiled from Great Britain, Board of Customs & Excise, Ledgers of Imports and Exports, 1696–1780, in the Public Records Office (PRO), London, reels 3–31. Data are missing for years 1705, 1712, and 1727. G. N. Clark, *Guide to English Commercial Statistics, 1696–1782* (London: Offices of the Royal Historical Society, 1938), 33–34, gives a good overview of PRO customs data, indicating that the records are more accurate for the quantity and weight of goods than for the value of goods. See also John J. McCusker and Russell R. Menard, *The Economy of British America, 1607–1789* (1985; rev. ed., Chapel Hill: University of North Carolina Press, 1991), 73–75.

demand, forcing the East India Company and its London agents to create a new market for tea at the colonial fringes of empire in North America and Ireland. The EIC, which accumulated increasing amounts of tea in warehouse during its attempts to corner the Canton market, turned first to Ireland as an outlet for the excess supply, especially as the European reexport market dried up (table 2.1). Between 1721 and 1725, English merchants reexported 213,353 pounds of EIC tea to Ireland, more than four times as much as the previous five years. During the subsequent five-year period, an additional 218,243 pounds reached Irish markets, and by the late 1730s reexportation of tea to Ireland had more than tripled. Reexports to the mainland and Caribbean American colonies, by contrast, increased more gradually, doubling every five years before leveling off in the mid-1740s. Interestingly, and pertinent to the question of consumer demand, reexports to the American colonies reached parity with those to Ireland by midcentury, even though the North American population remained about a third of Ireland's.[14]

The EIC focused on moving excess supplies of tea rather than fulfilling existing demand during the 1720s and 1730s for both economic and geopolitical reasons. Consider the context of the company's commercial activities and the intentions of merchant agents who purchased tea. First, the EIC was not involved in retail business. It had no reason to understand consumers, nor did it have a mechanism for responding to their demands, which the company left to private merchants, shopkeepers, and others who bought its goods at auction.[15] The EIC's Madras Council, which controlled the China trade, often lacked clear instructions from the Court of Directors in London and had to make judgments about purchasing tea for British markets from a distance. Only after tea shipments reached London could the company assess and manage its supply. During the early decades of the eighteenth century, the directors repeatedly voiced concerns about increasing amounts of surplus tea, even while insisting that company agents buy all available supply. As early as the 1715–16 season, the Court of Directors in London instructed EIC agents in Madras "to send no ship directly for China out and home because our markets are over-glutted with Tea as well by what we have in warehouse."[16] The EIC subsequently placed restrictions on private trade by ship captains and supercargoes, threatening to seize and forfeit any surplus tea company agents tried to bring home.[17] In the 1720s, the EIC worried far more about competition from European trade companies and the rise of smuggling across the Channel from French and Dutch suppliers than it did about the needs or desires of consumers. By the 1730s the Dutch had reestablished direct trade with China, which undermined the English reexport market to Holland and provided cheaper tea for the illegal trade. In response, the EIC lowered the auction price of Bohea to 5 shillings per pound, but excessive amounts of tea again clogged the London market, compelling the directors to warn agents in China that company warehouses contained at least two to three years worth of tea.[18] Paradoxically, the Dutch also had imported superfluous amounts of tea, overwhelming their own markets on the continent. The Dutch merchants Jacob Senserf & Son of Rotterdam lamented to their English partner Thomas Hall in 1731 that tea was hardly "worthwhile to engage in . . . at present as long as Europe is so vastly filled with said commodity."[19]

The corporate decision to "engross" Chinese tea in the 1720s and 1730s had lasting effects on the supply and pricing of tea at home. The EIC hoped that British colonial markets would provide new avenues for tea sales and potential profits for traders on both sides of the Atlantic. Still, the merchants who saw great opportunity in the sale of tea had to educate the public, to whet their appetite for an initially unfamiliar commodity. American merchants, for example, worked with their London correspondents to find marketing tricks that might make tea more attractive to or convenient for potential customers. Newspaper advertisements for East India goods, including tea, appeared for the first time in the 1720s. Philadelphia's *American Weekly Mercury* originally listed tea as one of many commodities in its "price currant" but then began to carry more specific announcements for it. In 1720, Andrew Bradford promoted the sale of "Super Fine Bohea Tea at 22 shillings per pound," in his Philadelphia store.[20] Peter Baynton lured customers in 1727 with "Choice Bohea Tea, and Mackrill newly imported and Double and Single refined Loaf-Sugar."[21] In 1738, Robert Strettell sold "Bohea Tea in Pound Cannisters" to make it more convenient for individual customers.[22] Boston traders, like those in Philadelphia, also dabbled in tea, and by the 1730s they were promoting their wares in local newspapers. Simple statements in the *Boston News-Letter* of 1730 informed consumers that Samuel Sleigh could provide "Excellent good Bohea Tea, lately Imported from London." Or that Mrs. Hannah Willard sold "Good Green and Bohea Tea, China Ware, and double refined Sugar."[23] While basic Bohea and green teas were most common, occasionally consumers could obtain "fine Imperial Green Tea."[24] Not until the late 1730s did American retailers and merchants begin to distinguish more varieties of tea, indicating gradations of green teas, such as fine Hyson and Singlo, or black teas beyond Bohea, such as Congou and Pekoe.[25] Longer advertisements with mixed font styles and woodblock illustrations became more common at midcentury, and handbills, broadsides, or almanac advertising supplemented newspapers. Merchants could not rely on demand alone to sell tea or any other foreign import; they had to entice potential customers to purchase their goods instead of a rival's.[26]

Indeed, during the 1720s and 1730s, American merchants showed more enthusiasm for tea than their customers did. By the early eighteenth century, colonial merchants sought goods, such as tea, which were portable, easy to transport and sell. Despite a confusing tangle of tax duties applied to the product, tea usually sold for "ready money" or on short credit (one to three months).[27] A lack of currency and the vagaries of credit could undo an otherwise solvent business; ready cash sales could assure a merchant's future commercial health. In October 1721, Thomas Lawrence complained to London agent Samuel Storke that Philadelphia had "neither money nor Creditt nor bills, ye Currant Cash of this place is so Clean gone that many people find itt Difficult to buy there dayly provisions," and he feared that his customers might turn to neighboring New York for cheaper goods.[28] The 1730s brought no relief to cash and credit markets. American merchants and shopkeepers often had to accept local produce such as pork, beef, dried cod, deerskins, bread, or flour in exchange for English goods. And, in turn, they had difficulty remitting payments to British suppliers, because London merchants often refused to take colonial produce in exchange for mercantile debts.[29]

Tea, however, provided merchants some liquidity and mobility of assets that may have been tied up longer if placed in financial instruments such as bills of exchange, letters of credit, or other products. John Reynell, a Philadelphia merchant, helped fellow Quaker Jane Fenn order a parcel of tea from London in November 1737. She submitted a series of credit instruments, including credit from the sale of a previous parcel tea, a bill of exchange for £35 and one for over £18, for which she asked English merchant John Hayward to "Invest in right good Bohea Tea" to be sent "the first Opportunity," along with an additional "parcel of Bohea & Green Tea on thy own Account," which she promised to sell on commission.[30] Fenn, at the time a single woman, then recruited the assistance of Reynell's partner and brother-in-law, Samuel Coates, to sell the tea on her behalf.[31] In this manner, she managed to convert book credit from London, a bill of exchange drawn on a third party, and a bill of exchange in her own name into a commodity that could yield ready cash income for her as she sold it in the colonies. Tea proved marketable, if not profitable, for some American merchants even during the economic volatility of the early eighteenth century. Between 1727, when he first arrived in Philadelphia, and 1747, Samuel Powel, a dedicated tea seller, worked as agent for three London firms—David Barclay & Sons, Thomas Hyam, and Benjamin & William Bell—usually commanding a commission of 5–10 percent on tea he sold at a nearly 100 percent markup for ready cash.[32] Boston merchant account books also indicate active tea orders, sales, and profits. Between late summer 1735 and 1751, Thomas Boylston and his son sold more than 1,500 pounds of tea in their busy Boston dry goods and grocery shop, bringing in £4,558 and making nearly £800 in profit from tea alone.[33]

Still, as the importation of EIC tea increased during the early decades of the eighteenth century, colonial merchants experienced familiar cycles of surplus and scarcity that plagued the company. Oversupply heightened problems with the flow of cash and credit, raising further questions about the nature and timing of consumer demand. As early as 1728 Samuel Powel felt the effects of commercial volatility: "our place is so extreamly overdone with English Goods," he complained to a London supplier, "that the pay is Grown so bad there is no doing any business with Creditt."[34] Throughout the 1730s, Powel grumbled to various correspondents that tea was, at times, a "drug" on the market and they should send no more. In November 1731 he warned Thomas

Hyam, "our Town has Tea Enough for these two years they say there is of last years Importation near 2000 lbs."[35] Two years later he complained to David Barclay, "Our town is so exceedingly overdone with tea that 'twill sell at no rate."[36] "I have Retailed a few Pounds of thy Tea," Powel protested to Benjamin Bell in March 1735, but "almost all of it un Paid for tis at Present a very Dull Comodity."[37] A month later, Powel noted that "there are now so many tea sellers here that the price is Run Down next to Nothing."[38] Jane Fenn also experienced the downside of surplus tea. Her 1737 order arrived "to a very Dull market" in Philadelphia, and over the next six months she "sold but little of it." She assured London merchant John Hayward that she would "Dispose of it as fast as I can," although in July 1738 she was still unable to send him remittance for her half of the original order.[39]

Besides excess inventory, inflated prices and unreliable quality also dampened the American merchant's ability to sell tea and further complicated the relationship between English supplier and American consumer. Many colonial merchants complained that London correspondents charged too much up front, forcing them to raise the retail price. Jane Fenn realized this only after she received her shipment; in light of a competitive tea market, she accused Hayward that he "has charg'd it rather too high, for it has been shipt by others Cheaper & believe full as good."[40] Product cost and pricing, in particular, fueled disagreements between American and London merchants. Samuel Powel complained in September 1735 that he had only sold about 240 pounds of Benjamin Bell's recent shipment of Bohea tea.[41] Four years later, Powel again grumbled, "I have sold but a few Pounds of yours" at 7 shillings a pound and would prefer to charge 6 shillings "tho your Letter seems to Expect more."[42] Of course, London suppliers had little control over the uncertain quality of product. The tea that Chinese merchants had pawned off to the EIC during its attempts to "engross" the market in the 1720s and 1730s, as well as the cheaper Bohea tea favored by Dutch smugglers, had begun to trickle into American markets. In 1735, Abigail Franks, wife of New York merchant Jacob Franks, complained to her son Naphtali in London that the green tea they received from merchants Simpson and Levy was "not worth drinking."[43] Although the supply of reexported tea to America undoubtedly rose prior to 1740 (see tables 2.1 and 2.2) and colonists participated in the consumption of luxury goods made available by Atlantic trade, the demand for tea by Americans still lagged behind the stock. In 1733 Powel agreed with Benjamin Bell's observation "that the Consumption of these Comidtys Increase in America." But he warned that "for some time Past the consumption

TABLE 2.2
EIC Tea Reexported to Select American Colonies, 1700–1750 (in lbs.)

Date	New England	New York	Pennsylvania	Maryland, Virginia, Carolinas, and Georgia	West Indies
1700–1705	40	35	6	56	1,847
1706–1710	186	82	8	104	1,947
1711–1715	530	649	106	1,681	6,637
1716–1720	1,117	2,213	216	4,135	10,529
1721–1725	3,927	8,620	236	10,194	20,175
1726–1730	15,686	25,156	2,349	21,802	41,872
1731–1735	26,028	44,809	6,857	63,536	63,124
1736–1740	53,404	145,281	23,227	90,074	147,793
1741–1745	99,123	264,661	49,670	137,924	212,149
1746–1750	93,102	176,478	104,786	108,418	170,379

Source: Compiled from Great Britain, Board of Customs & Excise, Ledgers of Imports and Exports, 1696–1780, in the Public Records Office, London, reels 3–31.

hath been vastly Less than the Importation. Here is now in town some thousand pounds value in tea. I suppose enough for 2 or 3 years."[44] The hope of profit and the lure of ready cash prompted merchants to order increasing amounts of tea from London. However, the persistent complaints about oversupply, the cost of product, and the reluctance of customers to pay the inflated retail price suggest that demand for tea had not yet caught up with inventory.

As tea became more readily available in America, more merchants entered the business, drawn by the potential profit. The increased intercolonial commercial competition, including an emergent smuggling trade, further squeezed retail prices. Samuel Powel, for instance, noted that a "variable" influx of tea into Philadelphia in the spring of 1734 "is thrust in here from the Islands, New England and [New] York in very large quantities."[45] The reexportation figures from England bear out Powel's observations on source and distribution, pointing to New York City as Philadelphia's toughest commercial rival for tea. According to British customs records, Pennsylvania merchants ordered relatively little tea directly from Great Britain until the late 1730s, far less than other colonial regions (table 2.2). Their tea supply, then, either came from legitimate or illegitimate sources shipped via New York or New England. Powel, a Quaker, simply blamed "outsiders" for hurting his business, noting in 1737, for instance, that the average sale price of Bohea tea had slid precipitously. Priced as high as 50 shillings per pound in the early 1720s, by the mid-1730s tea usually retailed for about 10 shillings per pound in Philadelphia, but Powel complained that it was sold for as little as 7 shillings 6 pence "by a Jew who has large Quantitys from another Jew of London, and 'tis a rule with them to undersell every body Else."[46] Most likely referring to fellow Philadelphia merchants David Franks and his uncle Nathan Levy, who were supplied by family in New York and London, Powel protested again several years later that "tea is drove in by the Jews of NYK in such prodigious Quantities that it never was so plenty and they will sell for almost any price they are bid."[47]

By the mid-1730s, New York merchants imported as much tea from England as the British Caribbean colonies, surpassing the rate of purchase in the southern colonies. In addition, tea came directly to New York from Amsterdam or the Dutch West Indies. New York merchants easily commanded enough tea to transship any excess to Philadelphia, at times oversupplying the market there. In 1737, Samuel Powel was unable to sell his latest tea shipment from London because "a great deal comes over land from New York and it is in so great a Number of Hands who are Continually undermining one another on the Price."[48] New York merchants sold Bohea tea at 5 shillings a pound and green tea at 8 shillings by 1738, undercutting Powel's attempts to retail his Bohea at more than 7 shillings per pound. He tried to attract more customers by extending short-term credit for cash sales to six or twelve months (instead of three) and at times kept his tea from market, hoping to create demand for it at a higher price.[49] Yet commercial competition and its negative impact on tea stock and prices did not stop Powel from ordering "a little more good green at a low Price" or "a small parcel of good rough imperial" from his London suppliers.[50] Tea provided American merchants some liquidity for their assets through relatively easy sale. Still, merchants searched endlessly for the delicate balance between cost and price that might whet the appetite of fickle or reluctant consumers.

Although demand did not necessarily precipitate the influx of tea from London, the subsequent glut proved a boon to American consumers and helped to habituate them to its taste. As the supply of tea and commercial competition grew in the 1730s, the price of tea dropped. By the early 1740s, its use had undeniably increased. But measuring increased use proves difficult when consumption figures are slippery at best. The demand for and consumption of tea was not necessarily equivalent to known supply or shipment, as some scholars have assumed.[51] Instead, examples of the ways that tea came into usage, how it was consumed, and by whom better demonstrate the relationship between supply and demand. Whether in New England, New York, Phil-

The Tea Party, ca. 1727. Richard Collins's painting depicts a fashionable young family at tea, which included porcelain cups without handles and an extensive silver tea set with canister, spoon boat, sugar dish, tongs, and warming platform for the teapot. The family appears relaxed and comfortable with the relatively new consumer activity. Another version of this painting, at the Victoria and Albert Museum in London, presents the family in a more formal posture without the young girl in the foreground. The Goldsmiths' Company, used with permission.

adelphia, Virginia, or South Carolina, colonial merchants supplied customers with tea, but they also had to provide the equipment needed to brew and drink it. During the early decades of the eighteenth century, when tea was expensive, only the elite could afford the leaf, let alone the special pots (most often silver or porcelain), caddies, and strainers for its preparation. These wealthy consumers only gradually adopted tea as "the preeminent genteel ritual," as one historian has called it. The presentation of tea for drinking called for proper teacups and saucers, silver spoons, and spoon trays, not to mention a porcelain bowl for sugar to be lifted with silver tongs to the cup. The warm liquid would then be diluted with milk or cream in its special vessel. And all the implements would be arranged nicely on a tea table.[52]

For British and American colonial elites, tea slowly became a daily ritual that punctuated a new leisure life marked by entertainments, visitations, and public celebrations. By the mid-eighteenth century tea had also become a staple for a surprising number of working people. But did the "lower sort" seek out tea from local shopkeepers as a means to imitate the lifestyle of their wealthier neighbors? Certainly as it became cheaper, it could have been a small luxury that represented aspirational consumption for some. More likely, however, tea was introduced to poorer consumers gradually through an exchange economy that paired customer book credit with shopkeeper commodities. Since hard currency was scarce, merchants usually kept running accounts for artisans and laborers, who often exchanged work for goods in kind. Merchants used consumables on hand, such as sugar, tea, or rum, to pay for work performed. By the 1730s in Boston, for instance, tea figured prominently for workers like bricklayer Samuel Brooks and barber Phillip Audeburt, who received tea regularly in exchange for their labor or, as in Audeburt's case, "By wiggs & Shaveing."[53] In early 1738, Thomas Boylston gave Benjamin Clough tea in exchange for an anchor; the following year Boylston paid Joseph Jackson, a milliner, some tea and other groceries for beaver hats.[54] Merchant Benjamin Greene noted in his Boston account books when artisans exchanged labor for tea as well. James Boyer, a jeweler, mended "a pair of Earrings" and exchanged "2 Mourning Rings" for goods including "1 pair of Tea Tongs" in October 1736 and for several pounds of tea in the fall of 1738.[55] Laborers chopped wood, mended clothing, built furniture, and shaped brass in exchange for tea.[56] Even the very poor drank tea. In 1738, New York's poorhouse spent 13.8 percent of its budget on sugar and caffeinated drinks, a much larger portion of total expenditures than its English counterpart, St. Andrew Holborn Workhouse, which spent only 4.5 percent on similar consumables in 1732.[57]

In fact, sugar and caffeinated beverages were becoming important parts of institutional as well as family budgets by the mid-eighteenth century. Whereas smuggling helped make cheap inventory of sugar and tea available, sugar made an otherwise bitter drink more palatable for European and American tastes. Indeed, the consumption of tea and sugar most likely rose together as both became more readily available and less expensive. Sugar prices dropped precipitously over the course of the seventeenth century, and by 1700 sugar consumption in Europe had risen to 4 pounds per capita per year, up from 2 pounds just forty years earlier. By 1720 Europeans consumed about 8 pounds of sugar per capita per year.[58] For American consumers, the price of British sugar declined between 1700 and the early 1730s, falling from over 50 shillings to around 10 shillings per hundredweight wholesale. The Molasses Act of 1733 had even greater effect on availability and price in North America, since it prompted a sharp rise in smuggling of sugar, molasses, and rum from less expensive French and Dutch Caribbean sources.[59] Similarly, the consumption of tea rose as the cost declined. Although it is nearly impossible to estimate how much tea the British purchased or drank, since illegal sales are not included in importation figures, some sources indicate that during the 1730s, the English and Welsh consumed about a half pound of tea per capita per year; this figure rose to at least 1 pound annually during the following decade.[60] At the same time, historians have placed annual consumption of tea in the British colonies at under a half pound per person, even though eighteenth-century observers estimated that by midcentury American consumers drank more than 2 pounds of tea a year, at least one cup a day.[61] By the late 1730s, with pressure from smugglers and nearby merchant competition, Bohea tea retailed in the mid-Atlantic for about 7 shillings per pound.

Gradual habituation and the addictive nature of sweetened caffeine created a growing demand for tea. The increase in consumer spending, however, presented a paradox to eighteenth-century society. Luxury consumption, which stimulated commercial empires, also raised questions and doubts about the consequences of human appetites. Skeptics asked whether luxury goods and new consumer activities could degrade individuals' moral virtues. Commercial success, the English came to believe, had a moral cost. Even if the laboring class did not aspire to imitate their betters by drinking tea, the elite worried incessantly that luxury goods, which had marked them as different, would do damage in the hands of the lower sort of consumer. Thus, it became important to regulate not the commercial markets themselves but the selfishness, irrationality, and appetites aroused by the proliferation of luxury commodities. British and colonial elites fretted that the new amenities of life would make men lazy; rather than putting idle men to work, as Richard Hakluyt had promised in the 1580s, consumption of foreign goods threatened to make working men idle.[62]

Seventeenth-century moralists accepted economic activity as part of God's larger providential plan. They worried, however, that increased commercial activity might lead to excessive acquisitiveness and dishonest practices, such as usury, that would harm society as a whole. Merchants might abuse credit, an essential component of their business, to the jeopardy of an individual's spiritual well-being.[63] Even Thomas Mun, a director of the EIC who championed the aggressive expansion of foreign trade, expressed concern that consumption of luxury items had deleterious effects. "The general leprosie of our piping, potting, feasting, fashion, and the mis-spending of our time in idleness and pleasure," Mun asserted, "hath made us effeminate in our bodies, weak in our knowledge, poor in our treasure, declined in our valour, unfortunate in our enterprises, and condemned by our enemies."[64] Social commentators of the eighteenth century still expressed concern that the growth of commercial markets might tempt individuals into sin. New Englanders, in particular, as heirs of the Puritans, wrestled with human behavior and its moral consequences. Early eighteenth-century jeremiads noted that accidents or natural disasters could be signs of economic misbehavior and idleness. After a *"Terrible Fire,"* Cotton Mather warned Bostonians in 1711 that to labor simply in order to buy things was vanity: *"O Uncertain Riches! O Deceitful Riches! What Fool will Trust in you!"*[65] The great New England earthquake of 1727 became an opportunity for clergy to warn congregations about the sins of "pride manifested in luxury and idleness."[66] By the 1720s and 1730s, with a proliferation of consumer goods, Boston newspapers regularly condemned "Luxury," "the Pleasures of Taste," "Superfluities," and "Extravigance in Apparel, and Luxury at our Tables" as equivalent to ungodliness and counter to God's plan.[67] Even though newspapers closely followed the business news of the day—stock prices, shipping news, and commodity sales—they criticized the consumption of foreign trade goods.

Generally, however, the eighteenth century brought less moralizing about consumer behavior and more modernizing of the economic lexicon. Terms such as "profit," "desire," "luxury," and "credit," once suspect for their negative implications, were redefined to neutralize moral overtones and to encourage or justify participation in the marketplace. Bernard Mandeville, in *The Fable of the Bees* (1714), most famously commented on the "Publick Benefits" of "Private Vices." He warned that self-denial could damage national prosperity by taking money out of circulation and slowing production; buying clothing, gloves, shoes, coaches, and imported commodities gave jobs to tailors, carpenters, dressmakers, and shopkeepers. "Frugality is, like Honesty, *a mean starving Virtue,*" Mandeville insisted, "that is only fit for small Societies of good peaceable Men, who are contented to be poor so they may be easy."[68] Similarly articulating a kind of early modern trickle-down theory, James

Steuart, in his midcentury essay "Of Luxury," maintained that the pursuit of luxury and consumption of harmless "superfluities" helped entire communities, rather than just individuals, because it gave "employment and bread to the industrious."[69] Whereas "ancient luxury" came at the expense of other people, "Modern luxury is *systematical*," he argued, employing a great number of people who manufactured goods but also were potential consumers.[70]

Still, tension remained between a modern concept of luxury's virtue and the perceived moral deficiencies that came with increased consumption, especially among the laboring class. Daniel Defoe, while an advocate of merchants and the commercial marketplace, expressed much more ambivalence about new consumer expenditure. He pointed out that what looked like economic virtue might, in fact, contain the seeds of moral downfall. He lamented that even though drinking ale or wearing elaborate and expensive fashions could provide a livelihood to grain farmers, brewers, spinners, weavers, and tailors, excessive use of spirits and fashionable goods could simultaneously take the food out of the mouths of "thousands of families" and turn them into beggars.[71] The proliferation of Chinese goods in the British Empire and increased interest in chinoiserie during the early eighteenth century often intersected with this ambivalent anxiety about luxury consumption. Anglo consumers bought textiles and chinaware covered with Asian design motifs, shaped their gardens based on fanciful Chinese landscapes, peppered their plays with Chinese characters, and even found republican virtue in Confucianism. Although Defoe thought China trade extremely important to the English economy, he also worried about the impact of exotic Chinese goods and ideas. By the 1720s, he had become somewhat hostile to Asia's role in foreign trade, depicting the Chinese in his works as petty, elite tyrants burdened by unbridled appetites.[72]

Tea, a seemingly innocuous luxury item, often figured prominently in the eighteenth century luxury debates. Indeed, the "Tea Table" as locus of luxury consumption and the presumed negative physical "properties of tea" concerned many on both sides of the Atlantic. More than any other beverage, tea became associated with luxury and the decline of individual virtue by the early eighteenth century. The Chinese had long considered tea as a cure for gout, indigestion, and "all Crudities from the Stomach," but European critics tended to be more skeptical of its medicinal applications.[73] In the early eighteenth century, the French writer Pierre Pomet conceded that tea had "a great many good Qualities, for it lightens and refreshes the Spirits, suppresses Vapours, prevents and drives away Drowsiness, strengthens the Brain and Heart, hastens Digestion, provokes Urine, cleanses or purifies the Blood, and is proper against the Scurvy."[74] According to one essayist, tea was a panacea—good for head colds, stomach disorders, lethargy, and "well adopted for consumptive, thin, and hectic, Persons, or that have Coughs, or profuse draining Ulcers, or an acrid Humour in their Blood."[75] Yet others cautioned that tea had a narcotic nature, like opium, and must be used with care. John Coakley Lettsom's midcentury experiments with tea, including the injection of distilled green tea into frogs, led him to determine it had "relaxing and sedative" qualities, which may cause "great uneasiness, anxiety and oppression" if overused.[76]

Beyond its physical effects, critics feared that tea, as a luxury item, would have a corrupting influence on an individual's morals and work habits. Perhaps because lower and laboring classes had begun to drink more tea in the eighteenth century, critics insisted it would undermine the industry of the working poor. Jonas Hanway, a merchant turned philanthropist, devoted a dozen or more pages to "Interest of Money paid to Strangers, and the Consumption of Tea, some of the Causes of the Beggary and Distress of a Part of the People." Referring to tea as "this Chinese drug," he asserted that the universal habit of tea drinking impoverished workers, drove the smuggling trade, and would eventually "prove extremely hurtful to this nation."[77] Duncan Forbes, a Scottish theologian, thought that the low price of tea allowed the "*meanest* labouring Man" to purchase it. Combined with sugar "the inseparable Companion of Tea," the drink "came to be in the possession of the very poorest Housewife, where formerly it had been a great Rarity."[78] Methodist minister John Wesley thought that if poor people "would save just the Price of the Tea," they could lessen their poverty.[79] Still, caffeinated stimulants benefited workers by providing a boost in energy; Thomas Short extolled tea's "eminent and unequalled Power to take off, or prevent Drowsiness and Dulness, Damps and Clouds on the Brain, and intellectual Faculties."[80] Tea and sugar also suppressed appetites, masking the fact that lower classes had less money to spend on food.[81] By the 1740s, working folk had become habituated to both tea and sugar. They tended to buy small quantities of tea, usually one-quarter to one-half pound at three-to-six-month intervals, though proportionally they spent a great deal of their wages on these small indulgences.[82] When strapped for cash, people in the early modern world tended to do without food before giving up new luxuries such as tea, sugar, or chocolate.[83] Despite the constraints on income and resources, purchase and consumption of sugar and tea increased.

Title page, *The Tea Drinking Wife, and Drunken Husband* ([Newcastle upon Tyne?], 1749). Courtesy of the British Library, Eighteenth Century Collections Online.

Although churchmen and philanthropists tied tea drinking to working-class vice, in the English-speaking world of literature, tea and tea drinking, especially its negative aspects, had become almost exclusively linked with the female domain. Popular and literary culture painted a picture of idle, elite, or social-climbing women gathered around the tea table, gossiping and dishing out scandal with tea and cakes. Daniel Defoe condemned "the tea-table among the ladies, and the coffee-house among the men," as places where the reputations of all people were eviscerated "in the most unchristian manner in the world."[84] English poets of the early eighteenth century made use of tea and tea-table etiquette to add dramatic domestic touches to their verse. Nicholas Amhurst, in *Poems on Several Occasions* (1723), warned his readers, "The fair one too perhaps on thee, Smiles, as she tattles o'er her Tea." Christopher Pitt, in "The Fable of the Young Man and his Cat," from *Poems and Translations* (1727) described scandal and gossip over tea as a form of "Female Politicks." William Shenstone, in *Poems upon Various Occasions* (1737) depicted slovenly women arising "near the Noon of Day; When rising Nymphs their

Fancy aid With Scandal—and *Bohea*."[85] In the 1730s and 1740s, Allan Ramsay devoted an entire volume of verse and song to "Tea-Table Miscellany," chronicling the rise of "A Tea-fac'd Generation" pleased by "Av'rice, Luxury and Ease" and "refresh'd with Scandal and with Tea."[86]

Even if they were unfamiliar with English poetry, American colonists were very familiar with the notion of tea-table gossip and its negative association with women's behavior. Colonial newspapers mocked women in satire as the center of scandal, especially because of their supposed idleness around the tea table and its effect on the family economy. The editor of the *New-England Courant* in March 1725 noted that he had received several letters from men "fill'd with bitter Complaints of the Idleness of their Wives. Whether this Idleness proceeds from the growing Custom of Tea-Drinking, is best known to the Purses of their Husbands."[87] Some newspaper critiques were penned by men writing as women who behaved badly. In the 1730s, Benjamin Franklin used his newspaper, the *Pennsylvania Gazette*, and his public personae as "Poor Richard" to espouse the cultural criticism of his day. Under the name of Alice Addertongue, he published several letters moralizing on the behavior of women at the tea table. "*Scandal*, like other Virtues," Addertongue wrote, "is in part its own Reward, as it gives us the Satisfaction of making our selves appear better than others, or others no better than ourselves."[88] In 1738, *Poor Richard's Almanack* included a preface by "Mistress Bridget Saunders," in which *she* declared "that Poor Dick's Wife has lately taken a fancy to drink a little Tea now and then," insinuating that the beverage had been a gift from a printer who had more than business on his mind.[89] Even though a few countercommentaries surfaced in the 1730s, acknowledging that tea drinking had more positive effects on the consuming public than, for example, alcohol, popular media tended to condemn tea and the women who drank it.[90]

Women may have borne the brunt of criticism for tea's supposed failings, but tea traders could little afford to alienate women consumers, let alone female shopkeepers, innkeepers, and merchants. For even though women's "consuming nature" seemed to threaten patriarchal control of the purse strings and virtuous female behavior, in the 1720s and 1730s women were central to the growth and strength of commercial markets in the colonies. Unlike poets, merchants aimed to sell merchandise; thus, they appealed to women shoppers in their selection and sale of goods. The historian Carl Robert Keyes notes that advertisements in eighteenth-century Pennsylvania generally portrayed female customers in a good light.[91] For example, John Sacheverell, a Philadel-

phia engraver and shopkeeper, drew on positive images of tea drinking when
he advertised in early 1733 his recently imported white-metal pewter teapots,
teaspoons, tea stands, and saucepans for "all Lovers of Decency, Neatness and
TEA-TABLE DECORUM."[92] Women bought tea and other goods in their own
right for home consumption and for resale.[93] John Reynell, who helped Jane
Fenn purchase tea, sold goods to many female customers, including Ann
Chandler, Mary Flower, Elizabeth Jones, "Widow Farrel," and Sarah James,
who all bought tea in small amounts during the 1730s and 1740s.[94] Samuel
Coates Sr., who facilitated the sale of Jane Fenn's tea, also noted a number
of women who frequented his shop, including Sarah Shoemaker, Grace Lloyd,
Beulah Coates, and Ann Widifield.[95] One of Benjamin Greene's most devoted
customers from 1738 to 1740 was Elizabeth Cowell of Boston, whom he identified as "Mrs. Elizabeth Cowell Tavernkeeper." She purchased 44.25 pounds
of tea over the course of two years, between July 1738 and October 1740, presumably to offer it as libation to her own paying customers.[96] In eighteenth-
century Philadelphia, women ran as many as half of all retail shops.[97]

New commodities brought into American households by women introduced new daily habits, inspiring consumers to experiment. By the 1740s, tea
was a relatively cheap way for people of all classes to participate in luxury
consumption, and the aspirational aspects of tea drinking—to imitate those
people one might see as social betters—helped transform a luxury into a necessity. Eighteenth-century contemporaries freely observed this aspirational
consumption. Samuel Johnson noted that tradesmen and merchants in London sought to improve their status through acquisitions, especially of novel
items. He remarked that "every man, in surveying the shops of London, sees
numberless instruments and conveniences, of which, while he did not know
them, he never felt the need; and yet when use has made them familiar, won-
ders how life could be supported without them."[98] Adam Smith, at the end of
The Theory of Moral Sentiments, asserted that vanity drove human actions:
"It is not wealth that men desire, but the consideration and good opinion that
wait upon riches."[99] Even in the colonies, aspirational consumption was at
work. Dr. Alexander Hamilton, a keen observer of consumer behavior in his
travels through rural Delaware and Pennsylvania in 1744, noted that a scruffy
land speculator, William Morison, who wished to "pass for a gentleman,"
deemed himself superior to a tavern keeper because he owned "good linen, . . .
a pair of silver buckles, silver clasps, and gold sleeve buttons, two Holland
shirts, and some neat nightcaps; and that his little woman att home drank tea

twice a day."[100] In other words, gradual habituation, fed by an oversupply of tea, and human vanity gave rise to increased demand.

By the 1740s, the so-called consumer revolution was well under way, propelled by expanded foreign trade, and had brought new goods and desires to Great Britain and its Atlantic colonies. The luxury debates of the 1720s and 1730s hashed out growing suspicions about the personal and moral implications of consumption. Still, commodities that were at first condemned as frivolous, even morally dangerous, eventually became ubiquitous necessities, used by men and women, rich and poor. The critique of luxury consumption, however, did not disappear. The criticism of tea in particular lingered, but it shifted from the personal moral cost to the broader political and economic consequences of consumer behavior. In 1734, "John Trusty," writing to *The New-York Weekly Journal*, noted foreign trade's personal impact on the household economy; spending what little they had, people who could least afford the expense bought "Tea and China Ware," pawning "their Rings and Plate to gratifie themselves in that Piece of Extravagance."[101] By the 1740s, however, critics made more pointed connections between luxury consumption and the economic health of the body politic. In 1744, Scotsman Duncan Forbes condemned the purchase of tea and "foreign spirits," which ravaged the working-class soul and bankrupted the nation by "the *Waste* of *Bullion* . . . and with it our *Trade* and *Credit*, are gone."[102] Americans also worried about consumption and its impact on national and local economies. An essay, "The Prevalence of Luxury, with a Burgo-master's excellent Admonitions against it," circulated in papers throughout the colonies, warning New Yorkers, Marylanders, and Bostonians that consumer spending would impoverish the empire and increase public debt: "Luxury is to Property, what a Plague is to Health; that 'tis equally contagious, and equally destructive."[103] Some colonists even proposed a boycott on tea to alleviate the personal debt its purchase engendered. In August 1746 the *Boston Evening Post* published a letter that warned, "The present exorbitant Price of Tea" should give individuals pause about the "absurd and destructive Practice" of drinking it. The author proposed that Bostonians "form and encourage a *Subscription* or *Association* against the Use of *Tea* and *all foreign Luxury*, as was done in most of the *Towns* and *Boroughs* of the *South Part of Scotland* the last Year."[104] But not until the 1760s did American colonists articulate the costs of consumption in real political terms. Tea, a commodity that lay on the edge between desire and restraint, would prove a key component.

CHAPTER THREE

Politicizing American Consumption

COMMERCE! We do thy num'rous Blessings own,
Thou bring'st the Fruit of other Nations Home:
The Taste of hot *Arabia's* Spice we know,
Nor feel the scorching Sun that makes it grow:
Without the Worm in *Persian* Silks we shine,
And without Planting, drink of every Vine.
—*Nathaniel Ames,* An Astronomical Diary; or, Almanack
for the Year of our Lord Christ, 1762

Nathaniel Ames's verses on commerce from his 1762 *Astronomical Diary,* published in Boston, celebrated America's ability to reap the benefits of foreign trade without having to plant, cultivate, or produce the commodities of that trade. But even as the lines extolled the "num'rous Blessings" of global exchange and the subsequent consumption of "the Fruit of other Nations Home," Ames implied an interdependence between colonial consumers and a far-flung British trade system that made those goods available.[1] By midcentury, America's colonial economy had expanded to embrace the empire's world trade. Nathaniel Ames's New England, for instance, experienced a renaissance that transformed smaller towns, such as New London and Hartford, Connecticut; Portsmouth, New Hampshire; Salem and Marblehead, Massachusetts; and Providence, Rhode Island, into provincial cities.[2] Large commercial centers such as Boston also expanded their business districts and modes of communication, increasing accessibility to foreign goods. In 1743 Faneuil Hall became a central marketplace, and merchants turned coffeehouses and taverns into places of business. Colonial newspapers helped to convey information of interest to merchants who traded within the Atlantic world, but they also advertised their wares to a new generation of consumers.[3] New England merchants transformed their commercial practices as well, establishing broader networks of trade that crossed colonial boundaries and incorporated the West Indies. Caribbean sugar fed the increasingly important rum distillation industry, which in turn paid for rice from South Carolina or English goods from London. The advent of paper money and other instruments of credit also expanded American merchant opportunities in trade; it helped to circulate goods between colonies, helped local industry flourish, and drew New England into transnational networks of trade. Although personal income in the northern colonies was on the rise, the period between 1745 and 1760 also saw volatility in commodity prices, making the cost of buying, selling, and consuming tea and sugar, for instance, unpredictable.[4]

Similarly, Philadelphia experienced the ebb and flow of economic tides between the 1740s and the Seven Years' War. Philadelphia had become the preeminent port city of the colonies—a center for business and soon-to-be center for politics. The rising demand for American grain fueled its economy. Philadelphia merchants began to ship produce directly to the West Indies and southern Europe.[5] Success in the provisions trade during the 1740s and 1750s increased the money in circulation, driving wages up for laborers and allowing them to participate in the so-called consumer revolution. Commercial success and consumer purchases, however, were also financed through debt and a growing imbalance of trade. By midcentury, Benjamin Franklin estimated that Britain exported nearly £500,000 worth of goods to Pennsylvania, with less than £40,000 worth of American commodities shipped in return.[6] Although new credit instruments greatly eased the process of doing cross-Atlantic business, scarce hard cash and restrictions on paper currency contributed to the difficulty of collecting debts, paying creditors, and, in turn, managing the supply, flow, and distribution of consumer goods. In early 1749, London merchant John Hunt wrote Israel Pemberton Jr. that he had been informed Philadelphia "had great Plenty of European Goods, & we Imagine the same will continue unless your Demand be very large." He worried that importing "such vast quantities of Goods" would affect the English economy because American merchants would be unable to sell enough to pay their debts.[7]

Midcentury economic expansion could be painful for the colonies, but tea could lubricate the credit markets. Increasing demand for, and potential high profits from, tea led American merchants to seek out new opportunities and build new commercial alliances, both legal and illegal. Despite Great Britain's attempts to control or eradicate illicit trade, some colonial merchants, who established and used intercolonial and transnational Atlantic commercial networks, made their fortunes smuggling foreign goods, such as tea and sugar.[8] Indeed, from the late 1740s to the 1760s, family and friends who shared religious views or social relations built trade ties among merchants in Philadelphia, Boston, and New York, in addition to London, Lisbon, Hamburg, and the Dutch and French West Indies. But foreign goods, tea in particular, were also highly politicized by the 1760s, a condition that manifested itself in the prerevolutionary nonimportation movement. Americans disputed the British tax structure and regulation of foreign imports, making tea a symbolic centerpiece of protests against the Stamp and Townshend Acts. The debates over luxury consumption of the 1720s and 1730s provided a moral vocabulary that Americans readily adopted as they began to debate the constitutionality of British economic sovereignty, the viability of trade monopolies, and the purpose of the political economy during the 1760s and 1770s. During the height of nonimportation, however, tensions rose between the growing political demands for consumer restraint and public desires to purchase a wide range of cheaper, available goods.[9] American traders and consumers may have acted politically by momentarily agreeing to not buy or not use tea, but the drink had already become a common habit for the "Tea-fac'd Generation" by the 1760s, and merchants profited from its sale. Staying the course of colonial boycotts proved difficult.

Faced with volatile economic cycles during the 1740s and 1750s, a dearth of hard currency, and unpaid debts, American merchants sought the best commercial markets in which to sell their products and purchase goods. The Navigation Acts limited American access to British ports alone, and since British merchants did not always take colonial goods in kind, merchants turned to alternative arenas in the Dutch and French West Indies, Holland, Hamburg, or Lisbon to sell American commodities. In exchange, they purchased easily mobile and saleable items such as sugar, molasses, rum, or tea. Indeed, the impulse to smuggle goods often arose from the need to sell provisions on hand—grains, timber, furs, or rum—rather than the desire to buy restricted or forbidden foreign goods. "Their chief Means of Purchasing vizt Their Corn and Flour *not* being . . . always admissible in England," London resident Samuel Wharton noted of Americans, "They have therefore, hitherto, been constrained, either to purchase their Teas from Foreigners, or to buy them on exorbitant Terms, from the Merchants in London."[10] Restrictions on the purchase and sale of legal tea put in place with the 1748 tax reform also encouraged the rise of tea smuggling. Although the British government had removed an onerous inland duty from any tea reexported to Ireland or America, after June 1748, tea purchased at the East India Company auction could only be reshipped in the original containers and only in large lots, "under the Penalty of the forfeiture of such Tea."[11] According to one London merchant, the new requirements made it difficult for small trade companies or individual merchants to buy tea directly from the EIC, since they would have to order an auction lot, consisting of 300–900 pounds of Bohea.[12] Although, London merchants saw some advantage in concentrating the wholesale tea trade into the hands of a few large merchant firms, reform placed the burden of certifying tea shipments on the shoulders of American merchants and gave custom officials greater powers to search and review ship manifests.

Smuggling in the American colonies also flourished in the wake of the trade wars between the EIC and the Dutch during the 1730s. Eventually shut out of Canton by the British, the Dutch continued to dominate trade in Indonesia, where they purchased cheap tea from itinerant Chinese merchants.[13] Unlike British regulation of the EIC, there were few restrictions on private Dutch trade in Asia, and merchant competition helped lower the cost of goods. British tax reform had done little to improve the price of EIC tea; thus, American merchants sought out cheaper product available through non-English sources. Although the EIC offered tea at auction for about 3 shillings a pound wholesale, the Dutch could still undercut the price, selling tea on the open market for about 1 shilling 11 pence per pound, easily infiltrating the colonial markets.[14] American merchants tracked closely the flow of Dutch tea from abroad. "According to our last Advices from Amsterdam," the *Boston Post Boy* reported in 1745, fifteen ships had landed in the Dutch port from the East Indies, bringing to sale 370,878 pounds of tea from the Dutch East India Company and 1,713,080 pounds from private merchants.[15] By the 1740s, merchants of all nationalities participated in the contraband trade especially across the porous international boundaries of the West Indies. Rich or poor, young or old, many British subjects (even government officials) in Jamaica and Bermuda smuggled goods through French and Dutch ports. Shippers from New England, New York, and Philadelphia joined an already active network of illicit trade in sugar, molasses, textiles, wine, gunpowder, paper, and tea. St. Eustatius emerged as the center of the Dutch smuggling trade, prompting Anglo-American agents to move there and to other free ports in the Caribbean, such as Spanish Monte Christi, to cash in on illicit trade.[16]

Although the Dutch provided cheap tea, North American merchants, using geography and family ties, also took advantage of haphazard British customs enforcement and the vagaries of war to smuggle goods. As early as 1737, Massachusetts governor Jonathan Belcher complained, "The Sea Coast of the Province is so extensive & has so many Commodious harbours, that the small number of Customs House Officers are often complaining they are not able to do much for preventing illegal Trade."[17] Merchants along the unguarded coastlines of Rhode Island, Connecticut, and New Jersey received illicit goods for shipment to Boston, New York, and even Philadelphia.[18] By the late 1750s and 1760s, the center of American smuggling had shifted away from New England to the mid-Atlantic, especially after Parliament placed the Customs Commission in Boston. Smuggling tea into Philadelphia was particularly easy. Like New England's geography, the banks of the Delaware River offered many places to land goods before entering the port. Indeed, the customs commissioners worried that "there are so many convenient Inlets & Harbours for Landing as well as smuggling of Contraband Goods, & no Custom House Officers near enough to prevent them."[19] The smuggler John Kidd assured one merchant house in Lisbon that "our officers are so indulgent here that I can land any other Goods without any risque in the worlde."[20] Another merchant celebrated "the freedom and Libarty of our Trade, being strangers to any interupsion from the Officers," allowing him to ply his trade between Philadelphia and the West Indies, as well as Ireland.[21] In the late 1760s the Philadelphia firm Orr, Dunlap, and Glenholme confirmed that tea was easily imported illegally "from Ireland & the West Indies owing to our want of Officers & no vessel of force lying here at present."[22]

Prolonged conflicts with the French during the 1740s and 1750s proved both profitable and challenging for some American merchants who, in order to find the best products and prices, combined legitimate mercantile orders from London suppliers with illicit trade. During King George's War, Thomas Hancock, a Boston merchant supplying Massachusetts soldiers at Louisbourg, used his connections in Lisbon, the West Indies, and Holland to develop a booming business in smuggled tea. By 1745, he was purchasing tea and other "Holland Goods" directly from the Dutch in Amsterdam or the West Indies and transporting them to Boston. Hancock instructed Martin Dubois Godet of St. Eustatius in March 1746 that his Amsterdam supplier had "shipt some Goods for my Accot, consigned you, to forward to me here," including two chests filled with 600 pounds of cheap Bohea tea.[23] The following year, Hancock ordered "Ten Chests more of the best Bohea tea" in August and another six chests of tea in November from merchants Thomas and Adrian Hope of Amsterdam, who shipped them to Godet at "Statia" for transshipment to Hancock in Boston.[24] Over the next twenty years Thomas Hancock received tea and textiles in this manner, to his great profit, especially during wartime. Indeed, merchants often complained that once conflict came to an end, business suffered. In November 1748, Thomas Hancock lamented to London

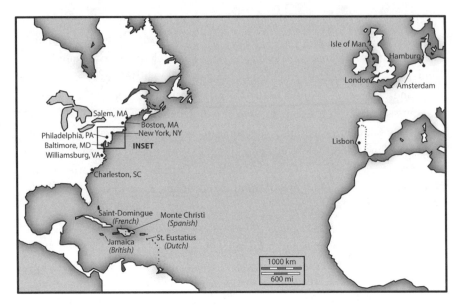

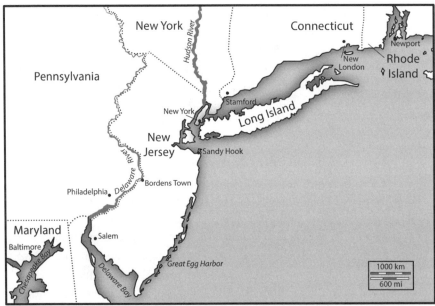

The Atlantic commercial world and ports of illegal trade, mid-eighteenth century, including smuggling networks from southern New England to the Mid-Atlantic (*inset*). Maps by Taya Barnett, Old Dominion University.

correspondents Kilby & Bernard that "peace hath put a stop to all Trade." Still, he added, "I must supply my Customers," implying that continuing demand would keep him searching for tea, whether through legal channels or not.[25]

As peacetime persisted, tea became a barometer for the volatility of local economic health. The early 1750s brought commercial malaise and a glut of goods to cities like Philadelphia, where the merchant John Kidd warned his London suppliers that tea was not selling: "We have had a large quantity of Tea in these 2 last ships which I am afraid will over Stock the Market."[26] Three years later, Kidd again observed that the tea market was saturated.[27] Like Samuel Powel in the 1730s, Kidd blamed the well-connected firm of Levy & Franks for importing tea from family in New York and flooding the market with smuggled product. Other Philadelphia merchants felt the impact of peace; oversupply put pressure on prices, which hurt all. As a new war loomed, John Reynell cautioned his cousin Thomas Sanders that trade had declined so much "that I can't encourage thy going into any Branch of it." He noted "such great Quantities of Goods Imported that large Parcells of 'em are sold almost every week at Public Vendue for less than they cost." Reynell concluded that only "a Warr with France" would mend Philadelphia's economic woes.[28]

As predicted, another "Warr with France" arrived the following year, ushering in embargos and commodity shortages from which merchants like Hancock, Kidd, and Reynell hoped to profit. In April 1755, William Gough, John Kidd's clerk, sent word to his employer then in London that the sale of tea had stopped simply because of rumors "that Madrass in the East Indies is taken by the French and that a War with France is inevitable."[29] Many hoped that a scarcity would drive up the long-deflated price of tea and even the possibility of profit drew several new players into the tea trade. Thomas Willing, who had taken over business in Philadelphia when his father Charles died in 1754, partnered with their one-time clerk Robert Morris and scrambled to stock up on tea. Willing told several of his British correspondents to purchase Bohea tea for him at the deflated price "If a War is inevitable," because he could sell it for more once fighting began.[30] Throughout the spring and summer of 1755 Willing anticipated a war that would advance his business, both legitimate and illegal.[31] Once the Seven Years' War began in earnest, American merchants regularly took risks, especially smuggling, and found ready partners in Lisbon and the Caribbean. Alongside their legal orders from London agents, Willing and Morris bought contraband tea throughout the war, taking advantage of embargos, which stopped all colonial trade for four months in the spring and summer of 1757. Thomas Willing sent his ship *The Nancy* to Europe in late summer 1757, instructing his uncle Thomas to purchase tea in Portugal.[32] In October, with great relief, Willing assured his Lisbon correspondents Mayne, Burn & Mayne that the tea had been "safely landed & will yield a very handsome Profitt & a speedy Remiss," since the price had risen back to 7 shillings per pound.[33]

Besides finding new partners in the Caribbean and Europe, mid-Atlantic merchants easily adapted smuggling to already existing intercolonial trade networks. Improved transportation helped connect Philadelphia and New York as a corridor for commerce, drawing in business from New Jersey and Delaware as well.[34] Many New York merchants had regular partners in Philadelphia who helped coordinate transportation of goods. Thomas Wharton of Philadelphia often received tea from New York merchant smuggler Captain John Waddell by way of Bordentown, New Jersey. In February 1756, Wharton instructed his courier, Joseph Borden Jr., to hold his crew "till after night & then they may come into the dock before my Store," where the tea chests could be carted through the streets under cover of darkness.[35] Some New York City firms, such as Greg & Cunningham, still turned to the southern New England coast for ports of entry between Stamford and New London, Connecticut. They had friends in the customs service and noted that many merchants carried on the Dutch trade "in so Publick a manner that all People in Trade was Obliged to be Concerned in it in their defence."[36] If southern New England proved too risky, smugglers could land at Sandy Hook, south of Manhattan at the mouth of New York Bay, and ferry goods into New York harbor in smaller boats.[37] From Stamford or Sandy Hook, goods would be shipped to Philadelphia by stage or by boat through Bordentown. After British customs seized some arms and tea in a 1756 shipment, Greg & Cunningham instructed their Rotterdam suppliers and the boatman "to take in the goods at Stamford & to proceed round Long Island to the River of Philadelphia," where they stored the goods for easy delivery to either New York or Philadelphia, depending on the demand.[38] Later that fall, Waddell Cunningham instructed his Belfast partner, Thomas Greg, to submit standing "orders in Amsterdam, Rotterdam, and Hamburgh to ship Eight Chests of Bohea Tea Cased in every Vessel that takes Freight to Rhode Island."[39]

As war raged and British naval ships searched for contraband, American merchants, once reluctant to participate in smuggling, changed their commercial habits to facilitate the storage and distribution of illegal goods, such as tea. In the early 1750s, Philadelphia merchant John Kidd regularly ordered

quantities of green and Bohea teas from legitimate London wholesalers. However, his frustration with unprofitable sales steadily grew as he noted a pleth-
ora of tea arriving "Via Irland," or "Imported in the Palantine Ships," or
"Dutch Tea from N York," or via the "Isle of Man."[40] Despite his fear that
smuggled tea might "intirely ruin the Trade of that Article, if it is not put a
stop to by some means or other," he also salivated at the thought of the potential gains that came with the illicit trade.[41] During the Seven Years' War, Kidd
regularly partnered with other merchants to ship tea as contraband. In spring
1757, Thomas Willing and Thomas Riché, two successful Philadelphia smugglers, joined Kidd in a "Tea Scheme." Willing asked his Lisbon supplier
Mayne, Burn & Mayne to ship up to £2,000 sterling worth of tea for no more
than 2 shillings 2 pence per pound. He added, with a note of caution, "as the
whole is Contraband pleasd to get Mr. Kids & my share fully insured where
you can depend most on the honour of the Assurers in case of loss."[42] When
the shipment arrived in Philadelphia, he sold most of the lot at 7 shillings per
pound, and by the summer of 1758 Willing and Kidd as partners had cleared
over £1,500 in net proceeds, with the same amount going to each Thomas
Riché and the Lisbon firm.[43] In October 1759, Riché partnered with Thomas
Willing and Robert Morris for a tea shipment directly from Amsterdam, both
realizing a gain of more than £2,700. Again in December 1759, Riché took a
lesser profit for his one-sixth stake in a Lisbon tea venture, whereas Willing
and Morris netted just over £3,058 for their half share.[44]

Even cautious Quaker merchants such as Abel James and Henry Drinker
of Philadelphia took advantage of wartime scarcity to profit from tea, although they were careful to avoid shipping smuggled goods. The partners had
invested heavily in naval stores and provisions, which they sent to the West
Indies in the 1750s, and when war was declared with France they found that
their trade continued to be "successful, having lost but one Vessel" in 1756.[45]
During the war they debated whether to allow their captains to capture enemy
ships, since Quakers openly condemned taking prize goods as unethical and
complained that prize and smuggled goods only provided cheap competing
merchandise at local vendue sales.[46] Although they occasionally captured
enemy ships, James & Drinker decided that buying and selling tea, spices, and
dry goods through known, legitimate sources would ease their consciences
but still provide profit. Noting a scarcity of tea by late 1757, over the next
three years they ordered Bohea, Hyson, and Congou in addition to an assortment of teacups, saucers, teapots, creamers, and other tea paraphernalia from
Neate & Neave (and its successor firm, Neate & Pigou) or David Barclay &

Sons, two London firms that provided tea to numerous clients in Philadelphia, New York, and Boston.[47] Still, by 1760, the partners struggled to find a market for their teas. As the Seven Years' War wound down in North America, the partners complained to suppliers of "so many Discouragements attending the Trade," since many goods from London "arrived to the most Glutted Market we ever knew."[48]

Once again, rumors of peace threatened to disrupt colonial commerce, in part because embargos were lifted, allowing a flood of new commodities onto the market. However, new powers granted the British Navy and customs service to control North American trade proved far more unsettling. Some of these efforts began during the conflict with France. New York governor Charles Hardy, appointed in 1755, called on the British Navy stationed in New York City to help locate and seize illicit goods. Greg & Cunningham, a New York firm involved in smuggling logwood and dry goods, complained in May 1756 that naval officers "were at last resolved to Seize every thing come in their way." Waddell Cunningham instructed Captain John Nealson, master of the snow *Prince of Wales,* to send word when they arrived from Rotterdam and he would retrieve the goods, including "three Chest of Arms & four Chests of Tea," to store safely in Philadelphia.[49] In Pennsylvania, however, Governor Robert Hunter Morris, exhorted by the Board of Trade to crack down on illegal trade practices, purportedly prowled wharfs along the Delaware River in the summer of 1756 to find hidden contraband.[50] Thomas Riché warned New York supplier Jacob VanZandt about the current risk in smuggling goods to Philadelphia, since the governor had "Orderd a Search Warrant with the Shirrif and his officers and Collecktar to Cease all they Came a Cross But in Particklar Tea . . . They Intend to Seize Tea where ever they see it & make the People Prove the importation."[51] By the end of the Seven Years' War, illicit traffic between New York and Philadelphia had become common, and customs officials had, in turn, become "much sharper than they formerly were," making smuggling a risky business according to Philadelphia trader Daniel Clark.[52] Indeed, the tax reform of 1748 required that American customs officials search ship cargos and review certificates of tea sales produced in London. Still, the system was underfunded and inefficient, and even after the war many customs officials were apt to shut their eyes to illegal trade.[53] For American merchants, smuggling had become an expedient alternative, especially useful during wartime, when legitimate trade routes had been stymied by embargos, and tea proved an easily purchased, transported, and saleable contraband product that they could turn into profit.

After 1763, a new enemy, British tax policy, emerged, and tea along with other consumer commodities became highly politicized. As Great Britain and France negotiated terms of peace, the British Treasury advised the king to reform trade duties in order to recover the cost of fighting in America and to pay salaries for an expanded imperial infrastructure. The war, which had ranged from the commercial territory of South Asia recently conquered by the EIC to the resource-rich North American continent, had been expensive, costing the empire £160 million.[54] To pay off the war debt, Parliament, with the support of powerful merchant and manufacturing lobbies, hoped to tap into colonial consumer demand, which made up at least one-third of all British foreign trade by midcentury.[55] New tax duties, however, had to be crafted carefully. Parliament had to balance the benefits of increased revenue against the potential squeeze of higher prices on consumers' ability to buy goods. Most of all, the Commissioners of Customs in London wanted to standardize and strengthen the powers of customs officials in America to prevent "the clandestine Importation of foreign Manufactures."[56] Two major reform measures got the attention of Americans. The Sugar Act, also known as the American Revenue Act of 1764, extended the Admiralty Court's ability to punish smugglers with the help of the British Navy, allowing customs to better collect tax duties.[57] Bostonians, especially, worried that restrictions on foreign molasses and sugars would strangle their provisions trade with the West Indies, not to mention making the primary ingredient for New England's rum distillation industry more expensive, and thus curtail their power of purchasing British goods.[58] The Stamp Act of 1765 placed a tax on paper products (newspapers, pamphlets, or playing cards) and required that any legal transactions (deeds, licenses, indentures, or decrees) be printed on stamped paper. The money would help to defray the cost of the late war and to pay for continued military defense of the North American colonies.

To members of Parliament, taxation was simply the quid pro quo of being British subjects. Charles Lloyd, secretary to George Grenville, the architect of the new tax policy, noted in his defense of the Stamp Act that "Americans, under the shade and protection of Great-Britain, have made rapid advances in population, commerce and wealth"; they owed a great debt to Britain in return.[59] Indeed, Grenville, who had supported a militarized EIC under Robert Clive, which had wrested parts of India away from potential French control during the late war, saw the American colonies in a similar light. By definition, imperial holdings provided revenue to be extracted with the help and administration of British armed forces.[60] Americans, of course, read their economic relationship to empire in a different light. John Dickinson, anonymously in *The Late Regulations Respecting the British Colonies on the Continent of America Considered*, agreed with Lloyd that previous "liberties" from tax duties and shipping restrictions had "enabled us to collect considerable sums of money for the joint benefit of ourselves and our mother country," in essence allowing Americans to participate in Atlantic commercial and consumer activities.[61] But, Dickinson emphasized, the mother country had already benefited from American prosperity through trade. The burden of further taxation would only threaten Americans' ability to maintain that commercial connection, taking cash out of consumers' pockets, cash they might use to purchase British manufactured goods.[62] In New England, critics of Grenville's new policies also perceived the broader commercial and imperial implications of taxes in America. Minister Ezra Stiles of Newport, Rhode Island, for instance, worried that the Stamp Act would turn the American colonies into just another exploited territory, like Bengal, under the sovereign care of an entity such as the EIC.[63]

Thus, when Americans developed a response to Grenville's tax policies, they did so in the context of global commercial activities and emerging anticorporate sentiments, and with support on both sides of the Atlantic. In late 1765 colonial merchants generally agreed that refusing to import British goods was an apt protest to what they saw as unfair taxation, and they asked their English commercial partners to pressure Parliament to repeal the act. Following the intercolonial Stamp Act Congress, two hundred New York merchants passed an agreement, in late October 1765, to instruct their British correspondents not to ship any goods "unless the Stamp Act be repealed."[64] Philadelphia merchants also supported nonimportation in principle, condemning the encroachment of Parliament on their rights to control colonial taxation. On November 7, 1765, a group of merchants, artisans, and shopkeepers signed an agreement to not import goods until the act was repealed— or at least "cancel future orders and countermand outstanding orders until the following May, at which time further action would be considered."[65] English merchants feared that by adding expense to cross-Atlantic legal documents and credit instruments in the form of a stamp tax, economic stability would be undermined and trade interrupted. With the support of British merchants, American colonists ultimately prevailed, and Parliament repealed the Stamp Act in 1766.[66]

Yet even as Parliament stood on the verge of repealing the Stamp Act, it debated a new "scheme" to raise revenue. "There is nothing produced in the

British colonies, in America," George Spencer reminded Parliament in January 1766, "that bears any resemblance [to tea]." A decade earlier he had informed against New York merchant smugglers and discovered that "people of all denominations, from the gentleman even to the slave" drank tea in America and would "not be satisfied without it." Spencer proposed that Great Britain leverage the demand for tea to procure a new tax of 12 pence per pound on its reexportation to America. He hoped the sale abroad of four thousand chests annually would reap revenue of £60,000. All told, for Americans at least, tea would still be "much cheaper than the consumer in England pays for that commodity."[67]

While the full extent of his suggestions did not come to fruition until 1773, the soon-passed Townshend Acts grasped the overwhelming importance of tea in Great Britain's search for a revenue source. Introduced by Chancellor of the Exchequer Charles Townshend, the Townshend Acts of 1767 placed new duties on enumerated trade goods—glass, lead, painter's colors, paper, and tea—and aimed to prevent "the clandestine running of goods in the colonies and plantations."[68] These taxes would provide salaries for newly appointed colonial customs and judicial officials, including an American Board of Customs based in Boston, to help with a "speedy and effectual collection" of import duties.[69] The Board of Customs and its agents would free up judges and civil officers from dependence on local legislatures and increase the use of writs of assistance to arrest suspected dealers in contraband.[70]

After the passage of the Townshend Acts in 1767, American colonists weighed how to respond. Boston, which had lagged behind other colonies in its reaction to the Stamp Act, proceeded quickly to boycott imported goods. In principle, Bostonians did not object to tax duties as long as they were limited to the regulation of trade and equally applied to all territories within the empire. But, the merchant Thomas Cushing, an early subscriber to nonimportation, complained in May 1767, "when Duties are laid with a view of raising a revenue out of the Colonies" to pay fixed salaries of British appointees, "this is looked upon to be unconstitutional" and could not be done "without vacating our Charter."[71] Many New Englanders were inspired by the moral issues raised by John Dickinson's "Letters from a Farmer in Pennsylvania," which called for steadfast resolve to use *"homespun clothes,"* in "reverence for the memory of our ancestors, who transmitted to us that freedom in which they have been blest."[72] However, Dickinson's economic, rather than ideological or constitutional, arguments resonated more loudly with the Boston merchants who eventually met and voted on the terms of nonimportation in early

March 1768.[73] A few years earlier, Dickinson had laid out the dire circumstances that commercial traders faced. Personal debt drove American merchants into bankruptcy since "Money is become extremely scarce" and credit tight. Then creditors sued for debtors' lands and personal effects but received little, which in turn ruined their business, "and the shock must be felt as far as *London*."[74] Still suffering from postwar stagnation and a cross-Atlantic credit crisis, New Englanders worried the Townshend Acts would further harm the broader economy. "Judicious Persons among us," wrote "S.X." in late 1767, were worried the new duties on tea, paper, glass, and paint would "soon drain all our Money, which will be quickly felt by the Rise of Interests, Fall of Landed Estates, Bankruptcies, Imprisonments, and the entire Ruin of Trade."[75] Hundreds of citizens attending the October 28, 1767, meeting of freeholders at Faneuil Hall signed subscriptions to "encourage the Use and Consumption of all Articles manufactured in any of the British American Colonies and more especially in this Province," while promising to not purchase a number of imported goods. They also lamented the scarcity of cash, Boston's declining trade, and the "heavy Debt, incurred in the Course of the late War."[76]

As they completed and approved a generally acceptable nonimportation agreement over the course of the spring and summer 1768, many Boston merchants (smugglers and legitimate traders alike) concluded that boycotts would not only send a political message but also alleviate their personal debt and benefit the colonial economy by allowing them to cease ordering new British goods and sell off their overstocked inventories of foreign goods on hand.[77] London and Bristol merchants had been eager to extend new lines of credit to peripheral participants in the Atlantic trade, such as shopkeepers and venduemasters, but their attempts to increase commercial interdependence between colonies and the mother country also added a growing amount of personal debt to British merchant creditors, which had reached about £2.9 million in 1766.[78] In March, the Boston merchants supporting nonimportation cited "the great Debt now standing against us, which if we go on Increasing by the excessive Import we have been accustomed to while our Sources of Remittance are daily drying up," threatening to ruin their own business and "that of many of our Creditors on the other side of the Water."[79] In a subsequent August 1768 agreement, Bostonians cited the heavy taxes imposed to pay off the war debt and the failure of cod fishing that year as reasons they struggled to pay "the debts we owe the merchants in Great Britain." They agreed to stop importing goods directly or on commission for one year (from January

Nicholas Boylston, 1769. Oil on canvas by John Singleton Copley. Indicative of a younger generation of merchants enamored of the East Indies and finding fortune in the tea and textile trade, Nicholas Boylston (1716–71) refashioned himself as a worldly trader with a prominent place in the global marketplace. Dressed in silk damask banyan (also known as an Indian gown) with a red velvet turban covering his wigless head, Boylston closely resembled an East India Company nabob. He refused to support the Boston nonimportation agreement. © Museum of Fine Arts, Boston.

1769 to January 1770), paying special attention to "any tea, glass, paper, or other goods commonly imported from Great Britain . . . until the Acts imposing duties on these articles have been repealed."[80]

Like Boston, merchants in Philadelphia hoped that nonimportation would help stabilize the colonial economy, allowing them to sell off inventory, collect from customers, and pay outstanding debts. For inspiration, advocates of nonimportation turned to John Dickinson, who argued that banishing a select number of British goods "will be universally beneficial, by inclining us to be more frugal, and affording our Merchants Time to collect their Debts, and enabling them to discharge those they owe to the Mother Country."[81] Indeed, in 1768 Pennsylvania merchants accumulated a trade deficit, importing £432,108 worth of goods from Britain while exporting only £59,406 worth of commodities.[82] The Pennsylvania Assembly, however, ignored requests to join Massachusetts, New York, and Virginia in support of nonimportation; instead they respectfully petitioned Parliament in September 1768 to reconsider the Townshend duties.[83] Only in early 1769, did Philadelphians finally take steps to join the colonial boycotts. Citizens initially promoted home manufacturing; some freeholders agreed not to consume lamb, hoping to increase the American woolen industry, and others chose to wear leather jackets instead of British-made cloth.[84] Perhaps driven by the threats of mob violence and boycotts of their individual shops, as well as the proliferation of threatening anonymous letters and pamphlets, an association of Philadelphia merchants agreed to stop importing goods on March 10, 1769.[85] Thomas Clifford assured a friend that the agreement was accepted "cooly & with great Unanimity."[86] Indeed, the following month, as a whole, the group of merchants wrote their London counterparts, warning them of the long-term consequences of the Townshend Acts. John Reynell, Abel James, Henry Drinker, William West, Thomas Mifflin, and Robert Morris, among others, noted that if the acts were not repealed, Americans were "determined not only to defeat the intent of the acts, by refraining from the use of those articles on which duties were laid, but to put a stop to the importation of [all] goods from Great-Britain."[87] Perhaps more true to merchant sentiment, Richard Waln, a Quaker, told one London firm soon after the resolutions went into effect that "it is a very general Wish amongst the Merchants that it may continue at least one Year in order that they may dispose of the great Quantity of Goods on hand, & contract their Affairs."[88]

Whereas American merchants worried about personal debt and unwinding inventory, colonial activists hoped to inspire consumers to support the boycotts on ideological grounds. Proponents of nonimportation borrowed from the rhetoric of virtue that permeated the luxury debates and critique of tea in the 1720s and 1730s. Calling on consumer restraint, boycott supporters blamed luxury consumption for threatening American liberties. The non-importation agreements reflected these moral arguments. Subscribers in Annapolis, Maryland, for instance, resolved in June 1769, "to discourage, and as much as may be, prevent the Use of foreign Luxuries and Superfluities," which contributed "to the great Detriment of our private Fortunes, and, in some Instances, to the Ruin of Families."[89] Similarly, Virginia's House of Burgesses, while acknowledging the dire economic impact of the Townshend Acts, called on a change in consumer behavior. In May 1769, they asked subscribers to use "their own Example, as all other legal Ways and Means in their Power, [to] promote and encourage Industry and Frugality, and discourage all Manner of Luxury and Extravagance."[90] Foregoing luxury was difficult for rising Virginia gentry, loath to give up their distinctions of rank as tobacco prices soared and markets boomed.[91] To many colonists, however, austerity appeared as a solution to both personal debt and moral failings. In October 1767, Boston subscribers hoped to "promote Industry, Oeconomy and Manufactures among ourselves, and by this Means prevent the unnecessary Importation of European Commodities, the excessive Use of which threatens the Country with Poverty and Ruin."[92] The exhortation to join subscriber lists helped unify consumers, in theory at least, letting the signers publicly acknowledge their shame and adhere to a new program of patriotic simplicity.[93]

Activists pressing for public support of nonimportation found an easy target, of course, in tea. They adapted the earlier generation's association of tea with luxury, scandal, and immorality to tea's new role as symbol of imperial tax policy. Critics of tea and foreign goods aimed to inspire consumers to change their habits or find alternatives. A gentleman "From Boston" called for colonial families to shift from tea to locally grown herbs. In December 1767, he noted an increased demand for "Labradore or Hyperion tea" supplied by local colonists: "Bohea tea is now wholly laid aside or used but sparingly in many of the best families in this town."[94] Publishers in Boston, New York, and Philadelphia circulated catchy verses to the "Young ladies in town," asking them to wear clothes "of your own make and spinning" and to "Throw aside your *Bohea*, and your *Green Hyson Tea*, and all things with new fashion duty."[95] "A number of young ladies," from Providence, Rhode Island, willing "to submit to frugality, and encourage industry," showed their patriotism by spinning more than forty skeins "of fine linen yarn, as a proof of their industry; and drank only LABRADORE TEA, and coffee, in testimony of their frugality."[96] In January 1768, at a Watertown, Massachusetts, town meeting, inhabitants agreed to do without enumerated articles but also "all Foreign Teas as Expensive & pernicious as well as unnecessary," replacing them with local "Herbs of a more Salubrious Quality."[97]

As in the early decades of the eighteenth century, critics watched women closely for their consumer behavior during the nonimportation boycotts. Women were berated as weak, easily swayed by their desires. Skeptics doubted that women could or would forgo tea. A pamphlet of 1770, *The Female Patriot, No. 1, Addressed to the Tea-Drinking Ladies of New-York*, mocked the commitment of women subscribers, calling them "not quite so compliant, If they want TEA, they'll storm and rave and rant."[98] However, between 1767 and the early 1770s, women were among those on the forefront of conspicuous nonconsumption. Milcah Martha Moore transcribed patriotic poems and essays in her commonplace book, which she exchanged with friends in Philadelphia. In "The Female Patriots. Address'd to the Daughters of Liberty in America. By the same 1768," she expressed the power of female consumer action, asking that "the Daughters of Liberty, nobly arise, / and tho' we've no Voice, but a negative here. / The use of the Taxables, let us forebear." Moore exhorted her friends to "Stand firmly resolved & bid Grenville to see / That rather than Freedom, we'll part with our Tea."[99] In February 1770, Boston women signed a pledge to join patriots "in denying ourselves the drinking of foreign tea, in hopes to frustrate a plan that tends to deprive a whole community of all that is valuable in life."[100]

Activists used ideological admonitions to shame female consumers into compliance, and many agreed to give up their foreign goods, such as tea. But the balance between restraint and desire was easily upset. The success of nonimportation agreements depended on the cooperation of merchants and their customers. Although many colonists signed subscriber agreements insisting that merchants not carry enumerated goods and agreed to stop using these goods, many also continued to purchase tea and other taxed items, not the least during those times that colonial nonimportation agreements were in effect. In other words, colonial consumers and merchants sometimes worked against nonimportation in practice even if they supported it in principle. For instance, plenty of dutied EIC tea was already available to consumers during nonimportation activities initiated by the Stamp Act and the Townshend Acts. By 1767, when the Townshend Acts went into effect, legal tea imports had rebounded substantially from the 1750s, surpassing imports from earlier years. Whereas the decade between 1751 and 1760 saw the importation of 1,492,496 pounds of tea to the mainland colonies, during the 1767 and 1768

TABLE 3.1
EIC Tea Reexported to Select American Colonies, 1740–1770 (in lbs.)

Date	New England	New York	Pennsylvania	Maryland, Virginia, Carolinas, and Georgia	West Indies
1741–1745	99,123	264,661	49,670	137,924	212,149
1746–1750	93,102	176,478	104,786	108,418	170,379
1751–1755	226,104	132,185	190,795	153,117	150,256
1756–1760	136,401	260,342	156,496	237,056	131,463
1761–1765	414,758	649,784	122,796	212,965	123,051
1766–1770	735,256	626,340	405,149	277,744	144,028

Source: Compiled from Great Britain, Board of Customs & Excise, Ledgers of Imports and Exports, 1696–1780, in the Public Records Office, London, reels 19–44.

seasons alone 1,400,000 pounds of tea arrived in America.[101] New England and Pennsylvania, in particular, rather than reducing tea imports, substantially increased the amount of tea accessible to consumers. From 1766 to 1770 New England imported 735,256 pounds of tea compared with 414,758 pounds for the preceding five years. Pennsylvania tea imports rose to 405,149 pounds from 122,796 pounds for the same five-year periods. Even New York imported over 600,000 pounds of tea during the politically active years between 1766 and 1770 (table 3.1).

American markets were well supplied with tea when nonimportation agreements went into effect, and merchants could forego new purchases for several years, thereby making it easy for some merchants to continue to sell, if not purchase, duties tea from British sources even while supporting nonimportation. Indeed, tea did not simply fill shopkeepers shelves; it found willing consumers after the Seven Years' War, despite the condemnation of new luxuries and the demand for self-restraint. Workers did participate in direct actions against merchants who imported from England; shop boycotts, tarring and feathering, riots, and burning a "wretched Importer" in effigy all served to express otherwise unarticulated political opinions on British tax law.[102] Still, between 1767 and 1773 (the height of prerevolutionary nonimportation activities), shallopmen, tailors, innkeepers, barbers, day laborers, ship captains, carpenters, merchant wholesalers, shoemakers, bricklayers, blockmakers, and plasterers who had become habituated to its use continued to buy tea from many of these same merchants. Merchant ledger books show that what had begun in the 1720s and 1730s as an occasional purchase or payment for work in kind had become by the 1750s and 1760s a routine practice among laborers and middling customers who purchased small amounts

Paul Revere, 1768. Oil on canvas by John Singleton Copley. Like many working Bostonians who supported nonimportation, silversmith Paul Revere is shown here in casual attire, surrounded by the tools of his trade. His plain linen shirt open at the collar, however, stands in contrast to the finely crafted silver teapot that he holds in his hand. Reflective of the new habits and accouterments of a rising middling class, the teapot speaks to the continued demand for tea. © Museum of Fine Arts, Boston.

of tea (usually one-half pound or less at three-to-six-month intervals) and sugar.[103] Even though their real wages had decreased 20–25 percent by the early 1760s, working people in Philadelphia continued to purchase sugar, molasses, spirits, and tea. In Massachusetts, by the 1770s, nearly 50 percent of "low-wealth" individuals owned pots and service equipment necessary to make and drink tea.[104]

Nonimportation agreements, which were coming into effect in the late 1760s, did not keep colonists from purchasing tea, and merchants carefully monitored their inventory so they could take advantage of consumer demand. For instance, between August 1768, when the details of the Boston non-importation agreement had been hammered out, and the end of 1769, John Tudor, a boycott supporter, sold 692.5 pounds of Bohea tea, mostly by the half-pound and for cash. In 1770 and 1771, as merchants weighed the agreement's effectiveness, Tudor sold another 140.5 pounds of tea, perhaps reflecting a decrease in his available inventory.[105] Samuel and Stephen Salisbury, brother merchants who lived in Boston and Worcester, Massachusetts, respectively, walked a fine line between consumer demand and compliance with nonimportation restrictions. Although Samuel generally supported the boycotts, Stephen had refused to sign any agreement and continued to offer tea for sale at their Worcester store. In February 1768, Stephen begged Samuel in Boston to "Send me Some Tea the Next Week as I find it is a damage to us to be out of that article." A month later, desperate to fill his customers' orders, he again scrawled a note to his brother: "Tea I am out off & by what I can learn there is none in Town."[106] Once the Boston agreement was signed in August 1768, the merchants' committee kept tabs on any imported goods and pressured outlying communities to comply with the resolutions. Samuel found that by periodically sending tea from their Boston store to Worcester, where the sale of tea had remained steady, they could stay out of trouble with the Boston committee and sell off supply at the same time. Indeed, in June 1769 Samuel sent a full chest (357 pounds) to their Worcester store even as he lambasted other merchants for selling enumerated goods.[107] Not so much an ideological as a practical position, Samuel (and eventually Stephen) came to believe nonimportation to be "the only thing to help us" alleviate colonial debt and stabilize the fluctuating value of stock they had on hand.[108] By late fall 1769, Samuel recommended that Stephen "sell as little [tea] as you can at present," not because it went against the Massachusetts merchant resolves but because he thought it would likely "grow very Dear" and bring a better profit in the spring.[109]

Similarly, Philadelphia merchants tried to balance nonimportation compliance with consumer demand for tea. But because their March 1769 agreement had no stipulation against selling enumerated goods already on hand, nor did it forbid trade with the West Indies, many merchants could supply

TABLE 3.2
EIC Tea Reexported to Select American Colonies, 1768–1772 (in lbs.)

Date	New England		New York		Pennsylvania	
	Customs 3	Customs 16	Customs 3	Customs 16	Customs 3	Customs 16
1767	152,435	—	177,111	—	87,741	—
1768	291,900	301,697	320,214	352,488	174,883	146,763
1769	86,004	110,960	4,282	16,986	81,729	112,159
1770	85,935	77,237	269	147	0	65
1771	282,857	283,638	1,035	344	495	0
1772	151,784	118,567	530	530	128	128

Source: Compiled from Great Britain, Board of Customs & Excise, Ledgers of Imports and Exports, 1696–1780, in the Public Records Office, London, reels 41–45 (also known as Customs 3); and Great Britain, Public Records Office, Commissioners of Customs in America, Customs 16 America, 1768–1772, in the Public Records Office, London, reel 1 (also known as Customs 16). Benjamin Woods Labaree, *The Boston Tea Party* (New York: Oxford University Press, 1961), 331, notes differently that New England imported 252,435 lbs. of tea in 1767, based on Customs 3 figures.
  Note: Em dash indicates data not available.

their customers even if they stopped ordering goods directly from Great Britain.[110] Between January 1767 and May 1770 Samuel Coates Jr. sold 208.75 pounds of legally purchased Bohea tea, mostly one pound at a time, for cash.[111] The dry goods merchant and wholesaler William West, who actively subscribed to nonimportation, continued to sell large amounts of his tea inventory; between May 1769 and February 1771, customers bought 1,271.5 pounds of Bohea tea from him.[112] Indeed, the ability to sell inventory on hand perhaps allowed Philadelphia merchants to cease purchasing dutied tea from Britain more effectively than in Boston. Although 1769 saw the influx of 81,729 pounds of legal tea into Pennsylvania, surprisingly the amount dropped to zero in 1770. New England tea imports, while dramatically reduced in weight from previous years, hit 86,004 pounds and 85,935 pounds during those same years (table 3.2). With strong ties to commercial networks in the Caribbean and well-established routes of trade from other colonies like New York, which also successfully cut orders for legal tea in 1769 and 1770, Philadelphia merchants could shut down the flow of legal tea and still fill consumer demand. Levi Hollingsworth, a Quaker from a politically connected family, used his brother in Baltimore and years of experience transporting provisions in the "shallop business" to smuggle and sell tea in Philadelphia. Between October 1768 and March 1771, he sold over 3,000 pounds of tea.[113]

To supply the demand for tea yet still comply with the provisions of nonimportation, Philadelphia merchants turned to illegal trade networks established during the 1740s and 1750s. In 1757, the merchant and smuggler John Kidd, urged by his London supplier to speculate on the "state of the Tea Trade of this Place," estimated that at least "40 Chests a year were Smugled" into Pennsylvania during 1750, 1751, and 1752, roughly equivalent to 36,000 pounds. With consumption of both legal and illegal tea "on an average 200 Chests Per Annum," Kidd figured that smuggling provided about 20 percent of tea used in the colony at that time.[114] Although legal tea imports made a comeback after the Seven Years' War, Thomas Hutchinson insisted in 1767 that smuggling still provided nearly three-fourths of all tea purchased in the North American colonies, despite powers granted to customs officials under the Townshend Acts. Pointing to America's "prodigious consumption" of tea, Hutchinson told his London supplier that "there does not come one fourth of it from England."[115] Indeed, if one looks at the commercial career of the Philadelphia smuggler Charles Wharton, who sold tea by the chest, keg, cask, hogshead, barrel, or any other container in which he could transport it, Hutchinson's Cassandra-like complaint seems less hyperbolic. From 1766, Wharton invested heavily in tea, especially through New York City sources, such as Benjamin and Amos Underhill or TenEyck & Seaman, where he could find illegal product at a better price. Between August 1768 and December 1769, Wharton sold 1,155.5 pounds of Bohea and Hyson tea to his Philadelphia customers. In 1770 alone, he sold 5,598 pounds and another 2,860.25 pounds of tea in 1771.[116] Wharton carefully instructed his suppliers to pack the tea "in Cleen floure Casks with Linneng hops Inside & out," to avoid detection, and to ship it "By way of Trentown with orders to Messrs Cox & Furman to send it by the First of their Shallops."[117]

Whether tea was smuggled or purchased legitimately, its source and sale produced conflict between and among American merchants. The politics of tea under the nonimportation agreements was particularly contentious in and around Boston. For example, between August 1768 and June 1769 Thomas Hutchinson and John Hancock aired their mutual rancor over presumed violations of nonimportation provisions in an all-out media war. With the help of John Mein, publisher of the *Boston Chronicle*, Thomas Hutchinson and his sons, who had invested heavily in legally sourced tea from 1766 on, targeted traders who had signed the Boston agreement but failed to follow it. In a series of newspaper issues, Mein printed the manifests of ships that arrived in Boston from Great Britain, noting the enumerated goods on board. He and Hutchinson hoped to expose John Hancock, in particular, who publicly encouraged merchants to hold fast to nonimportation resolutions even as he imported prodigious amounts of British tea.[118] Stephen Salisbury in Worcester called members of the Boston merchants' committee "*High handed Hellish*

Abominations," who "were Acting a *Deceitful part & deceiving the People."* He labeled John Hancock a *"Son of Liberty Son of Hell"* and accused others on the committee of making their livelihood by smuggling.[119]

In fact, John Hancock, John Rowe, and Jonathan and John Amory, all local proponents of the boycotts, ignored the strictures of nonimportation and received many goods directly from Britain between 1768 and 1770. According to British customs records, Boston merchants imported approximately 95,500 pounds of tea from British firms in 1769 alone. John Hancock's ships (*Boston Packet* and the *John*) carried over 18,000 pounds of tea in 1769 and another 17,121 pounds in 1770, which represented 36 percent of the total amount of tea legally imported to Boston that year. John Rowe also legally imported 24,754 pounds of tea in partnership with other Boston and London merchants during 1769.[120] Still, Hutchinson bitterly accused his competition of taking unfair advantage of illegal (as well as legal) sources of tea, undercutting the price. Far from stemming the tide of smuggling, the passage of the Townshend Acts had "not in any degree lessend the importation of Dutch Tea," Hutchinson complained to Thomas Pownall in early 1769.[121] In 1771, he increased his earlier estimates, claiming that the "consumption of Tea in America exceeds what any body in England imagines. Some person capable of judging suppose 5/6 of what has been consumed the two last years has been illegally imported."[122]

Internal conflicts between American merchants over the source of goods and the continued demand for tea undermined the unanimity and longevity of colonial boycotts. But rumors of parliamentary debates over the efficacy and potential repeal of the Townshend Acts in late 1769 also nudged American merchants cautiously back into commercial trade with London. Still, they were wary of the political implications of when, where, and how they purchased goods. Before Boston lifted its ban on British goods, the Amorys urgently turned to their contacts at Bruce, Wheeler & Higginson, where "we are told that one of your house is a director in the East India Company." They wanted to "make a trial" of fifty chests of Bohea tea during the coming spring and ordered an additional fifty chests for the fall of 1770.[123] William Dennie also hoped to jump back into the Atlantic trade as soon as possible. His London supplier, John Boylston, compiled an "Invoice of sundries to be Shipt Mr. Wm Dennie of Boston on the repeal of the Revenue Acts," including ten chests of Bohea tea.[124] By the spring of 1770, other merchants were acting quickly on rumors of repeal. New York merchants ordered goods for fear of losing customers. They learned from London suppliers that "large Quantities of Goods . . . are now daily shipping for Virginia, Maryland, Rhode Island, Boston, and Montreal, which will doubtless circulate all through the Colonies," taking potential business out of their hands.[125] In May 1770, Philadelphia merchant Richard Waln planned for every contingency. He instructed his ship's captain to sell his cargo at the first port of call "if the Markets are tolerable," and if he landed at St. Eustatius and "the Duty on Tea continues, lay out my money in that Article, procure Dutch Papers for the sloop, go to great Egg Harbour & apply to Richd Somers who will take charge of the Tea." If the tea duty were lifted, however, "bring Molasses or what thee may think best."[126] In other words, Waln thought carefully about how he could follow the spirit of the law, if not the letter. He would smuggle tea only if British tax duties and American nonimportation remained in place.

These tentative orders to London correspondents, although contingent on the tax law's repeal, set off a series of accusations and jealous acrimony, tearing asunder cooperation and partnership that once bolstered intercolonial commercial enterprise. New York merchants, who had supported nonimportation, waited anxiously in spring 1770 to hear of Parliament's repeal of the Revenue Acts, in particular, the tea duties. During the crisis, New York traders had carefully cultivated a reputation as sticklers for nonimportation, sending British goods back to New Haven in July 1769 with a curt warning: "many of our Enemies wish to see and would be pleased of reproaching us with, that the Colony of New York was become the common Receptacle of prohibited Goods from all parts of the Continent."[127] However, once Parliament agreed in April 1770 to repeal the Townshend Acts except the duty on tea, the New York merchant nonimportation committee quickly reconsidered the extent of its boycott. They agreed in mid-June that once the parliamentary repeal went into effect, December 1, they would begin importing British goods again, except "any Article or Articles upon which a Duty is laid or hereafter may be laid, for the Purpose of raising a Revenue in America," such as tea. But they also carefully stated that the agreement would not take effect until they heard of "the concurrence of Boston and Philadelphia."[128]

Fearing that the collapse of New York's nonimportation agreement would damage their market share, credit, and profits, some Philadelphia merchants argued for the right to revise or rescind their agreement. Those who favored rescinding the agreement complained largely of the commercial competition from colonies that had never agreed to nonimportation or whose merchants had ignored the resolutions. In May 1770, partners Abel James and Henry Drinker grumbled that "the little dirty Colony of Rhode Island has shamefully broken faith with the others, and has imported a ship load of goods as usual."[129] According to "A Freeholder," Pennsylvania's near neighbor Maryland had "imported, since their Association, three times the quantity of Goods which were necessary for their own consumption, and by those means supplied our back countries, and this city."[130] Philadelphia subscribers charged Boston, too, of making "large Importations, both contrary to the Spirit and Letter of their Agreement," thus undermining American unity and perhaps "preventing the Repeal of the Tea Act, last Sessions of Parliament."[131] But Philadelphia merchants especially condemned New York for its "sordid and wanton Defection from the common Cause" and threatened to "break off all commercial Intercourse with New York."[132] "The *New-Yorkers* have betrayed a Meanness and Cowardice in deserting us in the present important Juncture," accused "a Pennsylvanian," in July 1770.[133] Many feared that with the dissolution of New York's agreement, customers living in "the Jerseys" would turn to Manhattan rather than Philadelphia for goods and put further pressures on Pennsylvania's fragile economy.[134] John Reynell's nephew, Samuel Coates Jr., who had taken over management of his guardian uncle's business in the late 1760s, assured a friend in London that "New Yk gave Way" before Philadelphia merchants agreed to alter their agreement, and "Maryland was daily thriving at the Expence of this Province . . . for the Marylanders were deeply in debt here & the back part of Pennsylvania also."[135] At a general meeting in September 1770, most Philadelphia merchants agreed, at least in theory, to lift the ban on British goods except tea and a few other dutied articles.[136]

Boston merchants also debated whether to revise their original nonimportation agreement with an eye on the noncompliance of other colonies. In late 1769, the committee agreed to maintain the boycott "until the Acts imposing Duties in America for raising a Revenue, be totally repealed," and if any goods arrived, they would send them back or store them for future sale after the Townshend Acts were rescinded.[137] Still, Bostonians noted that "the Merchants of New York and Philadelphia, have already sent Orders for Goods to be shipped, in case the Acts should be repealed," reserving the right to send for goods as well.[138] Boston merchants especially complained that Philadelphia and New York could afford to maintain the boycott because both cities had better access to Dutch goods than Boston, which housed the king's Board of Custom Commissioners and their attendant security force. The Boston committee attempted to stem the influx of British goods. At a January 23, 1770, meeting of "Merchants & Traders," the group openly reprimanded several noncomplying merchants for being "obstinate and inveterate Enemies to their Country." Even though a few merchants stopped conforming to the agreement, the committee reiterated its objection to tea imports and voted to "strictly and religiously enjoin it upon our respective Families, totally to abstain from the Use of Tea upon *any Pretence whatever*." Further, they recommended to "Country Customers and Friends not to buy, sell or use it, until the said Duty shall be taken off."[139] Only after Philadelphia voted to rescind its support for continued boycotts in September, however, did Boston merchants follow suit.[140] Toward the end of 1770, colonial American merchants eagerly returned to business as usual.

Between 1769 and 1772, as Americans debated the Townshend Acts, nonimportation, and the impact of luxury consumption on America's virtue and economy, tea, while politically condemned by people participating in the boycotts, did not disappear from the tables of American consumers. In their debates over nonimportation and tea, in particular, merchants and their customers struggled with the political implications of consumption. Merchants, whether smugglers or not, veiled themselves in republican rhetoric to describe and protect their commercial reputations. They grumbled about imperial tax policies, thus supporting the principles of nonimportation. But they also feared that other merchants less scrupulous would use the opportunity to steal their business. Neither the Townshend Acts nor the nonimportation boycotts produced the result originally desired; they did not stem the tide of clandestine trade or raise the revenue expected. After heated debates about full or partial repeal, Parliament agreed in April 1770 to rescind the duties on enumerated trade goods effective December 1770, except for the tax on tea. Thomas Pownall, recently retired Massachusetts governor and member of Parliament, had argued before the Commons that Great Britain should consider full repeal of the acts, not for the sake of Americans but for the sake of the English merchant community. "THE REASONING AND THE ARGUMENTS FOR THE REPEAL OF THIS ACT," proclaimed Pownall, "STAND SOLELY ON THAT FACT, ITS ATTENDANT MISCHIEFS; AND ITS CONSEQUENCES TO THE COMMERICAL INTEREST OF GREAT BRITAIN." Pownall noted that despite the reduction of duties for the EIC tea reexported to America, the tax still provided an "advantage in favour of the Dutch teas imported into the colonies." He accused those who wanted to keep the tea tax of playing politics, simply to exercise their "right of taxing the Americans."[141] Similarly, Thomas Hutchinson, soon to become governor of Massachusetts, advocated repealing the tea tax. He was well aware of the burdens of Navigation Acts on American merchants, as his own business dealings had suffered. In October 1770, he lamented to Thomas Whately that although the nonimportation controversy was subsiding, he wished that Parliament had repealed the tea duty, for it gave American merchants "a better pretence for bringing [tea] from Holland" with support from the consuming public.[142] Despite the protests of Pownall and Hutchinson, Parliament kept the tax on tea.

CHAPTER FOUR

The Global Dimensions
of the American Tea Crisis

Tea is perhaps the most important object, taking it with its
necessary connections of any in the mighty circle of commerce.
If commercial principles had been the true motives to the repeal
[of the Townshend Acts], or had they been at all attended to, tea
would have been the last article we should have left taxed for a
subject of controversy.

—*Edmund Burke, "Speech on American Taxation,*
April 19, 1774"

Tea and its consumers helped to pay for the imperial ambitions of the East
India Company, which opened and dominated global commercial markets
throughout the eighteenth century. No wonder, then, that tea also triggered
a deep resentment of the British monopoly and its use of a private militia
supported by the British Army to conquer territory in South Asia. Even subjects residing in England began to question the corruption they discovered
in the company, revealed by the influence of Nabobs who could potentially
"easternize" the traditional values of empire.[1] By the early 1770s, the relationship between the EIC and Great Britain had become problematic. The
British government enjoyed the commercial fruits of East India; it supported
the company's exclusive rights to trade and became increasingly dependent
on the influx of tax revenues from the sale of tea and other foreign commodities. Conversely, the EIC, due to the increased cost of maintaining trade and
territory in Asia, relied on direct infusions of cash through short-term government loans. The company's distressed fiscal state in 1772, however, engendered fear of its imminent collapse. Some complained that the credit crisis
came about through mismanagement of funds, pushing the company near
bankruptcy, even as individual company agents amassed tremendous fortunes plundered from the wealth of India.

Beset by financial and public relations fiascos in 1772, the EIC and the British government negotiated a settlement that protected Great Britain's stream

of revenue from the sale of East India goods, bailed out the company by resolving immediate cash flow problems, and tackled competition from other nations and illegal trade networks. In the 1760s and early 1770s, the colonial critique of tea shifted subtly from the condemnation of luxury consumption and its physical and moral effects to a political critique of the people, companies, and imperial system that brought luxury goods to America. Thus, when the Tea Act was passed in 1773, American colonists were already suspicious of its purpose and supposed benefits. Although taxation appeared at the center of protests, Americans also feared the threat of the EIC's monopoly to their mercantile interests, whether they were importers, shippers, merchants, or shopkeepers. Americans criticized the privileges that the EIC agents enjoyed and the abuses that they inflicted on British territorial holdings. Company activity in India had engendered famine, land seizures, individual abuses of power, and tyranny of a far crueler sort than in the North American colonies. Colonial American critics recognized and feared that America's future might be similar. The EIC's new direct access to North American markets, much like their access to markets in India, would give them unprecedented commercial power, even potential sovereignty, over Americans.[2] Consequently, the Tea Act of 1773 inspired a torrent of patriotic actions, including a renewed cry to reject tea. Edmund Burke's lament about the political motives for keeping tax duties on tea in place came too late.[3] Just as the colonial trade in tea and its taxation had a broader global context, the colonial reaction to British tax policy was also part of a broader critique of empire.

By the mid-eighteenth century, the east coast of India had become central to the EIC's commercial empire abroad and an important staging ground for the China tea trade. English traders had established a permanent post in Bengal as early as 1636, and by the turn of the eighteenth century, the EIC held extensive powers over civil, legal, and military activities in the region. The company charter, renewed when the competing firms united in 1709, gave the EIC authority to wage war "with the Native Princes or States" for purposes of self-defense, to coin money for use in trade, and to establish a court system at Madras with civil powers over English subjects.[4] In 1714, George I gave the EIC additional defensive powers, including the ability to raise Indian troops (Sepoys) against outside invasion of occupied territory. The company needed permanent posts not only to maintain power in India but also to supply the China trade. India, in turn, became a staging ground for British competition with the French, Dutch, and Spanish. By 1717, the Mughal emperor at

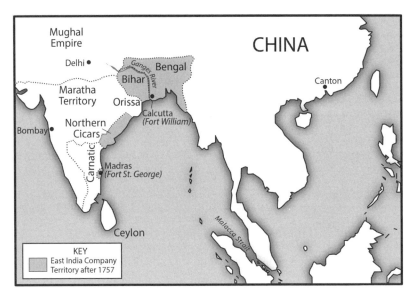

English East India Company territories in India after 1757. Map by Taya Barnett, Old Dominion University.

Delhi had granted the EIC a Phirmaund, or *farmān,* which, for a 3,000-rupee annual payment, conferred several open privileges, including freedom from local customs duties and the right to mint its own silver currency.[5]

When Mughal powers weakened after the Persian invasion of India in 1736, the English strengthened their commercial presence, but at a price. In Bengal, local leaders and native merchants demanded the company pay more for trading privileges, frustrating its efforts to establish permanent factories. By midcentury, the French threatened company access to the south, trying to dominate trade along the Coromandel Coast and the interior Deccan. During the Seven Years' War, both nations fought by proxy through competing native subahdars (Nawabs) for power, but eventually the English ousted the French from Pondicherry, the Deccan, and Golconda (later Hyderabad), reducing their European rivals to a small commercial presence in India.[6] Additionally, in 1757 under the leadership of Robert Clive, who had worked his way through the ranks of the EIC to become chief military and political strategist in India, the company recaptured Calcutta at the Battle of Plassey from the last independent Nawab, Siraj ud-Daulah.[7] This victory brought permanent control of territory in the provinces of Bengal, Bihar, and Orissa, as well as influence over rulers in the Carnatic and solidified the EIC's political power over a commercialized empire in India. The EIC insinuated itself into local politics by fighting, then negotiating peace directly with the Mughal emperor, who in April 1766 granted them a *diwani*. In exchange for military protection and a kickback payment, the emperor allowed the company, through the Nawab, administrative powers and rights to revenues from many commodities produced in Bengal. The EIC assured its commercial privileges by backing Mir Jafar, a compliant regional leader, as Nawab and eventually transformed itself from merely a merchant company to a powerful territorial state that governed the province through a native South Asian avatar. With the blessings of the British government, the company had become a commercial as well as sovereign power, exercising maritime and military authority over new colonial subjects.[8]

Despite receiving the *diwani* grant of Bengal from the Mughal emperor promising rent revenues and political powers, the EIC struggled financially following the Seven Years' War. The war and conquest of Bengal had been costly; the company recovered only half of the £8.5 million price tag from revenue collection or protection money paid by Indian allies. The British government threw in an additional £4.5 million in loans, but the EIC, faced with a corporate credit crisis and the expense of administrating its new commercial empire, had to find cash to keep afloat.[9] During the 1760s and 1770s, India proved an expensive piece of real estate to administrate and the company came to depend on the Canton trade to help pay for its efforts in South Asia. By midcentury, tea, which constituted an increasing portion of the EIC's foreign trade, provided necessary liquidity to weather the growing financial storm. Whereas tea made up about 25 percent of all East India goods sold at London auction in 1731, by the mid-1760s, tea accounted for nearly 50 percent of total company sales.[10] Simultaneously, however, the EIC worried that the tea trade drew increasing amounts of silver bullion from its coffers, even as it struggled to find markets for the *diwani* revenue, often collected in the form of Indian textiles, salt, or other commodities.[11] At home, England prohibited the sale of many India goods, such as cotton textiles, and other commodities did not sell in the British market. Instead, by the 1760s British traders began to exchange goods manufactured or grown in India for the more fungible Chinese tea, silk, and gold, which could be sold readily back home for British sterling, thus allowing company agents to extract an immense amount of wealth from India.[12]

In fact, the EIC depended greatly on trade with China to fund activities in India, even as the cash to facilitate this internal exchange was in short supply, creating precarious relations with Chinese officials and tensions within the company. By the 1760s, most of the EIC voyages sent to purchase tea in Canton came directly from Bombay, Bengal, or Fort St. George in Madras. The silver and produce of India that filled the ships bound for China steadily increased in value, from 455,630 tales (£151,877) in 1761 to more than 2 million tales (£770,148) in the 1767–68 season.[13] But the cost of tea in Canton had also risen, driven by increased demand in Europe and the financial needs of the Co-Hong merchants. The Co-Hong, now "an Association of Ten" merchants sanctioned by and indebted to the local Mandarins, had become very powerful and enjoyed a monopoly over all trade with foreigners.[14] The EIC went to great lengths to divide the interests of the Co-Hong merchants and protest their grant of privileges. James Flint, a supercargo who had served the company for decades in Canton, travelled to Peking in 1759 demanding that the emperor open trade; he was detained in Ning-po and threatened with deportation.[15] In response, the emperor published an edict to more closely regulate the activities of foreigners in Canton and to protect the Co-Hong merchants from debt to European traders. It curtailed the movement and residence of foreign traders and placed a regiment of soldiers to "control the riotous crews of the foreign ships anchored at Whampoa," just outside Canton.[16]

These strictures did not stop trade or curtail the financial interdependence of EIC agents and the Co-Hong. In 1765, company agents pressured Co-Hong merchants to curtail "their excessive presents to the Mandareens in power," in order to pay outstanding debts taken as advances on tea contracts with the EIC. The Co-Hong merchants, in turn, dragged their feet in negotiating new commercial contracts, hoping that competing traders from Holland or France would arrive so they could increase the price they asked for tea.[17] Panicked by the rising cost of trade, in 1767 the company reverted to its old practice of buying up as much surplus tea as possible with cash.[18] By early 1769, however, their cash reserves were dwindling; the company council at Fort St. George in Madras warned its counterparts in China that all available silver had been made "into Arcot Rupees for the expenses of our Army in the field"; thus, the annual ships were sent without any means to pay for tea in advance.[19] Late in the summer of 1769 council members unapologetically washed their hands of responsibility for funding the Canton trade, noting how "impoverished" the "Gentlemen of Bengall" had become "by the very heavy expences of the late War."[20] Company councils at Fort William, in Calcutta, and at Bombay Castle sent similar warnings to China. Company agents had to draw on London letters of credit and borrow cash from local sources to pay for tea because the sale of produce from India would not cover expenses. The Canton traders returned to Great Britain that year with "a more than usually large proportion" of cheap, low-grade teas.[21]

The ailing financial health of the company in India, along with its new political role in Asia, did not go unnoticed at home. The British government, fiscally dependent on the company's business, insisted that the nation benefited from the EIC's commercial empire abroad. In 1766 and 1767, the Chatham administration, led by William Pitt the elder, Earl of Chatham, hoping to stabilize the revenue stream from the sale of East India goods, struck a deal with the company.[22] In anticipation of sending nearly 1.5 million pounds of tea to the colonies in the coming year (nearly as much tea as had been reexported to America during the entire 1750s), the EIC lobbied Parliament in May 1767 to reduce inland duties and grant "a drawback on such teas as may be exported to Ireland, or to any of his Majesty's colonies."[23] Parliament complied, passing the Indemnity Act, which lowered duties on black and cheap green tea sold in England and allowed a drawback (or rebate) of the 25 percent ad valorem (value added) duty for tea sold in America. In exchange, the company agreed to pay an annual fee of £400,000 to the Exchequer (equal to 4 percent of government revenue) to cover any lost revenue from the drawback and reduction of the inland duty. In addition, Parliament, hoping to curtail speculation in and volatility of the company stock, passed the Dividend Bill in June 1767, which restricted the company's annual investor dividend to 10 percent or less.[24] The EIC was allowed to retain its territory in Bengal, but Parliament exerted new controls over company business.[25]

The 1767 deal, however, did not keep the EIC from financial crisis for long, or from further scrutiny. By 1772, the company had an abundance of goods and commodities, much of it stockpiled in warehouses, but little cash on hand. It had accumulated teas and silks from the China trade but also had stored goods as part of territorial revenues collected in Bengal, now administrated by the company. Despite parliamentary restrictions and its lack of cash, the company insisted on paying a high stock dividend of 12.5 percent to its shareholders. In order to maintain the dividend and operating cash flow, it sought loans from the British government through the Bank of England, from which the EIC borrowed £5.5 million between 1769 and 1772.[26] The subsequent investigation into the company's finances came as no surprise. An increasing number of MPs owned EIC stock by the early 1770s, ensuring their vested interest in the financial health of the company and its political future.[27] In April 1772, the House of Commons appointed General John Burgoyne to head a select committee to investigate charges of corruption. Burgoyne had his doubts about the company, noting a kind of "chaos where every element and principle of government, and charters, and firmauns, and the rights of conquests, and the rights of subjects, and the different functions and interests of merchants, and statesmen, and lawyers, and kings, are huddled together into one promiscuous tumult and confusion."[28] On trial were the EIC's mismanagement of operations in and revenues from Bengal. The *diwani* revenue had been estimated at £2–4 million a year, which many thought too optimistic, and little of it came in the form of hard currency.[29] When the House of Commons in late 1772 asked about the *diwani* revenue and its disbursement, the directors and company examiner admitted that most of the million rupees in taxes collected annually from the natives of India was parceled out to private individuals working for the EIC, such as the governor at Bengal, rather than reinvested in company operations or distributed to stockholders.[30] Many members of Parliament went on record to condemn the activities of the EIC in Bengal. Company agents were described as "Asiatic plunderers" who starved millions through their opulent manners, sucking the life out of India and its people. Recently retired MP Horace Walpole cryptically wrote a friend that the EIC raised "the price of everything, till the poor could not afford to purchase bread. Conquest, usurpation, wealth, luxury, famine."[31]

Perhaps Parliament took its cues from the increasing number of public critics. Political commentators puzzled over the unprecedented commercial and sovereign powers placed in the hands of the EIC. Could a private company, which was not part of a colonial settlement system such as North America, wield sovereign powers, in essence acting as a surrogate for the British government? The state had granted the EIC monopoly trading rights, enabling it to acquire territorial properties; consequently, critics argued, the state should have a say over the use and distribution of the company's revenues. For instance, one pamphlet author asserted in 1768 that the company "forfeited their charter, and consequently, their territorial acquisitions, by usurping the sovereign authority of making nabobs or potentates; and carrying on, without any authority from the British legislature." In essence, "Merchants have become warriors."[32] William Bolts, a former agent of the EIC and long-time resident of Calcutta, concurred, he warned that the company's private army often abused its power over "his Majesty's newly-acquired Asiatic subjects, as well as the British emigrant residing and established in India." The company had taken advantage of its privileged monopoly to raise an army of sixty thousand men and extended sovereignty over South Asia.[33]

The British public especially blamed individuals in the company who profited from trade for the corruption within the EIC. Critics at home despised the culpability and venality of company agents, whose role had radically changed from commercial trader to the face of British governance abroad. By midcentury, the stock figure of the Nabob (a term derived from *Nawab*, a Mughal aristocrat with regional power) referred specifically to the EIC agents who, according to one contemporary, "by art, fraud, cruelty, and imposition obtained the fortune of an Asiatic prince and returned to England to display his folly and vanity and ambition."[34] Indeed, many Englishmen feared that these Nabobs would impose similar strong-arm political force at home. Literature and the theater at times made fun of them as low-born, pompous, bumbling, nouveau riches—Samuel Foote's comedic play "The Nabob" was first performed in London the summer of 1772. But Britons also worried that company agents would use their wealth to buy political influence upon their return from India.[35] Although only a few ex-EIC employees were elected to Parliament in the 1760s, the widespread perception of corruption is instructive. In 1768, William Strahan, a London printer and MP, and a long-time critic of the EIC, assumed that "Immense Sums are daily given to secure Seats in Parliament and it is reckoned that not fewer than 30 or 40 Nabobs will get into the House this ensuing Election." Sharing his opinion with American friend and publisher David Hall, Strahan helped shape the image of the EIC agent that colonists came to know and loathe: "Men who in the East, by Rapine and Plunder, in most Cases attended with the most shocking Instances of Barbarity, have, suddenly acquired immense Wealth. Such you will perhaps think not the most proper Guardians of our Constitution and Liberties."[36]

Robert Clive, symbol of the EIC success in India and himself the recipient of immense personal wealth, became a lightning rod for controversy. Parliament began to investigate Clive's activities as early as 1766, but in 1772 the Burgoyne select committee reexamined Clive's privileges with more rigor. First they found that after taking Calcutta in 1757, Clive had signed a treaty with Mir Jafar, the Nawab, without the EIC directors or the British government having full knowledge, which bound the company to an alliance and granted great powers to Clive.[37] When put on the witness stand, Clive admitted receiving personal rewards of money and land from the Nawab, which "made my fortune easy." But he insisted that this personal wealth was simply "the reward of honourable services" to the company.[38] Indeed, Clive justified his actions by painting a picture of India in crisis and in need of outside intervention; the country, he insisted, was controlled by men who were "luxurious, effeminate, tyrannical, treacherous, venal, cruel." He claimed that although the company agents took advantage of the presents and graft that often flowed to people in power, the native leaders of India, without the EIC's knowledge and acting in the company's name, abused the poor and common laborers. In other words, young English traders were enticed by bribes of better living quarters, women, fine horses, carriages, and entertainments until they were trapped "in a state of dependence under the banyan, who commits acts of violence and oppression, as his interest prompts him to, under the pretended sanction and authority of the Company's servant."[39]

Parliament's investigation also brought astounding transparency to the EIC's murky financial structure, for the chancellor of the exchequer compelled the directors to open up and audit the accounts. In 1772, Mr. Hoole, a company auditor, prepared a set of records for the Court of Directors to present to the British Treasury and House of Commons. He included the company's cash balance and outstanding debts, sales from the previous ten years, customs duties collected, and estimates of stock on hand.[40] These accounts revealed a series of bad debts held by the company in Bengal, Madras, and Bombay, which had accumulated since the Seven Years' War. The EIC simply "wrote off" an increasing amount of debt each year. In 1766, for instance, £330,000 was written off "for Fortifications and Buildings at Bengal." In 1768, the company wrote off a total of £1,151,077, including uncollected debts at Fort St. George and Bombay, and £860,065 for "Fortifications and Buildings at Bengal, in which was included the sum of £6,145 for bad Debts at Dacca." With additional expenses carried forward from past years, by 1772 the company debt (at least the amount they were willing to report) had ballooned to over £1 million, mostly from the accumulated expense of the conquest and occupation of territory in Bengal. Indeed, the Committee of Proprietors appointed by the company's General Court expressed growing doubt that it would ever know how much the EIC owed or owned; the report concluded that no real value had been placed on the *diwani* at Bengal or the land and customs revenues collected at other EIC settlements, for "they cannot ascertain any specific Sum, which might be placed to the Company's Credit."[41]

Even as the EIC stood on the brink of financial disaster and public shame, the company directors optimistically insisted that investors had nothing to fear. But when Parliament's investigation revealed the extent of company debt, and investors noted the continued struggle to retain Madras against the French and the full impact of the 1769 Bengal famine, the stock price plummeted.[42] Still, the directors assured themselves, their stockholders, and the British government that they could relieve the current debt situation by borrowing cash rather than cutting the dividend, which they maintained at an unsustainable 12.5 percent. However, the directors also admitted that the company had to borrow money to make its £400,000 annual obligation to the national Treasury.[43] By early 1773, the EIC's troubled finances had become infamous on both sides of the Atlantic and fodder for speculation. Benjamin Franklin warned merchant Thomas Cushing in Boston that "the India Company is so out of Cash, that it cannot pay the bills drawn upon it, and its other Debts; and at the same time so out of Credit, that the Bank [of England] does not care to assist them, whence they find themselves obliged to lower their Dividend." At the same time, Franklin noted, the EIC had millions of pounds sterling worth of "Tea and other India Goods in their Warehouses" with no market and place to sell.[44] Paradoxically, the EIC had become too big to fail. If the company went bankrupt, then the cascade of ancillary business failures, investor losses, and lost revenue to the British Treasury would drag the nation's economy down.

The outcome of public criticism, financial crisis, and parliamentary investigation was nothing less than the reform and restructuring of the EIC. Between May and June 1773 Parliament passed three acts in succession to deal with the company's commercial operations, its fiscal health, and governance. The Loan Act and Regulating Act provided the EIC with an immediate secured loan of £1.4 million and the rights to retain its trade monopoly. In exchange, the EIC agreed to lower the dividend and limit voting rights in the company to those shareholders with at least £1,000 worth of stock. In addition, the Regulating Act required the company to provide its accounts to the Treasury and limit the terms for directors. Most importantly, Parliament placed the control of Bombay and Madras under the council at Bengal, headed by a state-sanctioned governor-general, Warren Hastings, to oversee the collection of revenue and perform diplomatic functions. In other words, the company could neither declare war nor negotiate "any treaty of peace, or other treaty, with any such *Indian* princes or powers," without the consent of a British imperial governing body.[45] Parliament now looked over the company's shoulder, prohibiting agents from receiving gifts and conducting private trade, even as it extended the court of law and civil service to British subjects abroad.

The net result, however, concentrated company power in the hands of a few wealthy stockholders.[46]

Not surprisingly, the EIC turned to tea as the cornerstone of its financial recovery plan. By the early 1770s, it was clear that the Townshend Acts and Indemnity Act had not worked as planned. The company directors calculated that when Parliament lowered the duty on all black and cheap green teas, the price per pound had fallen and the EIC had increased its sales. But since the remaining excise duties were based on the lower price, customs revenue "did not amount to more money on the increased quantity, than they would have amounted to on a lesser quantity sold at higher prices." Still, because the company was beholden to the Treasury for £400,000 a year, it could not afford to sell tea at a price competitive enough to stop the substantial trade in smuggled tea to Great Britain and the American colonies.[47] With 17 million pounds of tea stored in its warehouse and anticipation of another 14 million pounds to arrive from China in 1773 and 1774, the EIC held far more of the commodity than "the ordinary demand of twelve months."[48] The company expected to sell only 13 million pounds of tea over the next three years, sustaining an annual loss of £142,500.[49] The directors instructed the Canton council to cut back on tea contracts and concluded that it had to find ways of selling more tea, by expanding sales either in Europe or in the American colonies.[50] Amid continued debate over the EIC's trade monopoly, Parliament gave the company a chance to sell its surplus tea. Although it retained a three-penny per pound import duty paid in America, the Tea Act of 1773 allowed the EIC, free of other customs duties for five years, "to export tea, on their own account" directly to merchants in America, instead of through British wholesalers.[51] The company could export as much tea as it wanted, as long as it kept 10 million pounds in warehouse so that it would not overwhelm American markets.[52] Finally, and more important to the EIC, it would no longer be "liable for deficiencies in the revenue," saving £400,000 a year.[53]

Parliament and Prime Minister Lord North hoped not only to rescue the EIC, and consequently Great Britain, from financial ruin but also to combat smuggling and reap tax revenues by promoting tea sales in America.[54] William Palmer, a London tea merchant who took great interest in the American market, predicted 3 million pounds of tea would be sold annually. He encouraged the company directors to push the sale of Bohea but wanted to introduce new types of tea to American consumers, including Congou, Souchong, Singlo, and Twankay; Singlo tea, in particular, filled the EIC warehouses and was more likely to be "greatly damaged by age."[55] Palmer's recommendations came from the observations of merchants with cross-Atlantic interests. Gilbert Barclay of Philadelphia, for instance, suggested that direct sales to the colonies would be profitable for the company, and teas could be "sold cheaper than they can be smuggled from foreigners."[56] He hoped to profit as well with access to centrally located distribution centers and a patronage position from the company. He optimistically estimated an annual American demand of 6 million pounds of tea.[57] Samuel Wharton, another London merchant with Philadelphia ties, observed that repealing the three-penny duty on tea alone would not prevent Americans from purchasing teas from the Dutch or French. Instead, he believed that England could effectively command all the tea trade in North America only by sending a great "Quantity of Teas sufficient for the Consumption of that Continent."[58]

The Lords of the Treasury, who granted the EIC license to export tea, allowed for a few American "friends of government" to receive a commission to act as exclusive agents for the initial shipments under the Tea Act. When he heard about the consignments, Benjamin Franklin in London mused that other merchants "thus excluded from the tea trade" would likely be jealous.[59] The EIC directors looked to London merchants to nominate Americans for these commissions so that "satisfactory security" would be made for the transport and sale of the tea.[60] Indeed, the race to obtain company patronage began before the ink even dried on the Tea Act parchment. In May 1773, Gilbert Barclay of Philadelphia, who had suggested direct sales to America, received the first of four Philadelphia commissions to sell company tea.[61] Samuel Wharton, also a vocal proponent of having tea "annually landed immediately from China, in the most central Part of North America, and there being sold, at stated public Times," managed to get a commission for his brothers Thomas and Isaac Wharton.[62] Oddly enough, in the summer of 1773, Abel James and Henry Drinker were in the process of downsizing their Philadelphia business. They turned down a proposed trade partnership with William Henry, which they saw as "worthy the persuit of Men in the Prime of Life," rather than themselves.[63] Yet the following month they profusely thanked fellow Quaker Frederick Pigou in London and his partner Benjamin Booth for recommending them for a consignment of EIC tea.[64] The New York firm Pigou & Booth had also obtained a commission. With the chance to reap a 6 percent fee on the sales of their portion of 200,000 plus pounds of tea to be shipped to Philadelphia in the late fall, and with less than the usual shipping cost or risk, James and Drinker postponed retirement.[65] Similarly, consignees were selected for Boston and Charleston, with the first shipments of the EIC tea set to arrive in the colonies sometime in late November or early December 1773.[66] Soon, America would be awash in tea.

When news of the Tea Act reached the colonies, Americans generally despised it. Some colonists believed that by eliminating the English middleman, direct trade from the East Indies would give American merchants a new stature within British trading networks and consumers access to cheaper goods. A few even mustered sympathy and support for the EIC, since forced regulation was an infringement on its charter rights, a concern that the company shared with several American colonies. Most colonial political activists, however, worried that the Tea Act gave the EIC an unfair advantage within American commercial markets. They feared that once the EIC set up tea warehouses in America, the company would extend its monopoly to other East India goods or business practices.[67] "A Consistent Patriot" in Massachusetts thought the preference to appoint agents, "probably from North-Britain" (a reference to Scottish merchants and India-trained Nabobs), would allow outsiders to "thrive upon what are now the honest gains of *our own* Merchants."[68] A Pennsylvania pamphlet warned that if the EIC succeeded, "they will send their own Factors and Creatures, establish Houses amongst US, Ship US all other *East India* Goods . . . till they monopolize the whole Trade. Thus our Merchants are ruined, Ship Building ceases."[69] New York essayists also demanded protection for American merchants and markets. In October 1773, a series of five pamphlets written under the pen name HAMPDEN (in honor of John Hampden, who had died fighting the Stuart monarchs in the early 1640s) issued an *Alarm* to New York inhabitants about the "dreadful machinations" of the EIC and its attempt to force taxable tea on an unsuspecting public. Outlining the necessity of government to protect property rights and liberty of trade, HAMPDEN feared that American merchants teetered on the edge of a slippery slope. If the colonies accepted the shipment of company tea, he warned, "you will in Future, have an India Warehouse here; and the Trade of all the Commodities of that Country, will be lost to your Merchants, and carried on by the Company," which would control all pricing and sales.[70] Even British merchants feared that if colonists bought tea directly from the company at American warehouses with the little bit of hard currency they had, they would not be able to pay off their many English debts.[71]

Still, Americans tried to understand the intent and implication of the new tax duty under the Tea Act, to calculate their response. Inspired by the spirit of the nonimportation movement, many vocal colonists agreed that the EIC tea should not be accepted as long as the tax would be collected in America and the revenue paid salaries of British-appointed administrators. But even the American tea consignees seemed confused by the new tax structure and collection method. In August 1773, the EIC directors and Lord North suggested that the company pay the tea duties in London with bills of exchange, giving the appearance that America was not burdened with a new tax.[72] As late as November 1773, New York consignees Pigou & Booth thought the British Treasury had "taken great latitude" in explaining the Tea Act and wondered whether the law authorized the company "a Licence to send Tea to America *free of all Duties whatsoever.*" They assured James & Drinker in Philadelphia "that we have clear advices *that no duty will be paid here.*"[73] American political activists, however, were more skeptical. The Philadelphia "Mechanic" warned his readers not to believe "the artful Insinuation of our Enemies," when they insisted that "*the Duty will be paid in England*" rather than in the colonies.[74] Indeed, many Americans believed that the Tea Act simply masked the tea duty in a different guise; it allowed drawbacks in England yet maintained the three-penny tax in America, whether collected before, during, or after the sale.

The American tea consignees came to realize that their task would be complicated by the uncertain nature of the tax duty as well as the EIC's instructions, which narrowly restricted how individual merchants accepted, unloaded, secured, and sold their cargo. But they attempted to juggle their contractual obligations to the EIC and the demands of nonimportation committees with minimal conflict. Philadelphia activists reacted first, as news of the impending arrival of the EIC tea shipments spread along the East Coast. One faction, a self-appointed "Committee for Tarring and Feathering," threatened any Delaware River pilot who assisted the Philadelphia-bound tea ship with "A halter around your neck, ten gallons of liquid tar scattered on your pate, with the feathers of a dozen wild geese laid over." But in mid-October, citizens called for a meeting of the populace to discuss a more measured response. On October 16, 1773, they resolved that the duty on tea was "a tax on the Americans," levied without their consent. Within a week select members began to pressure the Philadelphia tea consignees to resign their commissions.[75] Activists called for action against the EIC, which, if allowed to land its tea "in this Land of Liberty," would effectively enslave "*American* Freemen."[76] When asked to resign their commission in October 1773, James and Drinker at first refused, citing the legal liabilities under which they acted; as

EIC consignees they would be responsible for protecting the tea under their care, as they would be for any private property in their possession.[77] Yet as they carefully danced around the letter of the law in their contracts, they also obfuscated their intentions. On October 17 and 19, the Philadelphia committee, after its daily pilgrimage to the merchants' doorstep, complained that James and Drinker's explanation of their refusal to resign was "neither candid nor Explicit."[78] No less opaque at the end of the week, the partners assured the crowd *that we neither meant nor intended to do any thing that would be disagreeable to our fellow Citizens.* " Hoping to appear "open and Friendly," they still refused to give the committee a definitive answer.[79]

As in Philadelphia, merchants prepared to receive tea shipments in New York worried about their liability under the EIC contract. Pigou & Booth resolutely declared: "With respect to ourselves as Agents to the Company, we mean to be very firm to the trust reposed in us, that we will neither be awed by the number of our opponents nor terrified by their threats, fully convinced that they act upon interested motives."[80] New York consignees faced their greatest resistance from smugglers and West Indies provisions traders, who supported the Sons of Liberty actions in late 1773.[81] Tea smugglers, in particular, threatened to disrupt the EIC shipments because they considered the company a commercial competitor, if not an enemy.[82] Benjamin Booth, hoping to garner sympathy from the public, accused those who opposed the consigned tea of rousing a mob, including maritime workers who profited from smuggling—"Boatmen, Along-shore men, Carmen and Porters, who are all paid highly for their services."[83] By mid-October, tradesmen began to pressure the New York consignees to resign their post "before the Tea comes," but Pigou and Booth insisted that they could not respond until they received instructions from the EIC.[84] Partially fearing that some of those who opposed them simply wanted "to wrest the Commission out of our hands," Pigou and Booth also hoped the vocal opposition would put them in better graces with the company. The firm confessed to fellow consignees in Philadelphia that they "pretend great fears" in order to maintain "an opposition sufficient to give us a claim of merit with the East India Company."[85]

By late November, the EIC-commissioned merchants in New York and Philadelphia offered to not sell the tea when it arrived but simply store it until they received further instructions from the company.[86] But local activists continued to pressure the consignees individually to send the cargo back to London. In Philadelphia, Abel James and Henry Drinker found "A Card" nailed to the door, informing them that the "TEA-SCHEME" meant to "enslave your native Country" would not be allowed: "we expect and desire you will immediately inform the PUBLIC . . . Whether you will, or will not, renounce all Pretensions to execute the Commission."[87] When threatened in a similar manner, Thomas and Isaac Wharton quickly resigned their commission, not wanting to lose "the affection of their fellow Citizens by their want of an explicit conduct."[88] Yet neither did they want to alienate the company that had hired them. In December, Thomas Wharton assured the merchant-banker Thomas Walpole that he gave up his EIC commission to distance himself from the growing controversy so he might "serve the Honable East India Company" more effectively.[89] A few days later he begged to be included in any future consignment of tea to Pennsylvania "after the Duty is repealed by Act of Parliament."[90] Indeed, by the time Captain Ayres, the commander of the ship *Polly*, arrived in Philadelphia with 568 chests and 130 quarter chests of tea, in mid-December, all the consignees—Thomas and Isaac Wharton, Abel James and Henry Drinker, Jonathan Brown, and Gilbert Barclay—had notarized affidavits refusing to accept the tea or even pay its freight charges, much to the captain's chagrin.[91] Although James & Drinker offered a compromise to receive and store the tea but not sell it, ultimately Captain Ayres, accompanied by Gilbert Barclay, returned peacefully to England with the controversial commodity still aboard.[92]

New York's "Tea Party" was a little more complicated. On November 29, 1773, when it became clear that both Philadelphia and Boston intended to refuse their shipments, the New York Association of the Sons of Liberty met "to prevent a Calamity," urging the tea consignees to resign their commissions. Like the Philadelphia resolves, New York activists also feared that the tea and its attendant tax duties would "sap the foundation of our freedom, whereby we should become slaves to our brethren and fellow subjects." Ominously, the Sons of Liberty warned that anyone who introduced "Tea from any Place whatsoever, into this Colony" that was subject to the new tax duty would "be deemed an Enemy to the liberties of *America*."[93] Although prepared to stop the tea from landing, the committee was probably disappointed when news arrived in late December that the New York–bound tea ship *Nancy*, under command of Captain Lockyer, had encountered a storm and lost its mizzenmast and anchor. Stuck on Sandy Hook at the mouth of New York Bay (a favorite unloading spot for smugglers), the captain entered the city to resupply. "We are now told that the Tea Ship will certainly go back, after being supplied with necessaries at the Hook," Pigou & Booth informed James & Drinker in Philadelphia. They hoped the governor and council would not attempt to land the tea, fearing it would "throw the Province into a Flame."[94] Wisely, the New York consignees sent Lockyer home to England, after briefly considering a plan to secretly forward the 698 chests of tea to Halifax.[95]

EIC-commissioned merchants in Philadelphia and New York were able to appease the committees and crowds to return the tea without unusual violence. Boston, however, experienced intense hostility between the consignees and political activists. Inspired by Philadelphia, Boston residents debated whether the tea should be landed in late October 1773. Thomas Peck, who, despite the rising controversy, had ordered several chests of tea from London merchants in mid-October, admitted the mistake to his suppliers within a week, since Philadelphia merchants had "voted unanimously that the tea shall not be landed and it is said that the Yorkers have concluded the same."[96] For the next two weeks, activists in Boston lobbied hard to get the merchants to resign their commissions and agree to return the tea. Protesters publicly boycotted the consignees' stores, attacked their homes, and held a series of town meetings. An advertisement posted November 2 invited all Bostonians to meet at the local Liberty Tree, where William Molineux, chairman of the "sons of freedom," along with Samuel Adams, William Dennie, Dr. Warren, and other committee members, confronted the consignees—Richard Clarke and his son Jonathan, Jonathan's cousin Joshua Winslow, Thomas and Elisha Hutchinson (the governor's sons), and Benjamin Faneuil—demanding that they resign. They refused.[97] Two meetings convened in early November, moderated by John Hancock, at which the members determined the Tea Act was "a political plan of the British administration" through which Boston's trade "is threatned to be totally destroyed" and America's liberty lost.[98] The "Freeholders and other Inhabitants" of Boston resolved, much like Philadelphians, that since the tea tax would be collected to pay government officials, court administrators, and military officers, it would, in essence supplant the colonial assemblies and "introduce arbitrary government and slavery."[99] They were determined to prevent the importation or sale of any tea.[100]

Like Philadelphia and New York, Boston consignees struggled to balance their responsibilities to the EIC with the demands of the Boston committee. In mid-November, as the mobs became more aggressive, the tea merchants became more obstinate. Governor Thomas Hutchinson insisted that he had done all he could to preserve "the peace and good Order of the Town." The governor's council, however, refused to back Hutchinson's efforts to suppress opposition.[101] A few days later, "a Considerable Body of People" paraded in front of and then attacked Richard Clark's house, where a family member fired a gun into the throng. The protesters broke windows but did "very little other Damage."[102] Confronted again at a town meeting November 18, the consignees assured John Hancock, the moderator, that they had "not yet received orders from the *East-India* Company respecting the expected *teas*," but they reminded the committee members that they had executed a legal bond with friends in London "of a commercial nature, which puts it out of our power to comply with the request of the town."[103] The nuance of their legal argument about contractual obligations, however, was lost on the crowd.

Once the *Dartmouth* arrived at the Boston Customs House with tea on November 28, the self-described patriots hastily called a town meeting for the following day. Faneuil Hall being too small, the crowd moved to the Old South Meeting House, where a thousand people gathered to demand that the ship be sent back to London.[104] With only twenty-one days to clear customs and unload the cargo, the merchant consignees suggested alternatives, such as letting the committee inspect and store the tea. But in the end they did nothing.[105] Francis Rotch, the ship owner, was loath to return to England, but he did not want to land the tea, fearing for his own safety. He thought it unfeasible to return the tea since the ship could not legally go back to England without being officially cleared at the Custom House.[106] Indeed, the consignees moved to the "Castle," a fortified structure in Boston harbor, for protection and to debate the demands of the committee. According to Governor Hutchinson, the activists first "resolved that the Tea should not be landed that no duty should be paid and that it should be sent back to England." The consignees, in turn, offered to suspend the sale of tea until the EIC could be consulted, but the committee rejected this proposal, demanding that the entire shipment be sent back to England. Hutchinson hoped to wait out the crowd since the tea "can neither be cleared here nor entered in England."[107]

However, when Captain Bruce arrived with the *Eleanor* and Captain Coffin's ship *Beaver* arrived "with the Small Pox & part of the Tea," the situation became extremely volatile.[108] Perhaps to save face, John Rowe, who owned the *Eleanor*, admitted to a town meeting on December 6 that he regretted "bringing any of that detestable and obnoxious Commodity" to town and wondered "Whether a little Salt Water would not do it good, or whether Salt Water would not make as good Tea as fresh."[109] Samuel Adams thought the situation more serious; indeed, he lamented the situation in Puritanical terms. Despite the nonimportation agreements and "to the Shame and Scandal of this Province," he argued, Boston merchants had continued to import taxed tea even though other colonies had stopped.[110] To rectify their sins, then, they should prevent the tea from landing. The governor refused the ships clearance to leave port, and the crowd blocked the ships from unloading their cargo. Looking back in sardonic understatement, Hutchinson informed Lord Dartmouth that by mid-December "the people in Boston and all the neighbouring Towns are raised to the highest degree of enthusiasm in opposition to the duty on Teas."[111]

What happened next any child could tell you, but contemporary witnesses described the scene with great economy. On the evening of December 16, 1773, "The Body meeting," as John Rowe dubbed it, dispersed, and "A number of People appearing in Indian Dresses went on board the three Ships Hall, Bruce & Coffin, they opened the Hatches, hoisted out the Tea & flung it overboard . . . Tis said near two thousand People were present at this affair."[112] John Tudor noted in his diary that it took "less then 3 some say 2 hours time" (Governor Hutchinson clocked it at "two hours time") to empty into the harbor 342 chests of tea worth £25,000 "without the least damage to the ships or other property."[113] Samuel Salisbury placed the deed at Griffin's wharf, where the three ships berthed. Before nine o'clock in the evening, "it was all destroy'd by breaking open the chest, & shovellg & Pouring out into the sea."[114] Most historians feel compelled to include the words of John Adams, who called the destruction of tea "so bold, so daring, so firm, intrepid and inflexible, and it must have so important consequences, and so lasting, that I cant but consider it as a Epocha in History." Still, the lawyer in him lamented that the mob action was "but an Attack upon Property. Another similar Exertion of popular Power, may produce the destruction of Lives."[115]

Perhaps this event can be viewed through another sort of prism—the global arena of commercial trade and a politicized consumer revolution. Indeed, those who condemned the 1773 Tea Act were far less provincial in their actions than assumed. Interestingly, the group who destroyed the tea in Boston came to be known as "MOHAWKS," a nod to the tribe of Iroquois warriors but also a reference to New York pamphleteers who first published their critique of the EIC tea in late November under that moniker.[116] Contemporary descriptions affirm the Boston activists' affinity to Native Americans. Several newspapers printed the minutes from "a Meeting of the PEOPLE of Boston," which noted that on December 16 "a number of brave and resolute men, dressed in the Indian manner, approached near the door of the assembly, and gave a war-whoop, which rang through the house, and was answered by some in the galleries." The group of "Indians" marched to the wharf "followed by hundreds of people" and dumped the tea in the harbor.[117] "An Impartial Observer,"

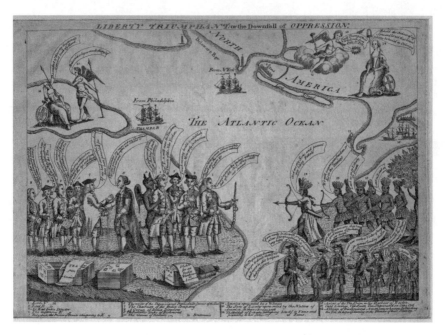

Liberty Triumphant; or, The Downfall of Oppression, engraving (Philadelphia, 1774).
In a "World Turned Upside Down," metaphorical Native American figures (Sons of
Liberty) on the right side of the print call for assistance from their fellow Americans
and promise to "secure your Freedom, or die in the Attempt." However, the Philadelphia engraver also downplayed the role of Boston during the 1773–74 tea crisis. The
rejected tea ships "From Philadelphia" (at the mouth of the Thames) and "From
N-York" are clearly marked, and the machinations between the East India Company,
the British ministry, the popular press, and the Devil to "establish our Monopoly
in America" take center stage. For a more detailed explanation of the image, see
E. P. Richardson, "Four American Political Prints," *American Art Journal* 6, no. 2
(November 1974): 36. The Library Company of Philadelphia.

in a letter to the *Boston Gazette* and *Boston Evening-Post*, also described the
appearance of "Aboriginal Natives" or "The Savages" who destroyed "the
pestilential Teas" even before the town meeting had adjourned.[118]

However, it seemed less clear what exactly white Americans thought a
"Mohawk" or "Aboriginal Native" might, in fact, look like. The haphazard disguises that the Bostonians threw together at the last minute may have masked
the true identity of men trying to evade possible arrest, but they also suggested another kind of exotic other. George Robert Twelves Hewes, who re-
counted his participation in the Boston Tea Party in his memoir at age ninety-

three, recalled that fifteen or twenty people donned "Indian dress," which simply entailed blackening their faces with soot from a blacksmith's shop and wrapping blankets around their shoulders.[119] Changing quickly at a neighbor's house, storefront, or tavern, they arrived at Griffin's wharf "with a company as fantastically arrayed in old frocks, red woolen caps, gowns, and all manner of like devices, as need be seen."[120] Although they may have been familiar with the use of the Indian figure as a metaphoric America fighting for its natural rights, as in the Philadelphia cartoonist's rendition of *Liberty Triumphant: or the Downfall of Oppression*, chances are that few of the men gathered to dump tea that evening had ever met or seen a Native American. However, through their labor on the waterfront as journeymen, apprentices, boatswains, or tradesmen, many would be familiar with the image of a Nabob or merchant agent trading in Asia, who were often portrayed in floppy caps and silken dressing gowns (banyans)—exotic garb of the East Indies. Indeed, many of these maritime laborers could have worked beside Asian sailors (lascars), who increasingly filled British merchant vessels that plied the Atlantic. By 1730, more than 25 percent of the crews in European-bound EIC ships were made up of lascars, mostly from Calcutta in Bengal. Lascars then became London-based sailors.[121] After all, marching alongside the Mohawk maiden in Carl Guttenberg's engraving *The Tea-Tax Tempest* were "East Indians" in the form of a turbaned and mounted Sepoy militiaman, both questioning the role of commercial empires in their colonized worlds.

Americans who opposed the Tea Act were especially aware of recent problems and abuses of the EIC in Asia and voiced sympathy for "East Indians." They did not just oppose the potential threat of tea taxes and the EIC's monopoly to American economic liberties; many condemned the company's imperial practices on the world stage. Even as early modern Anglo-Americans threw themselves wholeheartedly into a frenzy of consumption, they continued to express an underlying discomfort with the broader moral implications of commercial expansion and its political consequences. In 1773, some pamphleteers questioned the role of corporate entities within the empire, citing the unintended consequences of aggressive commercial expansion. A Philadelphia "Mechanic," for instance, warned that the EIC, once ensconced in America, would "leave no Stone unturned to become your Masters." Referring to the company's now notorious behavior in Bengal, the author argued that the EIC was "well versed in Tyranny, Plunder, Oppression, and Bloodshed. Whole Provinces labouring under the Distresses of Oppression, Slavery, Famine, and the Sword, are familiar to them. Thus they have enriched themselves,—thus they are become the most powerful Trading Company in the Universe."[122] Politically savvy Americans and merchants with cross-Atlantic ties were well aware of the rise of the EIC's corporate identity—the internal company tensions of the late seventeenth century, the emergence of an EIC-run militia to fend off interlopers and pirates of many nations, and finally, the sovereign powers that came with their entrenched presence in India.[123]

John Dickinson best articulated the moral outrage against the EIC after the passage of the Tea Act. Although he had earlier accepted a commercial codependence between Great Britain and its colonies, by late 1773 he had become more wary.[124] Writing as "Rusticus," he called on familiar linguistic riffs that equated economic regulation with colonial oppression. He noted with alarm that the five company tea ships then headed for America would "establish a Monopoly for the East-India Company, who have espoused the Cause of the Ministry; and hope to repair their broken Fortunes by the Ruin of *American* Freedom and Liberty!" Intriguingly, however, instead of picking apart the close ties between British tax policy and corporate power, he targeted the EIC's actions abroad as the source of America's fear. "Their conduct in *Asia*, for some Years past," he chided, disregarded the "Laws of Nations" as well as the rights of individuals. For the sake of profit, Dickinson argued, the EIC "levied War, excited Rebellions, dethroned lawful Princes," and "engrossed all the Necessaries of Life," allowing over a million residents of Bengal to starve during severe shortages in 1769.[125] Adam Smith similarly indicted the company for using their sovereign powers to squeeze "the little and transitory profit" from the natives of India, in essence acting against the best interest of those people for whom it served as civil administrator.[126] Dickinson, however, brought the argument home to America, warning, "The Monopoly of Tea, is . . . but a small Part of the Plan they have formed to strip us of our Property"; anyone who received company tea, or even assisted in unloading or storing it, would be an enemy of his country and no better than "a *Porter* to the *East-India Company.*" Dickinson asserted, as other Americans had, that he did not protest "the paltry Sum of Three-Pence which is now demanded, but the Principle upon which it is demanded"; he recognized that through a tangled network of global commercial concerns, an individual's purchase in the local marketplace affected the lives of those far beyond the shores of America.[127]

Just as Americans feared and loathed corporate sovereignty that might be used against them, British officials knew they depended greatly on the continued consumption of foreign goods by Americans and the revenue stream that trade produced. Even British supporters, who called for compromise and a looser tax policy, recognized the importance of the EIC in rectifying the political economy. Edmund Burke, for instance, exhorted Parliament to "Leave America, if she has taxable matter in her, to tax herself . . . Be content to bind America by laws of trade." He feared that, like a boar driven by a hunter, Americans might turn on Britain in anger.[128] He reminded Britons that the sale of tea, not taxes, provided the most important source of revenue from the colonies. Indeed, with millions of pounds "now locked up by the operation of an injudicious tax, and rotting in the warehouses of the Company," or dumped in Boston's harbor, Great Britain had lost its best chance of selling more tea in America. Still, he too thought in global terms and worried most about the cost of a burgeoning empire for a cash-strapped nation that had recently conquered parts of South Asia. Burke believed that tea held the key for alleviating the "crushing burden" of these "East India conquests."[129] Nevertheless, his hindsight in 1774 ignored the conclusions at which colonists had already arrived. Americans, who argued against the monopoly interests of the EIC, felt at a disadvantage in an increasingly global economy. They began to consider the British, like the French and Spanish, to be foreigners who limited their commercial rights. Advocacy for free trade as much as protests over the constitutionality of tax policy pushed Americans toward war.[130]

CHAPTER FIVE

Repatriating Tea in Revolutionary America

[Thomas] McKean informed the Congress that many Persons in
Pennsa, Maryland and Jersey sell Tea and drink Tea upon a
Report that Congress had granted Leave so to do and he doubted
Whether the Committees had Power to restrain them.
    —*Richard Smith, Diary, December 13, 1775*

At the height of the crisis that preceded the Boston Tea Party, Dr. Thomas
Young, known as a radical member of Boston's Committee of Correspondence, turned to published works by the French physicist Samuel Auguste
David Tissot and the English writer Thomas Short to condemn the use of tea
by American colonists—especially its presumed dangerous physical effects.
Ignoring Tissot's praise for its curative powers and Short's insistence that tea
had "eminent and unequalled Power to take off, or prevent Drowsiness and
Dulness, Damps and Clouds on the Brain and intellectual Facultie," Young
focused instead on the nervous disorders that both writers assumed stemmed
from the long-term use of the drink now common among the "Tea-fac'd Generation."[1] Dr. Young insisted tea was "a slow poison" that caused "the tremor
of the nerves" if one drank it strong. He included a cautionary tale of "an able
farmer's wife . . . whose ambition to ape high life, prompted her to drink Tea
so strong and unmixed, that in three or four years she lost the use of her
limbs, and died in a miserable condition." Although tea diminished the brain's
function, Young hoped it would not weaken the political resolve of patriots.[2]
Similarly, Dr. Benjamin Rush of Philadelphia warned of the physical and political consequences of consuming luxury commodities. In a February 1774
lecture Rush noted that tea had ravaging effects "upon the health and popu-
lousness of our country." He blamed tea for inducing a number of "political
evils" as well as "complicated diseases."[3] For both Young and Rush, tea cor-
roded the body and political virtue alike; it lulled Americans into a false ambition to imitate the fashionable "high life" before destroying their bodies
completely.

Young and Rush, however, were not articulating any new ideas; they wrote
out of critical habits held over from earlier luxury debates and nonimportation

A

S E R M O N

O N

T E A.

(✦✦✦✦✦✦✦✦✦✦✦✦✦✦✦✦✦✦✦✦✦✦✦✦)

" *Touch not, Taste not, Handle not.*"
ST. PAUL.

✦✦✦✦✦✦✦✦✦✦✦✦✦✦✦✦✦✦✦✦✦✦✦✦)

" *The Tea Pots full of warm Water, I see*
" *upon their Tables, put me in mind of* PANDO-
" RA's *Box, from whence all Sorts of Evil issue*
" *forth.*"
TISSOT.

✦✦✦✦✦✦✦✦✦✦✦✦✦✦✦✦✦✦✦✦✦✦✦✦)

L A N C A S T E R:
PRINTED BY F R A N C I S B A I L E Y.

Title page, *A Sermon on Tea*, printed by Francis Bailey (Lancaster, PA, 1774). This pamphlet addresses the physiological, cultural, and political criticisms of luxuries such as tea, which were common by the late eighteenth century. Courtesy of the Library of Congress.

arguments that were decades old. And tea, symbolic of the East India Company's trade monopoly and British parliamentary power, stood front and center in a new call for consumer restraint. In the aftermath of the Boston Tea Party and the broader colonial rejection of the EIC's monopoly powers, port cities, as well as small towns and local governments, took action to condemn the Coercive Acts imposed by Parliament in early 1774. Punitive in nature, these "Intolerable" Acts closed the port of Boston to trade but also placed control of Massachusetts's government and court system in the hands of British appointees until Americans agreed to pay compensation for the destroyed tea. Local committees throughout the mainland colonies, using a dose of moral language about the corrupting powers of luxury, called for limits on consumption, condemning the purchase and use of tea in particular to force Great Britain to lift its sanctions against Boston. By the fall of 1774, community resolves had persuaded the newly formed American Congress to establish the Continental Association, an organization that required national coordination and provincial committees of observation, inspection, and safety to oversee compliance with nonimportation and nonconsumption of all British goods and nonexportation of American produce.

Habits of censure, however, could not suppress habits of consumption. The closure of Boston's harbor followed by the near-universal acceptance of nonimportation disrupted Atlantic commerce, creating a scarcity of goods by late 1774 and early 1775. Despite the call for public virtue and consumer restraint, Americans' thirst for tea and other luxury goods to which they had grown accustomed had not diminished. Indeed, soon after the Continental Association went into effect, merchants and newly appointed provincial governments wrestled over provisions controlling tea still held from sale in America. Consumers rose up to action; rioting against merchant hoarders they demanded that tea and other scarce goods be made available to the public at a reasonable price. Even the Continental Congress had to rethink its trade policies in light of commercial demand and economic necessity. As the Massachusetts resistance became an American revolution in early 1776, Congress lifted its ban on exportations, allowing merchants to reestablish trade relations in the Dutch and French West Indies as an outlet for American provisions and once more to buy and sell tea. By the late 1770s, local and national politicians tasked with raising revenue to help pay the mounting cost of fighting a war even found tea the perfect commodity of exchange. Rather than eradicate luxury consumption, as Drs. Young and Rush suggested in 1774, Americans found ways to repatriate tea, to make it not only acceptable to drink once more but important to the budding commercial powers of a newly independent nation.

As news spread of the capsized tea in late 1773, Americans generally showed solidarity for the Boston patriots' actions. Several New England towns passed resolutions either during the tea crisis in December or immediately following. Lexington, Massachusetts (December 13, 1773), and Portsmouth, New Hampshire (December 16, 1773), resolved not to receive or sell tea, perhaps for fear that the EIC consignments might be diverted there.[4] But these communities also embraced nonimportation of British goods as a resounding political statement, equating tea with parliamentary taxes and its consumption as unpatriotic. Lexington, for instance, resolved to treat anyone who received, bought, or sold EIC tea "as enemies of their country," and if anyone purchased or consumed tea "in their families, such person shall be looked upon as an enemy to this Town, & to this country & shall, by this Town, be treated with neglect & contempt."[5] Rhode Island followed suit with a series of town meetings early the following year. On January 19, Providence condemned "the duty imposed by Parliament upon tea, landed in America" as a "tax on the Americans, or levying contributions on them, without their consent." Colonists were asked to oppose "this ministerial plan of governing America . . . to preserve even the shadow of liberty." The town ultimately resolved "That no tea belonging to the East India Company, or any other persons, subject to a duty, or duted tea, shall be unladed here, or brought to land." Supporting the opposition to tea in Boston, Philadelphia, and New York, Providence agreed to press all merchants to rescind any orders they may have placed for tea.[6] For the moment, at least, tea and its taxation, as well as suspicion of the EIC's monopoly and the anticipated repercussions in Boston, drove Americans to unite in condemning the luxury item.

Resolutions, however, hardly expressed the strong feelings in many American communities. The brash behavior of Bostonian patriots soon emboldened other colonists to devise "tea parties" of their own, setting off a chain of political actions from Massachusetts to South Carolina. Ten days after voting against the purchase and use of all tea, "the patriotic inhabitants of Lexington . . . brought together every ounce contained in the town, and committed it to one common bonfire."[7] On December 31, 1773, John Rowe noted that the people of Charlestown, Massachusetts, "collected what Tea they could find in the Town & burnt it in the view of a thousand Spectators"; at Dorchester the same day, a group seized a half chest of tea believed to be part of the original EIC consignment and "Brought it into the Common of Boston & Burnt it this night about eleven of Clock."[8] Well into 1774, tea in and around Boston, as well as up and down the Atlantic coast, was at risk of being destroyed. In January 1774, while at the College of New Jersey in Princeton, Charles Clinton Beatty and a group of high-spirited fellow students burned "all the Steward's winter store of Tea," along with an effigy of Thomas Hutchinson, to demonstrate their patriotism.[9]

Although the Princeton protest appeared a college prank, the violent con-

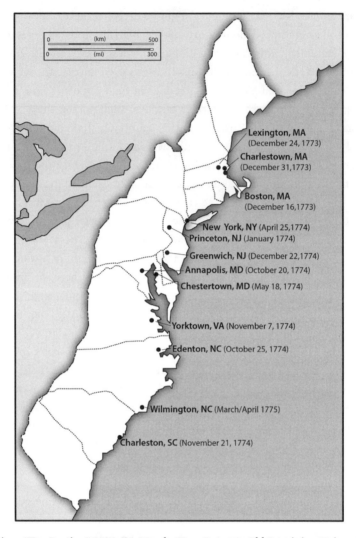

American "Tea Parties," 1773–75. Map by Taya Barnett, Old Dominion University.

demnation of tea also played out locally through the personal politics of small-town committees that had emerged during the preceding decade to oversee compliance to nonimportation agreements. When stopped in January 1774 by three or four men who "called themselves a Committee of suspicion for Charlestown," Cyrus Baldwin had to explain that in a pack of goods he was sending to his brother, he had stowed 26 pounds of Bohea tea "not for secrecy but for safety of conveyance." The self-appointed group broke open the cask and "carry'd off the bag with the Tea," as well as a few other articles.[10] When a portion of Boston's infamous tea consignment washed ashore on Cape Cod in Provincetown, the Wellfleet justice of the peace, John Greenough, helping merchant consignee Jonathan Clarke salvage his cargo, managed to get hold of two chests. His brother David warned him that the townspeople "are universally sett against it all our principal men seem to be in a Rage about it . . . that not only the Tea but your House & other effects will be destroyed with it & no body to pitty you."[11] Greenough was not dissuaded, however, and condemned the "absolute State of Tyrany and outrageous Cruelty" perpetuated by the Sons of Liberty, whom he called a "private gang of Plunderers & Assassins."[12] Greenough took one chest to Stephen Atwood in Provincetown, where it was destroyed the same night by townspeople, and he gave part of the other chest to Colonel Willard Knowles of Eastham, who fared no better.[13] When Knowles tried to sell a portion of the damaged tea in Eastham, "a Number of Persons trim'd in the modish or most devilish hew & Dress of barbarians with black faces & blacker Hearts" attempted to tar and feather him. But recognizing some of the men "by their voices he call'd them by Name" and begged to secure his health and life.[14] Tea and its consumption appeared to be universally condemned as unpatriotic. In the popular imagination, tea and those who sold it had become social pariahs.[15]

By the spring of 1774, Americans beyond New England faced the broader political implications of Boston's actions. Horrified by the potential repercussions of the Coercive Acts and fearful of parliamentary reprisal, many communities rallied against British policy, with tea the clear target of their anger. New Yorkers, whose EIC tea consignment had been stranded on Sandy Hook in late 1773, enjoyed a second chance to prove their patriotic bona fides. In April 1774, Captain Chambers, already rebuffed by a Philadelphia crowd, arrived in New York on the *London* with eighteen boxes of tea. Chambers had been "one of the first who refused to take the India Company's Tea on Freight the last Summer," for which he had been highly praised.[16] The New York Committee of Observation boarded the *London* to check the manifest and found not only the eighteen boxes of tea but the captain's own small stash of "20 small Boxes of fine Hyson tea," which he "positively denied having"; both were unceremoniously dumped into the harbor by an impatient crowd.[17] With the dramatic burning of the *Peggy Stewart* and its 2,320 pounds of "that detestable weed Tea" in Annapolis, Maryland, and smaller tea protests in Edenton, North Carolina; Yorktown, Virginia; and Charleston, South Carolina, by fall 1774 a boycott across the colonies of British goods, especially tea, was a foregone conclusion.[18]

Still, Americans had to translate local enthusiasm for burning tea into practical policy. The Continental Congress convened in September 1774 to debate a unified response to British sanctions in Massachusetts. The economic impact of the Coercive Acts and the efficacy of regulating importation were central to its deliberations. Although most members supported some form of economic protest, not everyone agreed that a ban on importation, let alone withholding American exports, would be effective. For example, John Adams argued for "a resolution against any tea, Dutch as well as English." However, he worried that a ban on exports would leave most Americans, especially his constituents in New England, without markets for their home-grown commodities and cut off from the Caribbean, where they traditionally sold fish, rye, wheat, or tobacco. "Could the people bear a total interruption of the West India trade?" Adams asked Congress. "Can they live without rum, sugar, and molasses? Will not this impatience and vexation defeat the measure? This would cut up the revenue by the roots, if wine, fruit, molasses, and sugar were discarded as well as tea."[19] In other words, like many merchants in the months prior, Adams worried that lost revenue from lack of trade abroad would do more economic damage than the Boston Port Bill itself. Nonetheless, in mid-October 1774, Congress adopted the Continental Association, which called for the complete cession of trade with Great Britain until Parliament lifted its restrictions on Boston. Citing the threat to life, liberty, and property implied in the recent parliamentary acts, Congress determined that "a non-importation, non-consumption, and non-exportation agreement, faithfully adhered to, will prove the most speedy, effectual, and peaceable measure." Tea, as symbol of British oppression, took center stage. From December first, Congress agreed that Americans should forgo the purchase of any "goods, wares, or merchandise" of Great Britain. More specifically, they agreed to "not purchase or use any tea imported on account of the East India Company, or any on which a duty hath been or shall be paid." Beginning March 1, 1775, the use or consumption of "any East India tea whatever" would be forbidden.[20] The more controversial policy, a ban on American exportation to Great Britain or the British West Indies, was to take effect September 10, 1775, in order to give merchants, farmers, manufacturers, and shippers time to plan for the disruption of trade.

Congress worried about the mechanics of complying with the Continental

Association, given the mixed success of nonimportation efforts during the prior decade. Although Americans were accustomed to nonimportation, Congress still had to urge colonists to practice "frugality, economy, and industry." It empowered county and local town committees "to observe the conduct of all persons touching this Association." Congress called on committees of observation and inspection to "discourage every species of extravagance and dissipation, especially all horse-racing, and all kinds of gaming, cock-fighting, exhibitions of shews, plays, and other expensive diversions and entertainments."[21] In addition, to coerce their fellow Americans, the local committees could use public shame, such as threatening to publish the names of consumers who did not comply. Changing long-established patterns of commercial autonomy, the committees could set prices and regulate the sale of confiscated goods, reimbursing the owner, but "the profit, if any," would be used to relieve the plight of the "poor inhabitants of the town of Boston," who suffered under the Coercive Acts.[22]

Empowered local committees especially tracked merchants, whom they often accused of wanton self-interest. In the wake of Congress's decree, the Massachusetts Provincial Congress, which sat at Cambridge, acted quickly to appoint a committee "to report a resolve recommending the total disuse of India teas."[23] In late October 1774 the committee recommended that every town and provincial district ban "all kinds of East India teas, as the baneful vehicle of a corrupt and venal administration, for the purpose of introducing despotism and slavery into this once happy country" and publish or post all the names of those "who shall sell or consume so extravagant and unnecessary an article of luxury."[24] Stephen Salisbury, in Worcester, Massachusetts, felt the sting of reprisal when he tried to remain neutral to nonimportation. As the deadline for compliance with the association drew near, local committee member Nathan Baldwin reminded "Friend Salisbury" that the Worcester nonconsumption and nonimportation agreement was already in effect, "which we have signed and are determined to abide by." Implying that Salisbury stood among "the *avoritious tory importers*" who had taken advantage of "Patriotick merchants who have countermanded their orders for goods," Baldwin called on Stephen to suspend trade "for the good of their Country."[25] Jonathan Amory in Boston also grumbled that the Massachusetts Provincial Congress resolved to seize merchant inventories "if our rights are not restored" by October 1775. He complained, "A very large Committee, no less than 63 have been chosen by the Town" to confiscate and store all British goods, including his.[26]

American merchants, attempting to balance the patriotic imperative of nonimportation with consumer demands for goods, scrambled to order items before Congress enacted the Continental Association. In June 1774, Samuel Salisbury "wrote an order to Mr. Waldo for a few goods" before Boston officially took a stance against importation.[27] The same month, Boston merchant William Barrell hoped to receive goods before the impending deadline. He warned his London correspondents Hayley & Hopkins that a nonimportation agreement would most likely "take place throughout the Continent this Fall" and begged them to ship his order without delay. He worried that Boston's committee of compliance would confiscate his goods if even "a few Hours" past the deadline.[28] But the rush to order goods before nonimportation took effect was even more pronounced in New York and Pennsylvania. In 1773, New Yorkers had imported £289,215 worth of goods from Great Britain, about half of the amount they took in two years earlier and slightly less than in 1772. However, in 1774 New York merchants increased the value of import orders to £437,938. Similarly, Philadelphia merchants ordered £426,449 worth of British imports in 1773, only £80,000 less than the year before, but increased their spending to £625,653 in 1774, hoping to beat the anticipated deadline for the Continental Association.[29] Even after its passage and despite the penalties of forfeiture and fines imposed by patriot governing bodies, American merchants continued to receive goods by alternative means. In New England, trade restrictions set by the Massachusetts Provincial Congress were undermined by "the practice of pedlers and petty chapmen," who brought British imports through smaller port towns such as Newport, Rhode Island, or Marblehead and Salem, Massachusetts, and traveled back roads "selling East India goods and teas, and various sorts of European manufactures, in direct opposition to the good and wholesome laws of this province."[30]

Merchant habits of self-interest also influenced Americans' response to new policies of nonexportation. American traders anxiously anticipated a drastic loss of business after September 1775, when the Continental Association cut off exportation of colonial produce. New York and Pennsylvania merchants carefully cultivated their trade networks in the Dutch West Indies, hoping to fill the expected decline in the provisions trade with Great Britain. They also wanted to show local committees of compliance, or committees of inspection and observation, that they were acting as patriots once war began in 1775. Still, New Yorkers exported £187,018 worth of goods to England during 1775, £100,000 more than the year before; Philadelphia merchants managed to export £175,963 worth of produce, over twice as much as the prior year. In other words, merchants still found ways to work with and around the Continental Association by timing their London orders, accelerating exportations, finding new networks of trade, or hoarding goods.[31]

Even amid the public displays of tea destruction and laws mandating nonimportation, nonconsumption, and nonexportation, tea played a complicated role in the political economy of revolutionary America. Pamphlets and broadsides like those by Drs. Young and Rush warned that tea, although an innocuous pleasure, might be America's political undoing. In the immediate aftermath of the Boston Tea Party, the demand for tea seemed to abate. Yet rhetoric and resolutions did not slow the circulation, sale, and consumption of tea for long. Throughout the 1770s merchants still ordered and offered tea for sale, and consumers still sought out and purchased tea. Samuel Wharton of London, a keen observer of American consumer trends, estimated in 1773 that 2 million Americans (whether urbanite or remote frontier dweller) drank tea daily, consuming about 5 million pounds a year.[32] New England merchants, however, complained they had little access to the cheap and politically acceptable Dutch tea that funneled through New York to Pennsylvania and New Jersey; thus they clung to British trade partners even as patriot activists demanded compliance with nonimportation. In 1771 and 1772, Bostonians legally imported a total of 373,077 pounds of tea; in 1774, anticipating its future scarcity, New England merchants ordered 30,161 pounds.[33] Indeed, tea made up a significant portion of last-minute orders prior to the embargo of British goods, at least in New England and the southern colonies. Maryland, Virginia, the Carolinas, and Georgia together imported 39,266 pounds of British tea in 1774, before Congress effectively cut off the supply (table 5.1).

As importation of British goods essentially ceased in the mid-Atlantic during 1774 and 1775, American merchants drew on well-used smuggling networks to find tea and other scarce commodities. Unlike New England and the South, the mid-Atlantic had better access to non-British goods, and merchants in Philadelphia and New York, once again working together, received, sold, and distributed tea from many alternative sources. For instance, large quantities of tea came into Philadelphia from New York smugglers, through wholesalers such as Charles Wharton, who offered tea to local shopkeepers and merchant firms by the hogshead, chest, and cask. Between January 1773 and December 1774, he sold over 44,000 pounds of tea.[34] Wharton, who began smuggling in the 1760s, sometimes partnered with other Philadelphia merchants but most often ordered tea from New York suppliers, who shipped goods "By way of Trentown," from which local shallop boats would ferry the

TABLE 5.1

EIC Tea Reexported to Select American Colonies, 1765–1776 (in lbs.)

Date	New England	New York	Pennsylvania	Maryland, Virginia, Carolinas, and Georgia
1765	175,389	226,232	54,538	65,265
1766	118,982	124,464	60,796	56,087
1767	152,435	177,111	87,741	62,674
1768	291,900	320,214	174,883	81,795
1769	86,004	4,282	81,729	54,763
1770	85,935	269	0	22,425
1771	282,857	1,035	495	74,766
1772	151,784	530	128	111,298
1773	206,312	208,385	208,191	115,520
1774	30,161	1,304	0	39,266
1775	8,005	0	0	0
1776	3,472	0	0	0

Source: Compiled from Great Britain, Board of Customs & Excise, Ledgers of Imports and Exports, 1696–1780, in the Public Records Office, London, reels 39–48 (also known as Customs 3). Great Britain, Public Records Office, Commissioners of Customs in America, Customs 16 America, 1768–1772, in the Public Records Office, London, reel 1, calculated slightly different figures for these regions; however, the general trends in importation of tea were the same.

Note: Figures for 1773 include the EIC tea that was turned away or destroyed in December.

tea to Philadelphia.[35] Wharton could resell tea smuggled via New York for a commission of 2.5–5 percent. In May 1774 alone he grossed over £230 on four lots of tea worth £6,000 that he sold for New York merchants John Vanderbilt, Cornelius and John Sebring, and VanEyck & Seaman.[36] Throughout 1774, Wharton's sales were brisk and cash his preferred mode of payment. Fellow Philadelphia merchant William Smith, a sometime co-conspirator of Wharton, had less luck with his New York tea connections. During late 1773, Smith tried to capitalize on the high demand he anticipated once the EIC boycott stopped the flow of tea. In mid-December, Smith ordered 1,500 pounds of tea from the New York firm Mercer & Ramsay, observing, "We have been so bare of Tea that all that is come or may be comeing will not last above 2 Weeks."[37] Unfortunately, many other merchants who had spare cash had ordered tea for precisely the same reason as Smith, and by January 1774, Philadelphia was awash in the beverage.[38] Circulation and sale of tea continued through late 1774 and 1775, although complicated by the boycotts and nonconsumption agreements. Smugglers supported the Continental Association when it coincided with their commercial interests but worried when nonconsumption clauses targeted even Dutch tea, in which they were heavily invested. In New York, for instance, less wealthy merchants known as "Holland free traders" flocked to the Sons of Liberty during 1774, hoping to control the committee system, while large dry goods importers fled. Still, when the New York Provincial Congress and Committee of Safety tried to shut down the consumption of all teas the following year, smugglers of Dutch tea demanded exemptions from the new laws.[39]

During 1775 and 1776, as fighting broke out in Massachusetts, newly established governing bodies carefully threaded their way between the economic needs of merchant communities (who had products to sell) and the demands of a consuming public. The Second Continental Congress, burdened with the implementation of nonexportation, had great difficulty enforcing commercial regulation as merchants called for open American ports and free trade. Some members of Congress fell back on the familiar rhetoric of restraint born of the luxury debates and earlier attempts at nonimportation. During the summer of 1775, for instance, Benjamin Franklin urged Americans to remain vigilant against importing foreign "Luxuries and Superfluities." He believed that the extensive boycotts had been beneficial to America's wartime economy: "By the present Stoppage of our Trade we save between four and five Millions per annum which will do something towards the Expense of the War."[40] However, Congress also began to take into account local economies and habits of consumption as they made commercial decisions for the new nation. In the fall of 1775, John Adams, recently appointed to a committee investigating complaints from New York and Philadelphia merchants about restrictions on the sale of tea inventories, wondered whether an America at war could survive without trade. Although he criticized mercantile self-interest as "mercenary and avaricious," he was a practical man and worried that commercial embargos would exacerbate unemployment or even food scarcity. "Shall We be able to maintain the War, wholly without Trade?" he asked his fellow delegates. "Can We support the Credit of our Currency, without it?"[41]

Merchants thought not. Early the next year they pressured Congress, Adams, and his committee to overturn policies restricting the sale and use of tea, indicating a subtle shift in the public's attitude about tea and its place in America's commercial markets.[42] In February some provincial governments sought direction from Congress about the sale and use of tea. Uncertain about its course of action, the legislative body instructed all local committees of inspection and observation "not to proceed in passing any censures on the venders, and users of Tea, till farther orders from Congress."[43] Congress finally lifted the ban on exportations and opened American ports to trade in April 1776. Extremely unpopular, nonexportation had cut off crucial provisions trade with the West Indies, along with exportation to Great Britain. Yet

America at war needed materials as well as European allies, and it could best find both through commercial treaties. Congress continued to ban all goods "of the growth, production, or manufacture of, or brought from any country under the dominion of the King of Great Britain" but allowed imports, subject to American duties, "from any other parts of the world to the thirteen United Colonies . . . except East India Tea."[44] However, tea was not dismissed out of hand. The same day that Congress opened ports to trade it appointed a new committee, which included Robert Morris, John Jay, and Thomas McKean, to decide how Americans should use or distribute tea already in the country.[45] The Continental Association of 1774, the committee argued, had not given the public enough time to sell or consume tea on hand, leaving "many zealous friends to the American cause" with large quantities. These patriot merchants stood to lose a great deal of money, thus "rendered incapable not only of paying their debts and maintaining their families, but also of vigourously exerting themselves in the service of their country." Consequently, the committee recommended that only teas imported on account of the EIC be excluded from sale, unless such tea had been taken by wartime privateers aboard prize ships; all other teas, especially those bought through the Dutch West Indies, could be sold and used. However, the congressional committee wanted to protect the interests of tea consumers as well; they required local town associations to cap the sales price for Bohea tea at 6 shillings per pound. They condemned any person who asked more for tea "as enemies to the American cause."[46] A relieved Connecticut congressional delegate, Oliver Wolcott, assured his wife by letter that "The Tea now in the Country will undoubtedly in a Very few days (by Resolve of Congress) be permitted to be consumed."[47]

Predictably, tensions soon arose between merchants ("zealous friends to the American cause") who wanted to control pricing and distribution of goods, local committees who had been granted powers by Congress to oversee commercial activities, and new state governments that tried to benefit from the regulated resale of tea. When fighting began, tea merchants complained that Congress did not give them enough time to sell their stock before the original Continental Association went into effect. When Congress reopened markets to tea in April 1776, merchants still complained, particularly about the powers placed in the hands of local committees to control prices and limit hoarding.[48] Backing away from its original mandate, the congressional committee appointed to investigate the tea trade in Philadelphia reported that since only traders who "took a lot of risk to bring goods into the city" had the knowledge and right to set commodity prices, "the power of committees of inspection and observation to regulate the prices of goods . . . ought to cease."[49] Still, a stagnant economy and inflated continental currency called for some form of intervention. In mid-1775 the New York Provincial Congress considered how tea might help the state recover some of the "very large expense" that the Continental Army owed. "Sundry of our merchants have on hand a considerable quantity of tea, imported from Holland, which cannot be sold," they informed their congressional delegation in July 1775. By consequence, they were unable to raise the cash to buy other needed goods for wartime, such as "sail duck, Russia drilling, Osnaburgs, arms and ammunition, all of them highly necessary for us, and easily to be obtained from Holland." The Provincial Congress recognized that tea, an easily transported and sold commodity of exchange, could provide needed tax revenue for the new state. But it also wanted to apply the tax "in the manner least liable to popular disgust, or perhaps, opposition." New York proposed, in essence, to fix the sales price of Bohea and green teas with a tax of one shilling per pound so that "we might raise a considerable sum from the obstinate consumers of this article." The state warned Congress that tea would make its way into New York whether they banned it or not; only by regulation and taxation could "the general consumption of it throughout the Colony" be used for a greater good.[50]

Throughout 1776, the New York provincial government and regional committees of compliance mediated conflicts between merchants and their customers over hoarding and price-gouging, thus helping to repatriate tea, despite occasional patriotic backlash. That summer the New-Windsor Committee of Safety in Ulster County complained that Jonathan Lawrence's wife sold tea at 8 shillings per pound, 2 shillings above the limit set by Congress.[51] In August, a similar complaint surfaced in New York City, where consumers were "reduced to great difficulties by the frequent sales of Bohea tea at higher prices than that limited by the Congress." The petitioners warned the New York provincial government about the "growing evil" and demanded quick action.[52] Although the New York committees still drew on language that condemned tea as a "useless herb," it is less clear whether the "growing evil" they referred to was the return of tea to the consumer market or the greed displayed by tea merchants. During the fall, the New York State Committee of Safety complained that when granted permission to sell tea, merchants had assured the state "that they would be content to sell the remaining stock on hand at the former current price," promising to use "the moneys arising from the sale of it in importing divers commodities very necessary to the defence of the Colonies." However, New York merchants scoffed at the price cap placed on a commodity that Congress had only recently condemned as unpatriotic. Instead, they threatened to stockpile tea "until such time as an artificial scarcity" would force consumers to buy at "exorbitant prices." The New York Committee of Safety, angry at monopolizers intent on creating "an artificial scarcity," resolved to confiscate Bohea tea from "every tea merchant, shop keeper, or other person or persons whatsoever in this State" who held more than 25 pounds. After reimbursing the merchants at 6 shillings per pound, including "a commission of 3 d per lb," the committee would make sure that the tea was made widely available to consumers and sold in a fair manner.[53]

Military suppliers in New York also battled merchants over price-gouging and stockpiling tea. In May 1776, for instance, Isaac Sears, a merchant shipper stationed in New Haven and zealous patriot who supplied the Continental Army, complained to George Washington that New York merchants threatened to charge as much as "a dollar per pound for their tea" and others had started selling their tea at 8 shillings, compelling New Haven merchants "to refuse selling their tea till they see what New-York intends to do." Sears assured General Washington that the thirty-nine chests of tea, which he held in New Haven, would be opened for "sale by the small quantity, at 6 s[hillings] New-York currency." Still, he worried that his tea might subsequently be re-sold at a much higher price.[54] That same month, cartmen Samuel Ward and Cornelius Van Horne entered the "Ten Eyck and Seaman's store" to purchase tea and supplies for the army in New York and faced another reluctant merchant. As the men later complained, storekeeper Andrew Gautier Jr. demanded "hard money for the tea, gold or silver, for that he would not sell an ounce of it for Continental money." After calling the two men "good for nothing rascals," Gautier's clerk, Zacharias Sickles, ordered them out of the store without the tea. Van Horne threatened to "raise a posse and take the tea by force," whereupon Sickles retorted, "if he did he would blow his brains out." Van Horne backed down but sardonically asked "where should cartmen get hard money; we work for the Continent and get Continental money," with which he could barely "purchase . . . the necessaries for his family."[55] Presumably the army, along with provincial governments, was beginning to agree with American consumers. Tea had become a necessity and should be priced so a common soldier or laborer like Van Horne could afford it.

Throughout the mid-1770s debate over the pricing and distribution of tea, consumers played the most important role in efforts to reintroduce the commodity to America. Women, in particular, voiced their concerns about importation, along with their desire for consumer goods, as store shelves emptied of British merchandise. Because they purchased the majority of household goods, women drove markets, but they also became easy targets for the rhetoric of restraint that still permeated the nonimportation and nonconsumption movement. Under the Continental Association in 1774 and 1775, ardent patriots condemned the use of tea by criticizing women for their supposed weakness in the face of luxury. In *A Sermon on Tea*, published in Lancaster, Pennsylvania, in 1774, women were warned that the letters TEA represented Tattling, Extravagance, and Absurdity, and that tea drinking would lead to scandal, excess, and disorders "worse than Pandora's Box." One of these disorders, Hysteria, was "peculiar to the fair sex," but tea would go so far as to turn "men into women, and the women into—God knows what."[56] Indeed, for women, the political calamity produced by tea drinking may have been secondary to its physical and spiritual damages, the author argued, strong green tea, having "powerful effects on the nerves," caused "tremors" and rendered a woman unattractive to the opposite sex.[57] Even when women publicly supported nonimportation, men found reasons to mock or question their motives. A few months after North Carolina's Provincial Congress at New Bern resolved to "not use nor suffer East India Tea to be used in our Families," in late summer 1774, the "Patriotic Ladies" of Edenton made a dramatically public promise "not to Conform to that Pernicious Custom of Drinking Tea" or to wear any clothing manufactured in England until the Coercive Acts were repealed.[58] The pictorial record of their action showed women as frivolous and fickle consumers, careless, even disorderly, in the company of leering men. In *A Society of Patriotic Ladies at Edenton, North Carolina*, by Philip Dawe, a child sits neglected on the floor amid domestic chaos. However, the women also display their political acumen; some dump tea from canisters, and others sign a petition. Even the child throws a small tea set on the floor in a fit, while a dog urinates on a pile of tea canisters nearby.

Yet American women also expressed ambivalence about nonconsumption, and their actions in the mid-1770s helped to repatriate tea to American stores and homes. In early 1775, Eliza Farmer of Philadelphia lamented that "the Non Importation is strictly adheard to and after this month no Tea is to be bought sold or drank." She worried the town committees might mark her and her family as "Enimies to America."[59] Young women of means tried to encourage each other to stay the course of the boycott, exchanging verse and prose in their commonplace books. In February 1775, Milcah Martha Moore and her friends were prepared to "sacrifice to Patriot Fame" and "give up Tea by way of healing." The poem she commemorated defiantly declared to "Let

A Society of Patriotic Ladies at Edenton in North Carolina, mezzotint, Philip Dawe (London, March 25, 1775). Courtesy Library of Congress.

the proud Nabobs storm & fret, / They cannot force our Throats to swallow." Still, Moore's hesitance about giving up a pleasant, daily social ritual rever- berated in her next commonplace entry. "The Ladies Lamentation over an empty Cannister" asked plaintively, "Why all their Malice shewn to Tea / So near, so dear-belov'd by me, / Reviving Draught, when I am dry— / Tea I must have, or I shall dye." Moore's friend "S.W." added a marginal note to the book: "Alas! How could the wise & generous gent. Who compos'd the Congress so cruel to the whole female World, to debar them so totally of their favourite Potation?—& does not this, largely partake of that Sp[iri]t of D[e]spotism, so loudly complain'd of in America." By 1777, Moore, reflecting a shift in public sentiment, had returned to open praise of tea: "Blest Leaf whose aromatic

Gales dispence, / To Men, Politeness, & to Ladies Sense / Gay Wit, good-Nature, circulate with thee, / Doctors & Misers, only rail at Tea."[60]

Clearly, Americans bristled at a "spirit of despotism" that touched their political economy as much as their politics. Rather than condemning the sale and consumption of tea, however, during the American Revolution more consumers, especially women, demanded access to commodities at a fair price and hounded the merchants who acted in self-interest. Taking up where committees and state governments left off, women took direct action against merchants who stockpiled or charged too much for tea and other scarce provisions. In August 1776, a group of women at Fishkill, New York, complained of the "most exorbitant price" that Jacobus Lefferts demanded for his tea; they formed their own committee, marched on his store, and proceeded to weigh, measure, and sell the tea for the congressionally sanctioned 6 shillings per pound. Instead of paying Lefferts, they "planned to send the proceeds from their sale to the Revolutionary county committee."[61] That same month, John Sleght, chairman of the Kingston, New York, Committee of Safety noted that an angry group of women had surrounded "the committee chamber, and say if they cannot have *tea*, their husbands and sons shall fight no more."[62] In the spring of 1777, near Poughkeepsie, New York, a crowd of women took tea from Peter Messier's store and sold it after determining their own price.[63] At New-Windsor, New York, James H. Kip warned merchant James Caldwell in July 1777 "that the women ! in this place have risen in a mob, and are now selling a box of tea of yours at 6s. per pound." He seemed quite surprised about "How they knew or got intelligence of it," but they had seized and broken open the boxes, forcing Caldwell to plead before the Council of Safety for assistance.[64] Although the New York Council of Safety disapproved of the "violent and disorderly proceedings" that threatened private property, the members acknowledged that the female rioters were following current laws in place; Caldwell would have to petition a higher authority.[65] All told, eight riots took place during 1776 and 1777 in New York alone to protest the excessive price or artificial scarcity of tea.[66]

Similar tensions played out between government regulations, consumer demands, and merchant self-interest in New England and Pennsylvania. In June 1776, the Committee of Correspondence, Inspection, and Safety of Worcester County, Massachusetts, followed Congress's lead and resolved to punish anyone who bought or sold Bohea tea for more than the congressionally sanctioned price.[67] In late 1776, Connecticut grappled with inflation, taxation, price controls, and scarcity. The state legislature worried about the "rapid and exorbitant rise upon the necessaries and conveniences of life" instigated "by monopolizers, the great pest of society, who prefer their own private gain to the interest and safety of their country." It passed an act to restrict prices on certain commodities, including Bohea tea.[68] The Philadelphia Committee of Inspection also reiterated the need to regulate the sale of both green and Bohea teas, warning merchants that if they refused to sell tea at a limited price, "they may depend upon being held up as enemies to their country."[69] Patriots turned republican critiques of luxury consumption on their head; they now condemned those merchants who charged too much for their foreign imports. Indeed, although they complained about their right to free trade, merchants began advertising their compliance to the law; Attmore & Hellings "at their store on the wharf, a few doors below Chestnut-street" assured customers that, in addition to "Bar Iron . . . Dutch Ovens, Pots, Kettles . . . brown Sugars, Molasses, French Brandy . . . Nutmegs, Spermaceti and Whale Oil," they offered "Tea at the price limited by Congress."[70] And consumers, especially women, in New England, New York, and Pennsylvania made clear their demands for a moral economy (or at least one that curtailed undue profit from the privation of others) by seizing goods from greedy merchants, petitioning for price caps, and taking public action when they thought it necessary.[71]

During the American Revolution, merchants and their customers quarreled over tea's price and availability, even as self-interest and the habits of consumption converged to reintroduce tea to store shelves. But the repatriation of tea also came about by actions of the Continental Congress, which sought to revive commercial credit abroad and extend diplomacy to finance the war. Individuals such as Robert Morris used personal fortunes to help purchase materials for the Continental Army, but Congress also encouraged participation of other merchants in foreign commerce to jump-start an independent economy and raise revenue.[72] Between 1775 and 1777, Congress commissioned a "Committee of Secret Correspondence" (later the Committee of Foreign Affairs) to negotiate commercial treaties in Europe. The committee granted its members Robert Morris, John Alsop, Francis Lewis, Philip Livingston, and Silas Deane a 5 percent commission to purchase an array of American produce, ship the commodities to friendly European ports ("Great Britain and the British Isles excepted"), and sell them at the best price. Any net proceeds from the sale of those commodities were to be invested in other "goods, wares or merchandise as the said Committee of Secrecy shall direct" and brought back to America.[73] France was particularly important to this commercial diplomacy. Members of the Committee of Secret Correspondence turned to French mercantile connections in the Caribbean for assistance even before the formal military alliance was agreed and the Treaty of Amity and Commerce signed. Robert Morris and his Philadelphia trade partner Thomas Willing purchased muskets and gunpowder to arm the Continental Army and found the French eager to provide any marketable commodities to American merchants in support of America's military needs. Estienne de Cathalan of Marseille assured Willing and Morris in January 1776 that besides the thousand muskets he shipped them via Bermuda vessels at Saint-Domingue, he could easily provide them "any other Articles they might be readily procured here, and conveyed to you by way of the West Indies."[74]

For war financiers like Willing and Morris, self-interest served a larger national purpose, and tea furnished an opportunity to pursue private fortunes that could be made in the name of public financing. Merchants in New York tapped into already established transnational networks in the Dutch West Indies, using their prerevolutionary talents as smugglers to avoid British blockades. In the summer of 1778, Gerard W. Beekman turned to trade partners in both St. Eustatius and Curaçao who supplied him with "Goods of all kinds," which were scarce and in great demand throughout America. Tea, in particular, interested him; he noted to his brother that he had one ship taken at Egg Harbor, "But I had Three Vessels Arrived Safe at Said place With Tea etc.," which sold for about £14,000.[75] No longer hampered by restrictions on its price and sale, Gerard worried that tea, which could command over £4 per pound late in the war, had become too valuable to risk its transport by wagon to New York markets.[76] Indeed, in late 1779, Beekman lost £28,000 to £30,000 worth of tea he had shipped via Virginia and Baltimore and another £10,000 in tea confiscated by the British.[77] Still, the rewards appeared to outweigh the risks for Beekman, who continued to order green and Bohea tea through his Dutch connections. By summer 1780, he parlayed his tea into "Bills on Spain" and "Bills on France," or simply cash on hand that could be used once more to purchase tea or other saleable goods.[78] Beekman, along with other American merchants, assisted by transnational commercial treaties and informal commercial connections, were crucial to reviving the flow of goods and credit to and from an emerging independent nation.

Yet tea still elicited familiar criticisms from the men tasked to revive American commerce. Benjamin Franklin, the American ambassador to France during the war, lamented the moral implications of the renewed demand for tea in America. In March 1779, Franklin's grandnephew Jonathan Williams Jr., a merchant and former congressional commissioner living in Nantes, informed him of several orders for goods he had received from America. Aside from "necessarys for Familys" more than half of the purchases consisted of Bohea tea.[79] Franklin was horrified and ashamed of the consuming behavior of Americans "when necessaries are wanting for Cloathing and defending!"[80] In a letter to Josiah Quincy Sr., Franklin berated his fellow countrymen for asking their money be laid out "for Superfluities," especially tea. He calculated that before the war Americans drank upward of £500,000 worth of tea annually. He worried the expense would continue to "weaken & impoverish our Country!"[81] Franklin's habit of extolling the so-called virtues of a republican political economy and condemning American luxury consumption, however, rings hollow, for Franklin failed to refuse himself any number of luxuries.[82] Always a man of paradox, he spent many an afternoon, whether in America or on diplomatic mission in France, entertaining friends, mistresses, or political envoys over a cup of tea.[83]

Despite Franklin's faux moral umbrage, American orders for tea made a sort of political and economic sense. American merchants and political leaders hoped to reestablish trade with the Dutch and French as part of broader diplomatic overtures. In October 1779, for instance, Franklin warned the president of Congress, John Jay, they could "have no expectations [of aid] from Holland" as long as "our credit there [is] so low." Indeed, the merchant orders for "superfluities" that he received were funded "with Congress interest bills of exchange," an attempt by the fledgling American government to establish credit and subsequent economic independence through commercial markets.[84] As Continental currency depreciated, however, foreign credit became more scarce. John Adams, openly courting the commercial favor of the French, worried late in the war that because American bills of exchange had depreciated, the public, as well as foreign traders, might lose faith in their value. In June 1780, Adams reprimanded the French foreign minister Charles Gravier, comte de Vergennes, that his countrymen, having profited greatly from American trade, were now unwilling to accept the depreciated rate of exchange that the Congress Plan of Finance had set in March. He noted that the commodity prices of salt, linens, broadcloth, iron, and millinery supplies had all been in France's favor. On top of his list was Bohea tea, which cost "forty sous a pound at L'Orient and Nantes" but could be sold for "forty-five dollars" in American ports like Boston or Philadelphia.[85]

Whereas the government under the Articles of Confederation struggled to establish a stable form of commercial credit internationally, emerging states began to pursue their own trade agreements directly with European nations. In July 1780, for instance, Pennsylvania appointed James Searle, one of its delegates in Congress and "late Chairman of the Commercial Committee of the said Congress," to negotiate a £200,000 loan with any willing nation at no more than 5 percent interest. If successful, the Pennsylvania Executive Council instructed Searle to use the money first to "purchase cloathing and Military Stores," then to send one-fourth of the remaining cash to the state president and council. More importantly, cash was to be "laid out in such articles of Merchandize as will be most usefull and profitable, such as Coarse Linnens and Woollens, Sail-duck, Osnabrigs, one hundred chests of Bohea Tea, & twenty-five chests of Green," to be shipped "in Dutch bottoms" by way of St. Eustatius.[86] Pennsylvania, like New York, used these goods, including the tea, not only to provision their troops but also to sell for a profit to pay for the expenses of war.[87] Clearly, the emerging American states no longer worried about the moral failings of luxury consumption. They hoped, instead, to harness consumer demand in order to pay off the growing debt brought on by war and the cost of newfound independence.

During and immediately after the Revolution, Americans tread carefully between the rhetoric of nonconsumption as the last bastion of liberty, the demands of the consumer marketplace, and the desire to establish an independent commercial empire on their own terms. Tea often triggered these contentious debates within local and state governments, as committees of compliance and legislatures haggled with merchants and consumers over the sale, price, and use of the commodity. Americans, long used to drinking the caffeinated beverage sweetened with sugar, demanded to have access to tea at a reasonable price. Merchants, with markets restricted by the war and congressional fiat, tried to maximize the price paid by artificially manipulating the supply of tea. State governments and Congress hoped that they could reap revenue to pay for a long and expensive war by selling or taxing tea. Still, a few political activists and writers on the American side of the Atlantic clung to the blatantly moral language of the earlier luxury debates to paint a negative picture of the new American consumer. "In vain we sought to check the growth of luxury, by sumptuary laws," wrote David Ramsay in 1778. Equating the consumer revolution that Americans had happily participated in with the tyranny of British rule, Ramsay blamed merchants or fashion-forward Londoners for enticing Americans "to copy the dissipated manners of the country from which we sprung. If therefore, we had continued dependent, our frugality, industry, and simplicity of manners, would have been lost in an imitation of British extravagance, idleness, and false refinements."[88] Only with the end of war could statesmen again promote the cultivation of useful knowledge, arts, and sciences, uplifting Americans to virtue. Interestingly, Ramsay anticipated an American future that included a global commercial presence as significant as Great Britain. He envisioned an empire where "Our stately oaks . . . will now be converted into ships of war, to ride triumphant on the ocean, and to carry American thunder around the world." With new "vessels of commerce, enriching this independent continent with the produce of every clime and every soil. The wealth of Europe, Asia, and Africa, will flow in upon America." Ramsay imagined a global trade unencumbered by restraints; free trade essentially would provide better prices for American produce and easier access to foreign goods "than we ever could, while we were subject to a British monopoly."[89]

By the end of the Revolution, Congress saw even greater advantages in the imported "wealth of Europe, Asia, and Africa"—a flood of goods that would provide a means to rebalance American trade and raise revenue for governmental operations. In December 1780, Congress urged the states to grant it the right to place duties on imported goods. Although it recommended that state assemblies pass laws to curtail "the importation of Foreign articles of luxury; as the most effectual means for encouraging industry, bringing the balance of trade in favor of the United States and increasing the national wealth," Congress also recognized that these same luxuries could provide much-needed revenue to pay off enormous debts after the war. Indeed, Congress provided a template for state importation tax laws to be enacted in April 1781 "for the purposes of redeeming the paper Bills of Credit issued for defraying the public expence." Among the first enumerated items were Madeira wine, port, rum, and green and Bohea teas. In return for this revenue stream, the states would allow Congress to erect "Custom Houses and appoint such officers to collect said duties."[90] Paradoxically, repatriated tea and the tax duties imposed on it would make American commercial independence possible. Yet, in fact, Americans would establish a commercial system somewhat similar to the hated British customs authority, which would require cargo manifests and grant agents the powers to board vessels, to inspect, search, and seize contraband.

CHAPTER SIX

Chinese Tea and American Commercial Independence

In our last we announced the arrival of the sloop Harriot,
captain Hallet, from the Cape of Good Hope; which event must
fill with sensible pleasure the breast of every American, and
cause their hearts to expand with gratitude to the Supreme Ruler
of the universe, by whose beneficence our commerce is freed
from those shackles it used to be cramped with, and bids fair to
extend to every part of the globe, without passing through the
medium of England, that rotten island, absorbed in debt, and
crumbling fast to annihilation.

— Pennsylvania Packet, *July 15, 1784*

After Rev. William Rogers of the Reformed Calvinist Church blessed the federal constitutional convention assembled at Philadelphia in the summer of 1787, James Campbell, the main orator at the Fourth of July commemoration, took the podium to praise the new nation and its economic future. "Our national Independence has opened the avenues of commerce with every part of the world," Campbell extolled, "and thereby not only lessened the price of our imports, but added to the value of our products." Like other proponents of free trade, he envisioned a diplomatic commercial spirit that would spread America's "civilizing virtues" by way of international trade treaties. More than economic independence, the defeat of Great Britain had helped America shake off "national prejudices," Campbell continued, "and we now view the whole human race as members of one great and extensive family, however much they may be distinguished from us by the circumstances of distance, colour, or religion."[1] Rather than a call to erase racial or religious bigotries, however, Campbell perceived this new unity as necessary for an open global marketplace: "the inhabitants of China, Bengal, and the United States, have met together on the sands of India; and by the influence of commerce have added the ties of interest to the obligations of universal benevolence."[2] He believed that American commercial self-interest contained moral elements that justified the quest for profits abroad.

Campbell and other American boosters heralded an age of economic optimism for America. Whereas Great Britain wrestled with the scandal of recent and continuing East India Company abuses and moved to rein in its corporate powers under Pitt's India Act of 1784, Americans imagined a bright, prosperous economic future that included free and open trade with Asia and the world. Also with the constitutional convention in mind, Tench Coxe, the political economist and delegate from Pennsylvania, addressed the Society for Political Enquiries meeting at Benjamin Franklin's Philadelphia house in 1787 to explore the role that commerce and industry would take in a new United States. "The revolution has opened to us some new branches of valuable commerce," Coxe reminded his audience. He envisioned that America could expand direct trade with known commercial allies, such as France, but also find new trade partners in Russia and Asia, thus paying off debts to "Europe with some of the *produce* of India." In this way, America could become a major shipper of commodities to and from Europe's West Indian and South American colonies.[3] Coxe, soon to become the assistant secretary of the Treasury under Alexander Hamilton, encouraged commercial expansion and direct trade with those nations whose commodities Americans had previously purchased from Great Britain. Unfettered by the taxes and mercantile restrictions of the British Empire, America would become an independent commercial nation, as well as a hub for trading Asian goods in the Western Hemisphere. Free and open trade between nations would usher in a new diplomatic era, binding America and Europe together in peace.[4]

Still, there was wariness embedded in the optimism of early national America; those with powers to shape a new political economy faced the conundrum of how to balance economic growth and commercial security. Coxe, for instance, mused that commercial expansion could only occur "if we do not over-regulate trade," yet he also knew that in order to take advantage of "the original market for the supplies of which we stand in need," American merchants required the protection of a strong federal government.[5] The emergence of direct trade between the United States and Asia in the 1780s and 1790s had a significant influence on the politics of consumption in America. Debates over the role of free trade and protectionism within an independent political economy divided state and national leaders, as well as merchant traders. During the Revolution, self-interest had been a necessity; privateering merchants took personal risks to maintain a flow of foodstuffs, war matériel, and cash to American markets. Yet their unconventional trading practices also threatened the success of the Revolution, which called for sacrifice to a common cause.[6] Merchants who hoped to profit by stockpiling tea or raising commodity prices had been reprimanded and reined in by the Continental Association and revolutionary committees of compliance. As the Revolution came to a close and the domestic economy stagnated, merchants sought to trade freely once more, first in exports to the West Indies, then directly with Asia, the source of many desirable consumer luxury goods. Hardly a new thought, as Coxe implied, direct trade with Asia had long captivated the American commercial imagination. By the mid-1780s, merchants in Philadelphia, New York, and New England were using the West Indies trade networks established by Europeans in the early eighteenth century, as well as money they made in those markets, to access the lucrative commerce of India and China. The ideals of free and open trade, born of contempt for British mercantilist monopolies and honed by merchant smugglers and wartime privateers, drove Americans to seek equal access to foreign markets.[7]

Political and economic necessity at home, however, forced Americans to adapt familiar mercantile policies to reap revenue from expanded maritime trade and protect American commercial interests. After the war, the tensions between self-interested freedom to trade and regulation of trade for tax revenues were at the forefront of political debates leading up to the constitutional convention and during the first session of the federal Congress in 1789. The Constitution granted Congress greater powers to create a uniform impost system, setting standard tariffs and duties on imports and exports in every state and allowing the federal government to collect revenue as well as protect American interests abroad. Still, most merchants hoped that commercial law would do more to encourage an entrepreneurial spirit rather than regulate with a heavy mercantilist hand like Great Britain. By the 1790s, the US government managed to find a balance with the passage of an initial Impost Bill. Rather than establishing American monopolies that would limit commercial participation, Congress used discriminating tariffs to favor any American merchant and ship over foreign competition.

Tea and the China trade framed the debates and outcome of these policies because tea reflected the importance of the global marketplace to the new American nation and the importance of consumer activities to the political economy. Although American consumers were mired in recession and slow to find the cash to pay for luxury goods after the Revolution, American taste for tea had not abated. Even during the Revolution, consumers bought, sold, traded, demanded, and drank tea. After the Revolution, Americans became even more enamored of the brew. Their tastes had expanded beyond Bohea, the staple coarse black tea of the colonial period, to a more varied palate; Souchong, Congou, Hyson, Hyson Skin, and Pekoe made their way into American households. Merchants used new marketing and packaging to entice American consumers and competed within a burgeoning host of tea sellers. As a commodity in demand, tea shaped early national debates over imposts, tariffs, and commercial diplomacy. National and state governments, saddled with war debts, hoped to tap into American consumer desires by enacting tariffs and tax duties on foreign imports. By the early 1790s, imposts on tea imports had become a cornerstone for new tax policy. Even though few merchants successfully participated in direct trade with China before the nineteenth century, tea merchants lobbied Congress for tax structures that favored their activities. Asia also played an oversized role in the American political vision as a symbol of the new nation's future commercial potential; if American merchants could compete favorably with the English East India Company without the benefit of monopoly rights, the United States could escape economic dependence. In fact, the first Congress specified tea for discriminating tariffs that favored American shippers over non-American importers, thus protecting American profits and encouraging direct trade to China by American merchants.

In the aftermath of the Revolution, Americans attempted to restore economic normalcy. Currency and credit were in short supply as states and individuals struggled with debt. Although a few commercial markets, such as Philadelphia dry goods, revived for a brief time with the help of French trade partners, business was volatile in the 1780s; moments of economic boom, especially during the latter years of the war and first years of peace, led to spectacular busts and bankruptcies. Abel James, for instance, once the successful partner of Henry Drinker, lost much of his fortune in real estate speculation; other Philadelphia firms collapsed along with the city's import business between 1783 and 1787. Sixty-eight Philadelphia firms failed during the 1780s, and the city directories record a steady decline in the number of businesses.[8] The credit crisis that undermined city mercantile firms also hurt ordinary Pennsylvania farmers who, unable to pay their taxes or provide crops for sale, suffered from a round of foreclosures.[9] New York markets proved equally insecure. Transnational partnerships helped goods flow to and from the West Indies; however, British suppliers had pulled out of New York at the end of the war and were forbidden to do business with US citizens in the Caribbean, forcing American merchants to seek out Dutch, French, and Spanish avenues of trade.[10] New England, which had excelled in wartime privateering, lagged behind Philadelphia and New York in the revival of its credit markets and foreign shipping. Fishing and farming had been disrupted, so the provisions trade was slow to recover. Many wealthy merchants fled during the war to Halifax along with British troops, leaving the commercial landscape in shambles. Troubling economic circumstances, centered on debt and lack of liquidity, tempered commercial optimism in the early 1780s.[11]

Britain still considered itself a major player in American markets and hoped to quickly restore credit and commercial ties across the Atlantic after the Treaty of Paris. However, British reluctance to accept American commercial independence created diplomatic tensions. Although Prime Minister Shelburne, negotiating for Great Britain at Paris in 1782, believed in the principles of free trade, he left the resolution of an initial postwar trade agreement ambiguous. Americans hoped for their old privileges of access to all British ports and normalization of previous trade patterns, without the restrictions of Navigation Acts. The British wanted renewed access to American "colonial" commodities in order to compete with French Caribbean produce. But by 1783, with Shelburne's removal, Parliament banned American ships from British colonies, excluding them from Caribbean ports, threatening the American provisions trade.[12] Great Britain worried most about potential competition from independent American merchants who bought and sold luxury imports. If some American shippers were "admitted into the ports of the West-India islands," reasoned one British commentator, then others would seek profit there, trading goods freely between European sources and British consumers. "Thus the American citizens will supply the West-India planters with the silks of France, with the groceries of Holland, and with the linens of Germany, in opposition to the manufactures of Great-Britain," unless Parliament took measures to stop trade between the United States and the British West Indies.[13] In essence, American free trade worried Great Britain immensely.

Although American diplomats such as John Adams hoped to restore "the intercourse between the United States, and the British islands in the West-Indies," US merchants calculated that they were perhaps more important to British trade than Britain was to reviving American commerce.[14] British merchants wanted desperately to recover outstanding debts from American correspondents and were confident that Americans in need of immediate easy credit and a sure market for their agricultural products would seek out the comfort of known trade partners. During one week in November 1782, Richard Waln of Philadelphia received nearly identical letters from merchant companies David & John Barclay and Harford & Powell touting the "pleasing prospect of the revival of an Intercourse with your Continent" and "the happy period of returning Peace." Both London firms quickly came to the point. The Barclays submitted a detailed account, asking for an outstanding balance of nearly £400, which they hoped the merchant would "embrace the earliest Opportunity to discharge."[15] Harford & Powell likewise demanded that Waln refer back to the balance due they had sent "in our Letter of 11 June 1776," and pay immediate and "frindly attention to the liquidation of thy account with us."[16]

Many Americans hoped to avoid British creditors, however, and instead pursued alternative markets in the Dutch, French, and Spanish West Indies. St. Eustatius, which had been important to American smugglers from the mid-eighteenth century, continued to provide cheaper and more expedient access to the consumer goods that Americans demanded. James Beekman and his brother Gerard W. Beekman of New York ordered goods, especially tea, from St. Eustatius and directly from Amsterdam in the 1780s.[17] "Independent" assured readers of *South-Carolina Gazette and General Advertiser* that the Dutch would gladly provide an assortment of Madeira wines, French brandy, Irish linens, silks, lace, sugar, and spices. And in exchange for ship timber, dried codfish, tobacco, tar, or turpentine, merchants in Lisbon, Portugal, could offer "teas much cheaper than from England."[18] The Spanish West Indies had also become an important market for American exports during the Revolution. By the early 1780s, Philadelphia merchants such as Robert Morris turned to Havana to secure hard currency. Silver Spanish pesos helped pay for war matériel and troop wages, but Cuba also purchased Pennsylvania flour and tentatively opened trade for American provisions, at least until 1785 when access to Spanish American ports was heavily restricted.[19] All told, the newly independent United States relied on trade with Caribbean islands as an outlet for American commodities and natural resources.

France in particular welcomed America's willingness to abandon old British trade partners. Within a year or two of the Treaty of Paris, diplomats had successfully negotiated access for American merchant ships to several free ports in the French Caribbean and along the French Atlantic coast. The French monarch, to promote trade, ordered that the ports of Dunkirk, Marseilles, L'Orient, Bayonne, and St. Jean de Luce "have full liberty of receiving the ships and merchandise of all nations, and to export all kinds of productions and goods."[20] A reporter from Languedoc in southern France insisted, "The town of L'Orient has immense markets in every article imported from

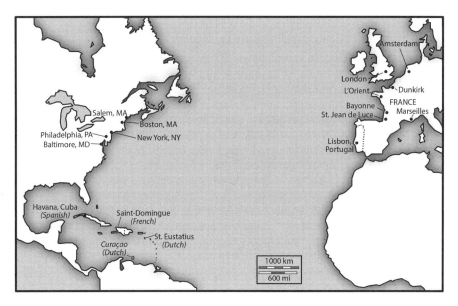

Ports of Trade for American Merchants, 1776–1790. Map by Taya Barnett, Old Dominion University.

India and China; America can always get from there great assortments of linens, silks, muslins, coffee, teas, pepper, and china-ware, at the same prices and credit, or discount, as England can give."[21] In 1784, after the arrival of congressional diplomatic commissioners Thomas Jefferson, Benjamin Franklin, and John Adams, France expanded its commercial agreement with the United States to include free exchange of goods at the Mauritius islands (the Isle de France), allowing Americans to purchase East India goods without investing in the longer voyage to Asia and drawing them closer to their ambition of direct trade with China.[22] Many US merchants agreed that French ports had advantages. The Amory brothers of Boston tried to revive their trade in the waning days of the Revolution. Jonathan wrote John, who had fled to London early in the war, that he thought "it better to ship from France than Holland," since the North Sea held greater risks than other Atlantic ports. More importantly, the cost of tea was reportedly higher in Holland than France.[23] Still, the French limited importation of trade items from America to those goods that French merchants could not provide themselves. Complete commercial equity was hard to attain.[24]

American merchants welcomed access to familiar Atlantic markets, such as Lisbon and St. Eustatius, and to new ports in Havana, Cuba, or L'Orient, because they were vital outlets for American commodity exports. However, Americans had a commercial vision that encompassed global interests; never simply Atlantic-centric, merchants soon sought direct access to Asian markets with desirable luxury commodities as a means for national economic recovery and assurance of commercial independence. In London, John Adams predicted a bright economic future in Asia, where commerce would secure America's "rising Empire," and, in turn, stimulate domestic manufacturing and agricultural output. Worried that Great Britain planned to restore the paternal controls of the Navigation Acts in America and that France also wished to undercut American free trade, Adams advocated, as he had since the 1770s, that Americans steer their own course. "There is no better advice to be given to the merchants of the United States," he told Secretary of Foreign Affairs John Jay in November 1785, "than to push their commerce to the East Indies as fast and as far as it will go." Noting that tobacco, animal furs, and ginseng "have been found to answer very well" in the Chinese market, he tied the nation's plentiful natural resources to foreign commerce.[25] Adams knew that direct trade abroad could function diplomatically as well. The presence of American merchants in Asia would signify American power and could be used to pressure Great Britain or France to deal favorably with the United States. News of the first Asian venture embarking from New York City brought images of proud Americans who congratulated "each other on the pleasing prospect of so many large ships being under sail in the bay." After a long, hard-fought war, many believed that the initiation of American commercial trade in the East Indies was a source of national pride, if not a potential "new source of riches."[26] William Grayson, a Virginia senator living in New York, where Congress convened, remarked that while in Canton "our country men had as much respect & civility shewn them as those of any other nation. The opinion here is that trade can be carried on to great advantage."[27]

Indeed, considering the recent war, commercial disruption, and credit restraints, Americans made a relatively speedy transition to direct Asian trade in the mid-1780s. Although the West Indies proved a better market for American goods, the challenge of competing globally drove the first generation of China traders. Using New England maritime skills and mid-Atlantic money, American merchants built or purchased foreign vessels large enough for long voyages. At first, merchant shippers returned to familiar networks in the West Indies for East India goods but added a few new ports that took them closer to Asia. The Cape of Good Hope and the Mauritius islands became early testing grounds for the marketability of American commodities—tobacco, flour, butter, dried cod, naval stores, and beef.[28] A Boston sloop, the *Harriet*, in late 1783, and the Salem-built *Grand Turks*, in late 1784, made initial excursions. Both carried crews and captains experienced with privateering and trade in the West Indies during the Revolution. Captain Hallet, on the *Harriet*, would have sailed farther East but was persuaded to sell the ship's cargo of American ginseng to British traders at the Cape of Good Hope in exchange for Hyson tea.[29] Elias Hasket Derby's *Grand Turks*, a fully armed 300-ton merchantman, had little luck selling its cargo of West Indian rum, sugar, and Virginia tobacco to the Dutch at the cape but managed to exchange it for £3,000 worth of Hyson tea at St. Helena. The captain returned to the French Caribbean where he traded the tea for more rum, thus making a small profit when he returned to Salem.[30]

Personal profit was elusive for some early traders, but a few transformed their China experience into acts of public diplomacy—commanding respect among the community of nations trading abroad. Within a year of the *Harriet*'s voyage, the *Empress of China*, a ship built in Baltimore and funded by Robert Morris of Philadelphia and Daniel Parker & Company of New York, completed the first American trip to China at a total cost of about $119,000.[31] Welcomed by the French and Portuguese when the ship arrived at Canton in August 1784, Samuel Shaw, hired as supercargo, insisted that Americans be considered equal trading partners. The Chinese merchants, government officials, and other European traders treated "them, in all respects, as a free and independent nation," Shaw noted in his journal. "The Chinese themselves were very indulgent towards us, and happy in the contemplation of a new people, opening to view a fresh force of commerce to their extensive empire."[32] All told, between 1784 and 1790, forty-one American maritime ventures exchanged goods in Canton markets; some ships, such as the *Empress of China*, made several voyages. Over the next decade (1791–1800) another 166 American vessels sailed directly to China. By the turn of the nineteenth century, Americans, using smaller, maneuverable ships with a minimal number of crewmembers, provided the EIC fierce competition for trade in Asia.[33]

Despite the growing presence of experienced "China hands" and merchant firms, Americans, like their European predecessors, struggled to find commodities other than hard currency as medium of exchange. Initially, as John Adams had suggested, Americans brought ginseng to Canton, since it was highly prized by the Chinese for its medicinal properties. One newspaper editor advised that Congress "encourage the cultivation and proper curing of ginseng, to prevent its exportation to any other country than China (and that in our own vessels)." He hoped that American merchants would "soon be enabled without the aid of specie, to receive in return every *necessary* oriental commodity," profiting greatly from "this lucrative trade."[34] Indeed, beginning in 1783, many shopkeepers in the United States accepted ginseng in lieu of currency or even offered to purchase it outright for resale in China.[35] Ginseng, however, quickly flooded the Asian market. In 1784, John White Swift, the purser on the *Empress of China*, worried that the ship's cargo included "too much Ginseng. A little of the best kind will yield an immense profit, but all the European Nations trading here bring this Article, and unfortunately this year ten times as much arrived as ever did before."[36] By 1786, Chinese merchants and other European traders complained that the Americans had so depreciated the price of ginseng as to bankrupt those who still held it.[37] British traders also complained that since the *Empress of China*'s arrival, the surplus of ginseng had made it "unsaleable." By the late 1780s, American merchants had to sell their ginseng in Canton at a loss.[38]

As the ginseng market collapsed, merchants turned to another plentiful North American natural resource, animal furs and skins, to bankroll the early China trade with mixed results. American agents in Canton tried to guide merchants through the commercial landscape of China to sell their furs at a good price. Samuel Shaw, supercargo of the *Empress of China*, was among the first Americans to establish a permanent China firm, in partnership with Thomas Randall of New York. They assured potential clients and investors that their collective experience from two voyages to China and Shaw's permanent residence in Canton enabled them to "do the business of any vessel in the most advantageous manner."[39] In his combined capacity as American consul to China (1786–1789) and veteran trader, Shaw seemed uniquely situated to negotiate a working relationship with Chinese merchants and to prepare the necessary paperwork to engage linguists (translators), pilots, and sponsors in Canton. In late 1789, for instance, Joseph Barrell & Company, the owners of the *Columbia* and the *Washington* enlisted the services of Shaw & Randall to dispose of the ships' furs and purchase goods for a return trip. The *Columbia*, however, had far more trouble selling its cargo than anticipated. Captain Robert Gray had arrived in China by way of the Pacific Northwest coast and Sandwich Islands with otter skins to sell. First, he failed to follow the advice of Shaw & Randall, who strongly suggested that he either sell the skins in Macao before sailing to Canton or hide the cargo from the local Mandarins to avoid the requisite shipping duties. Consequently, at Canton Captain

Gray and Richard Howe, the supercargo, could not find a buyer for his "seven hundred Indifferent Skins and three hundred pieces."[40] Shaw & Randall assured Joseph Barrell & Company that they would make every effort to find a full return cargo for the ship, but the lack of funds left few options except to purchase some poor quality Bohea tea, of which they secured contracts for six hundred chests.[41] Chinese officials delayed the ship further by refusing it permission to land. When Gray's compatriot, Captain John Kendrick, arrived on the *Washington* in late January 1790, he faced even greater problems finding a market for his American furs. Unable to leave Macao, Kendrick begged Gray and Howe for assistance, "being entirely destitute of every necessary or Cash to purchase unless I dispose of my furrs."[42] Shaw & Randall, exasperated by the American crew's lack of preparation or understanding of the China market, refused to assist them further. "We have endeavored to help the voyage buy a freight of Bohea teas on the same terms that other American vessels offered to take them," they wrote ship owner Joseph Barrell, but they had already loaned a good deal of cash to the crew and merchant agents without any assurance that the "Skin Cargo" would find a buyer in Canton.[43]

Prior to the nineteenth century, the American China trade floundered because, like the EIC before and other foreign traders in Canton, American merchants had to supplement their cargos with cold, hard cash when ginseng, sandalwood, and otter skins proved to be unreliable and unwanted commodities. Even during the first American voyages, merchants recognized the limitations of the Asian trade; John White Swift, of the *Empress of China*, knowingly wrote that the best cargo consisted of "A little Tar, a little Ginseng, a little Wine, and a great many Dollars."[44] Perhaps two-thirds of American purchases in China were made with silver coins during the late eighteenth century.[45] In fact, American commercial expansion in the Caribbean and to new ports in South America made it possible to capitalize ventures to Asia with Spanish silver.[46] The cash that Shaw & Randall loaned to struggling American traders in China always came in the form of Spanish dollars. Even though the *Columbia* and the *Washington* had trouble selling all their furs in 1790, the owner of the ships had to pay the firm $3,386 (in Spanish dollars) for the services of a Co-Hong merchant, Piqua, and presents to the local Hoppo, $216 for a linguist with an additional $44 for his transportation. For their work, China agents Shaw & Randall received a $1,605 commission on a $21,400 cargo that was eventually sold in Canton. After selling the cargo, paying the commission, and covering "Factory expences," the balance of $11,241.57 purchased a return cargo of Bohea tea for the *Columbia*, and Shaw & Randall retained enough cash for additional loans the firm could make to other American merchants arriving in China.[47]

Silver linked Atlantic trade networks with new Asian markets and allowed American traders to participate in a vibrant global economy, although they did not always profit. Still, despite their initial missteps or difficulties in finding viable commodities to exchange, Americans returned to China again and again to purchase an important commodity for home consumption: tea. "The inhabitants of America must have tea," Samuel Shaw purportedly proclaimed in the 1780s, "the consumption of which will necessarily increase with the increasing population of our country . . . and the otherwise useless produce of her mountains and forests will in a considerable degree supply her with this elegant luxury."[48] In the 1784–85 season, only two American ships sailed directly to China but they returned with 880,100 pounds of tea. The *Empress of China* alone transported 327,918 pounds of Bohea and Souchong and 74,915 pounds of green tea, from which Robert Morris and Daniel Parker realized a 25 percent return on their investment.[49] Over the next decade, American merchants purchased a prodigious amount of tea directly from China, averaging over 1 million pounds annually (table 6.1). Merchants instructed their agents trading at Canton to purchase tea, and lots of it. The supercargoes of the *Grand Turks*, which reached China on its second voyage, informed Salem merchant investor Elias Hasket Derby in November 1786 that they were taking a cargo to America, including porcelain cups and saucers and $21,000 worth of Bohea, Hyson, Singlo, and Congou teas.[50] During their first China voyage, in 1787, Joseph Barrell directed Captains Gray and Kendrick to sell both ships and the small sloop if need be and invest the proceeds in good quality Hyson tea.[51] Even when the bottom fell out of the ginseng market, supercargoes managed to purchase tea. Four American ships owned by Derby— the *Astrea*, *Atlantic*, *Light Horse*, and *Three Sisters*—arrived in Canton in 1789, loaded with ginseng. Disappointed with the resale value offered, the supercargoes sold two ships, netting $94,000; the remaining vessels *Astrea* and *Light Horse* sailed away with 728,871 pounds of tea.[52] Into the 1790s, tea made up at least half of the cargo value for most American ships trading in China.[53]

Americans did not simply import increasing amounts of tea in the 1780s and 1790s; the domestic markets for tea and availability of varietal teas also expanded. Once tea became more readily available to American consumers in the late 1780s, consumption met, and in some cases exceeded, prerevolution-

TABLE 6.1
Tea Imported to the United States from China on American Ships (in lbs.)

Date	Milburn Figures	Downs/Pitkin Figures
1784–85	880,100	—
1785–86	695,000	—
1786–87	1,181,860	—
1787–88	750,900	—
1788–89	1,188,800	—
1789–90	3,093,200	—
1790–91	743,100	3,047,242
1791–92	1,863,200	985,997
1792–93	1,538,400	2,614,008
1793–94	1,974,130	2,009,509
1794–95	1,438,270	2,460,914

Source: William Milburn, *Oriental Commerce* (London: Black, Parry, 1813), 2:486. Jacques M. Downs, *The Golden Ghetto: The American Commercial Community at Canton and the Shaping of American China Policy, 1784–1844* (Bethlehem, PA: Lehigh University Press, 1997), 353, provides alternate figures for 1790 on, based on Timothy Pitkin, *A Statistical View of the Commerce of the United States of America* (Hartford, CT, 1835), 246–47, which deduct teas reexported, perhaps reflecting domestic consumption more accurately. Nevertheless, James Fichter, *So Great a Profit: How the East Indies Trade Transformed Anglo-American Capitalism* (Cambridge, MA: Harvard University Press, 2010), 88, argues that very little tea purchased by American merchants was reexported to Europe until after 1800.
Note: Em dash indicates data not available.

ary estimates. Whereas Samuel Wharton had reckoned that Americans drank 2 pounds of tea annually in the 1770s, a typical family of the 1790s might purchase and drink 4 to 5 pounds each year. Boston merchant David S. Greenough kept careful records of his family budget between 1787 and 1789, buying 16 pounds of various teas for consumption. Over the course of the next four years (1790–1793), the family purchased just over 18 pounds of tea.[54] American consumer tastes for tea also became more sophisticated in the postwar period. Rather than the ubiquitous Bohea (a cheap, ordinary black tea), by the late eighteenth century Americans were drinking teas considered more subtle in taste. Souchong, Pekoe, and Congou could command higher prices, as could the green teas like Hyson, Young Hyson, Singlo, Gunpowder, and Bing. The refining of the American palette was partly due to the influence of merchants themselves, who pioneered techniques for the evaluation and marketing of tea. Merchants became connoisseurs of quality, hiring supercargoes for their experience not only in negotiating a deal in Canton but also in discerning the merits of various types of tea. Samuel Salisbury asked for feedback from his customers to determine what type of tea to purchase for his stores in Boston and Worcester. "The Chest of Tea I now send you is very much approv'd of," he told his brother Stephen in October 1785; he had rejected a cheaper variety because "it was not lik'd."[55]

Merchants, recognizing more sophisticated consumer tastes, tried to distinguish their goods from competitors' through newspaper advertisements and packaging, which grew more elaborate in the postwar period. Merchants also competed with public auctions and vendue sales that often sold larger quantities of goods at deep discounts. Thus they might use block letters or larger fonts to highlight the most popular items that drew customers. In 1789, Joseph Peirce in Boston proclaimed, "His Goods are purchased from first Hands, and the Prices of them compared with the Quality," which he assured his customers was worth the money. He sold "Hyson and Souchong Tea of the finest Flavor, in Cannisters or without," along with the "best Bohea Tea" at his shop on King Street.[56] On the front page of the *Pennsylvania Packet and Daily Advertiser*, merchants repeatedly informed consumers of "the best quality, imported" or "the first quality" of "Fresh Hyson, Tonkay, Souchong, and Bohea Teas."[57] By the 1790s, newspapers carried prominent advertisements for "India Goods." The *Salem Gazette* of March 22, 1791, emblazoned its front page with a lengthy column advertisement for a new cargo of goods from Bengal, Madras, and China to be sold at Elias Hasket Derby's store. The Chinese teas "of the best qualities" included seventy-five chests of Bohea, thirty chests of Hyson, and thirty chests of Souchong.[58] Merchants also played on the exotic nature of the East Indies to lure consumers, emphasizing the sophistication of American tastes to appeal to their vanity. Thomas Hare of Baltimore included an elaborate woodcut of the "Emperor of China" holding an umbrella to announce his "New Tea Store" with the "freshest Green and Black Teas, of every denomination."[59]

Urban commercial marketplaces and shopkeepers catered to rising consumer demands by becoming more specialized in tea sales. During the 1780s, city directories from New York, Boston, and Philadelphia make no mention of "tea merchants" among the ranks of well-known businesspeople. By the 1790s, however, many individuals identified themselves as "tea merchants." In Philadelphia, for instance, Ann Powel, situated at 15 South Third Street, distinguished herself as a simple "shopkeeper" in 1791, whereas two years later, she had become proprietor of her own "tea shop."[60] During that same year, three other individuals—John Campbell, William Whiteside, and William Redwood—were listed as tea merchants. Redwood had participated in the tea and grocery business from the 1770s and sold tea in small quantities, but he also bought and sold tea in bulk at vendue sales.[61] Originally from Rhode

New Tea Store.
Thomas Hare

At his Store *at the sign of the* Emperor *of* China, *and nearly op-posite the* Branch Bank, *has just received per the* Sarah and Elifa-beth *from* Nantz.

A QUANTITY OF
High flavoured and freſh Figs, Prunes, ſoft ſhelled Almonds and Raiſins—the Prunes are in ſmall baſkets of 6lb. each, which he can ſell at one dollar each.

A L S O,
A well choſen aſſortment of the beſt and freſheſt

Green and Black Teas,
of every denomination.

, G R O C E R I E S,
OF EVERY DESCRIPTION.

The quality of all will be found good, the whole of which will be ſold wholeſale or retail for *caſh* or *grain*, at as ſmall a profit as the buſineſs can poſſibly afford—He will not pre-ſume to promiſe too much, he is very ſenſible that the beſt way of expreſſing his gratitude for paſt favours, is by ſup-plying his cuſtomers with goods of the beſt quality, and at the moſt moderate prices —And the daily increaſe of buſi-neſs at the *New Store,* furniſhes him with humble hopes, that his friends and cuſtomers do not think him inattentive to thoſe conſiderations.

Baltimore, July 19, 1793.

Advertisement for the Thomas Hare Tea Store, *Baltimore Evening Post*, July 19, 1793.

Island, he moved to Philadelphia and by the 1770s was doing a brisk business in tea until the nonimportation boycotts of 1773 and 1774. In 1788, Redwood revived his business and for the next decade traded almost exclusively in tea. He supplied a wide range of teas to an increasingly discriminating clientele. Although Redwood sold Bohea in chests to storekeepers, individual consumers tended to buy more expensive varieties directly from him in smaller containers, such as a quarter chest or canister.[62] Philadelphia's booming tea market sported a number of competing merchants. In 1795, William Whiteside upgraded his listing at 99 North Second Street from tea merchant to "Whitesides Tea Warehouse," indicating that his business had expanded. Only a block away, "Joseph Wynkoop Tea Warehouse" set up shop.[63] By 1798, Whiteside's wife, Elizabeth, had taken over management of the warehouse, competing with Hannah Baker, Nathaniel Thomas, and John Barnes, all "dealers in tea," and the "tea warehouse" of Eaton & Co.[64]

Advertisement, specialization, and the influence of the merchant sales pitch could only account for some of the increase in tea sales and usage during the 1780s and 1790s. In the postwar period, domestic markets also expanded well beyond the usual port cities and their peripheries. Bostonians, Philadelphians, and New Yorkers had always had access to tea and other luxury consumer goods. But after the Revolution, country folk in townships far beyond urban America became significant consumers of tea. For instance, Stephen and Samuel Salisbury sold goods in their Boston and Worcester, Massachusetts, stores, but they also extended commercial networks into the rural communities of Grafton, Sutton, Leicester, Shrewsbury, Paxton, Amherst, Spencer, and Holden. Their tea sales had revived in the latter years of the Revolutionary War, and by 1781 the scale and breadth of their sales had increased significantly.[65] In 1786, John Hinckley of Leicester ordered "40 lb of good bohea tea" from Stephen Salisbury in Worcester, noting that he was "going to have a team goin to the Country to moro" where he would try to resell the tea: "I will Pay you the balance Next week," he promised—"p.s. need some squirrel shot as well."[66] In light of the newly opened China trade, Benjamin Gorton of Vermont advertised to purchase "Ginseng that is well washed, and dried in the air, and not by fire or in an oven," which he offered "in exchange for Bohea Tea, or Dry Goods."[67] Even as far north as Falmouth, Maine, storekeeper John Quinby kept his customers supplied with tea between 1784 and the 1790s. In exchange for their hard labor and resources, such as pine timber, shingles, or "1 pair Dear Skin Glove," Quinby sold small amounts of tea to townsfolk for a total of 90 pounds over the course of seven years.[68] Similar scenes played out in rural New York and the South as revolutionary restraint gave way to the comforts of daily tea consumption.[69]

As consumers shed the moral misgivings of buying and drinking tea, American governmental bodies also turned away from nonimportation and nonconsumption policies. After the war, the United States needed practical political solutions to economic problems; encouraging commercial enterprise abroad, for instance, could stimulate negotiation of international trade agreements, and tariffs on imported goods could provide a source of revenue. Rather than debating the ethical nature of economic policies, American statesmen more often disputed whether and under what circumstances to allow free trade or how to apply protective trade regulations. Granted, a few critics still warned of the physical, moral, and political failings brought on by luxury consumption. In early 1784, a Philadelphia newspaper alerted its readers that tea and the tea trade injured the physical health of American consumers by "enfeebling and enervating the bodies of people, and introducing several disorders that arise from laxity and debility." Tea would "corrupt the morals of the people" and affect the nerves so as "to abate courage, vigour and steadiness of mind."[70] Indeed, the renewed luxury debates drew on a moral language familiar to Americans. New England commentators, reiterating the Puritan jeremiad, renewed their calls for frugality and vigilance. In the mid-1780s, Noah Webster, Massachusetts essayist and educator, warned that American farmers lacked the moral restraint to forego luxury, which "rages among you." Many ministers and moralists fretted that excessive consumption of luxury goods would undermine Americans' hard-won political liberties.[71]

Still, postrevolutionary concerns leaned more toward the fiscal consequences of luxury consumption than the moral arguments of human failings. Americans worried that their nation's economic health could be susceptible to unrestrained market behavior. Even Webster emphasized that consumer desires, while morally suspect, could potentially bankrupt Americans, saddling them with crippling debt. In the mid-1780s, Massachusetts citizens created "anti-extravagance associations"—akin to the nonimportation and nonconsumption associations of the 1770s—that urged people to reduce luxury consumption in order to deal with personal financial problems and to live within their means.[72] American merchants, however, feared that British traders would take advantage of American desires and restrictions on American ships at British ports to dominate the import trade. In late 1785, New York merchant James Beekman blamed the "vast Importations since the Peace" on "the Number of British Merchants residing here, who have it in their power to undersell us to the allowed Detriment of Trade." Multiple vendue auctions, where shopkeepers could supply themselves with cheap goods, also made American merchants nervous. James Beekman even blamed the influx of low-priced bulk goods for creating a scarcity of cash.[73] Some critics pointed to the fate of Great Britain in Asia as a cautionary tale for America's new global commercial interests. The trade of foreign luxury goods, "A Citizen of New-York" warned in 1786, would corrupt Americans as it had Europeans, leaving the United States in debt and ruined financially. The writer argued that, like the Egyptians, Grecians, and Romans before, England had been sucked into the trap of conquest and commerce in India "by the sword of *violence*" at a great financial and political cost. Abusing credit and depleting the British nation of hard currency, the EIC had drained national wealth while its stock fell in London and it accrued "immense sums in debt in *India*."[74] America might just as easily succumb to commercial folly in foreign trade. Instead, the New York critic suggested that Americans forego foreign luxuries, such as silk, muslin, and tea, using instead "native commodities," lest they become degenerate and indebted like the EIC and Great Britain.[75]

But consumers returned readily to aspirational goods and spending, providing the states a new means for possible economic stability at home. Burdened with debt after the war, new state governments enthusiastically embraced taxes on luxury imports such as tea to raise revenue to fund state budgets and meet the requisitions demanded for the national war debt, which in 1785 was $3 million.[76] Prior to the Constitution's ratification, however, the states rejected attempts by the Continental Congress to impose a national tariff, insisting that it would unfairly burden states with busy commercial ports, such as Rhode Island. In 1781 Congress proposed a 5 percent impost on foreign imports, but there was no means to collect it.[77] A few years later, Congress tried again to secure the power to regulate foreign trade as part of broader commercial treaties. The appointed finance committee assessed the potential tax revenues on tea separate from "the imports of all goods from Europe," to better quantify an ad valorem (value-added) tax, and estimated that an expected importation of 300,000 pounds of Bohea and 25,000 pounds of other teas that year could yield $26,666 in import duties, or about 3 percent of total tax revenue.[78] Still, delegates from both New York and Rhode Island delayed these measures, since a national impost would nullify the states' own revenue provisions.

The states adopted a hodge-podge of trade regulations and tariffs on import commodities that set up competing commercial interests and sometimes countermanded or threatened to undermine international commercial treaties between the United States and foreign nations.[79] For instance, from 1783 to 1787 Massachusetts enforced "Articles of Impost and Excise," which charged an excise of 6 pence per pound on Bohea tea and 1 shilling for "every pound of other India Tea."[80] Georgia's 1786 "Act to Revise and Amend an Act for regulating the Trade" included import duties on Jamaica rum, molasses, beer, porter, ale, ciders, sugars, cocoa, pimento, coffee, and "On every pound of Bohea tea, four pence. On every pound of tea of any other kind, one shilling." The state required an additional 2 shillings per ton of cargo from "all British vessels" and 9 pence per ton for all others, giving preference to any vessel "wholly the property of any citizen or citizens of the United States."[81]

In fact, several state impost laws included discriminating tariffs that favored American merchants. Despite perennial rejection of proposed national tariffs, Rhode Island had a complicated system of "duties and imposts" in place by the late 1780s. It separated imposts on "all teas imported from China or India, in ships built in the thirteen states of North America," from those goods imported in foreign vessels. As late as September 1789, Rhode Island collected 6 cents a pound for Bohea, 10 cents a pound for Souchong or other black teas, and 20 cents a pound for Hyson, if imported directly by American merchants on American ships. "On all teas imported from Europe," however, the duties increased by 2 to 8 cents per pound.[82]

By the late 1780s the politics of consumption had evolved from the earlier luxury debates that questioned the moral character of the individual consumer to a broader discussion of the political economy. Americans pondered how to turn luxury consumption to its best political purpose in a way that benefited the nation as a whole. Politicians and economic pundits wondered how the United States could protect American trade without reproducing the mercantilist and monopolistic policies that had prompted their resistance to British rule a decade earlier. In fact, arguments that pitted free trade against protectionist regulation nudged Americans toward ratifying the Constitution, and the tea trade played a major role in these debates, since Asian trade represented a key component of America's participation in the global economy and a potential source of revenue. Some in the public still hoped that a stronger central government might use imposts on foreign goods to "check and prohibit an intemperate, impolitic, and luxurious commerce," in the words of the New York author of *The Commercial Conduct of the United States of American Considered*.[83] But more often, with the initiation of direct trade to Asia, observers promoted the use of discriminating tariffs that allowed American shippers freedom to import goods. John Adams, in 1785, suggested a balanced approach to tax duties that might discourage luxury consumption at home but also stem European commercial competition. He believed that the states could encourage direct trade between America and Asia "by laying on duties upon the importation of all East India goods from Europe," which may in turn lessen the demand for these goods. "Duties judiciously calculated," Adams wrote John Jay from London, "and made high enough to give a clear advantage to the direct importer from India, will answer the end as effectually as prohibitions, and are less odious, and less liable to exceptions."[84] The editor of the *Connecticut Courant* used the *Empress of China*'s second voyage in 1786 to urge Congress "to impose a heavy duty on the produce of the

East, unless imported directly from there in ships which are the property of citizens of the United States," in order to make sure "the profits of this lucrative trade will rest entirely among ourselves."[85]

Only after the Constitution was ratified, eliminating interstate trade restrictions, could Congress levy a uniform impost and create a Customs Office that had the powers to collect duties and enforce its laws.[86] The first session of Congress took up the issue of commercial regulation immediately, with a heated debate over tariffs and trade protections. Those who argued for free trade, such as James Madison, acknowledged the need to raise revenue for the "deficiency in our Treasury," but with laws that were not "oppressive to our constituents."[87] Madison believed that limited imposts on goods from China, which he described as mere luxuries, could accomplish both without favoring one region of the country over another or threatening the commercial treaties already in place. However, protectionists knew that commodities like tea were in high demand and thus it would be best for consumers to get tea from American merchants "first hand" rather than permit Britain to dominate the market. Robert Morris, who sought his own profits from the China trade, pressed the Pennsylvania delegation to incorporate discriminating tariffs, which gave preference to tea shipped directly from China on American vessels, into the Impost Bill that came before Congress for debate in April 1789.[88] Despite his past experience in privateering, Morris argued that the penalties against smuggling should be substantial enough to dissuade merchants from evading the import duties. Still, both free trade advocates and protectionists believed that some form of the bill should be put in place quickly. American merchants had already factored new tariffs into the price they charged for goods; they planned to profit before Congress acted and customs officials could collect the revenue on imports. Both Congress and the merchant community assumed consumers would bear the additional cost of taxes when they bought luxury goods like tea.[89]

In the end, the first Impost Bill included measures that protected American commercial interests in the tea trade and benefited the new federal government almost immediately. Even though it was never a substantial source of revenue, the duties "On tea imported direct from India or China in American ships" were surprisingly specific and reflected the growing refinement of American consumer tastes: 6 cents per pound assessed for Bohea, 10 cents per pound for Souchong and other black teas, 20 cents per pound on all green teas. If imported on foreign ships, the tea tariffs rose an additional 2 to 10 cents per pound.[90] Thus in 1790 alone the United States presumably collected

TABLE 6.2
Tea Imported to the United States from China and Europe, 1789–1794 (in lbs.)

Date	Type of Tea	From China	From Europe and Elsewhere
1789	Bohea	—	172,866
	Souchong	—	38,773
	Hyson	—	17,263
	Other green tea	—	23,345
1790	Bohea	1,503,293	565,938
	Souchong	378,683	55,974
	Hyson	637,904	19,992
	Other green tea	89,515	10,110
1791	Bohea	353,652	420,780
	Souchong	97,785	27,722
	Hyson	166,047	3,575
	Other green tea	53,206	473
1792	Bohea	1,250,261	1,098,513
	Souchong	87,024	49,499
	Hyson	134,277	15,808
	Other green tea	25,730	8,991
1793	Bohea	1,182,860	385,740
	Souchong	179,348	198,344
	Hyson	101,321	21,869
	Other green tea	112,467	22,497
1794	Bohea	1,397,901	737,615
	Souchong	286,856	48,866
	Hyson	94,893	5,593
	Other green tea	50,206	1,335

Source: "Value of Imports paying ad valorem, and quantities subject to specific duties, from 1789 to 1794," January 26, 1796, *American State Papers, Commerce and Navigation*, vol. 1, House, 4th Cong., 1st sess., no. 20, table p. 324.
   Note: Em dash indicates data not available.

$273,549.68 in tax revenue on all teas imported directly from China in American ships; nearly $60,000 more came from teas brought from Europe, far more than estimated seven years earlier (table 6.2).

Regrettably, discriminating tea tariffs on non-American shippers did not eliminate foreign competition. European traders continued to fulfill increasing demand for a variety of teas in the 1790s (see table 6.2). One commentator estimated that American merchants imported over 2.6 million pounds of tea directly from China in 1790, "which is fully equal to our consumption." However, Europeans (not including the British) shipped an additional 416,652 pounds of tea that year, "to the great injury of our merchants."[91] As the American markets overflowed with tea, some traders could not sell enough inventory to pay their tax bills. In 1791, Elias Hasket Derby of Salem, estimating a tea supply of "at least three Years Consumption," and a group of other wealthy merchants in New England, New York, and Philadelphia who depended on the emergent China trade, petitioned Congress for federal protections against both foreign shippers and customs duties.[92] Alexander Hamilton, then secretary of the Treasury, supported their cause. He assured Congress in early 1791 that he would never act "in favor of an individual" but "that the importers of teas" as a group had difficulty covering the tax duties since the commodity price had dropped. Hamilton asked Congress to consider extending a credit "upon the impost on teas" to all American importers. He noted that European traders had introduced "considerable quantities of Bohea tea" in the United States despite discriminating tariffs, which "contributed both to overstock the market and to reduce the price below the standard at which it can be afforded by the merchants trading to China." Because he believed the China trade remained vital to the American economy, Hamilton also suggested an additional 3 cents per pound duty be added to foreign importation of Bohea tea.[93] In March 1791, Congress passed a "Tea Act," which gave American tea importers two years to pay import duties if they put up a bond and deposited their wares in storage under supervision of a customs inspector.[94] Government leaders had learned hard lessons from the inflexible, contentious tax policies of their youth; bending to merchant interests now could prevent a future break in the fragile American political economy.

Consumer Desires

The potential rewards of trade with Asia, through the purchase and sale of tea in particular, drove enterprising American merchants to take risks and try their luck in China. Prior to the nineteenth century, however, these efforts disappointed more often than not. American products did not always work in the Canton marketplace, and cash was scarce. Profits from the produce of China and the tax revenue it generated remained relatively minor during the first decades of independence, when West Indies trade proved far more important. By 1790, nearly a third of all American exports—especially provisions such as flour, beef, pork, fish, and corn—landed in the West Indies. This trade expanded tremendously after 1793, with the outbreak of war between France and Great Britain. French Caribbean islands like Saint-Domingue welcomed trade with the United States to the amount of $8 million a year until Jay's Treaty dampened commercial goodwill between the two nations.[1] Still, the China trade and tea continued to play a key role in the politics of consumption. Tea promised all that America had fought for commercially. Consumers could fulfill their desires without limitations. The United States could command respect from Great Britain and challenge the East India Company's monopoly in Asia, stimulating economic growth and the assurance of free and open trade that allowed merchants to demonstrate their bona fides as global players within a rising American empire.

For a second generation of American merchants in China, the tea trade provided greater rewards as their expertise grew. Thomas Handasyd Perkins, a Boston merchant whose family had been extensively involved in the West Indian provisions trade after the Revolutionary War, turned to China in the 1790s. Perkins came to know all aspects of the tea trade. In 1798, he instructed his ship captain to deal with the Hong merchant Pankequa, whom he believed "the most reputable of the Colony for a number of years," but to withhold payment until the teas were stowed on board. He recommended purchasing only fresh teas, which could be judged by their heaviness "in the hand, greenish, with no red leaves," but warned not to buy from "Foreigners in Canton," who would "try to put off old teas on you. Better deal with the Chinese."[2] By the early nineteenth century, in partnership with his brother

James, Thomas created Perkins & Company, which operated out of Canton, and sent an apprentice, Ephraim Bumstead, and distant nephew, Frederick William Paine, to run the business. They made a tidy fortune in tea.[3]

However, potential profits induced some to make unethical commercial choices, raising new questions about corporate accountability. Like other American merchants in China, Perkins & Company tested out new trade routes and new commodities to exchange for tea. Bombay and Calcutta became way stations for American ships where "a load of Cotton" or "Black Wood" could be purchased for the China trade.[4] More risky, but increasingly lucrative, was the sale of opium. Smyrna, in present-day Turkey, and Bengal provided the drug to American merchants, who could sell it in Batavia "for Dollars" or trade it in Borneo for pepper. But more often, opium was taken to China in exchange for tea. Even after China outlawed opium imports in 1800, American traders smuggled opium into Canton with the help of a well-armed vessel and "subaltern Mandarins."[5] Besides Perkins & Company, Philadelphia merchant Stephen Girard and the firm Willings & Francis, as well as Christopher Gantt of Baltimore joined this illegal trade, creating a series of "opium rushes," similar to the boom and bust cycles that ginseng and otter skins had generated in prior decades.[6] The EIC and other European trade companies also flooded the market at Canton with opium, which soon outpaced any other item as a commodity of exchange between India and China, leading to increased addiction among the Chinese population, open conflict between Britain and China, and the forced concession of Hong Kong in the early 1840s.[7] Although Americans of an earlier generation had complained about the EIC abuse of corporate powers in South Asia, nineteenth-century American merchants profited from illegal sales of opium and, because of British military threats, the United States received similar commercial concessions from China in 1844.

Consumer markets and behavior had also changed by the turn of the nineteenth century. Habituation had created more demand for tea, putting pressure on the chain of production and distribution in China. Thus merchants purchased and sold increasing quantities of cheap black teas offered in Canton. But American tastes had become more refined; tea merchants, like Thomas Handasyd Perkins, lamented that even the buying habits of less wealthy consumers precluded cheap teas. "It is not that the rich have abandoned Hyson and substituted Hyson Skins," he warned his agent in Canton, "but that the Farmers have given up Bohea and other inferior teas and taken to Skin teas." Evoking the moral arguments of the previous century, Perkins added: "As population and its handmaid luxury are increasing, we expect that Bohea will be out of use in a few years."[8] Some merchants attempted to dress up cheaper teas to look more expensive. Edward Carrington, a Rhode Island merchant doing business in Canton determined that "the American Market does not require the best qualities of tea, nor, will the consumers *here* pay a price for them." Instead, he packed his "fair quality" teas "in handsome chests & boxes" in order to sell more.[9] Still, merchants had to stock a far greater variety of teas to please the American palate. During the 1805–6 season, Willings & Francis purchased 5,000 quarter chests of tea in Canton, including Congo, Campoy, Souchong, Pekoe, Hyson, Hyson Skin, Tonkay, Singlo, Young Hyson, Padre Souchong, Black Gunpowder, and Fine Gunpowder.[10] And advertisements for an array of global goods featured patriotic images of eagles with talons clutching arrows or American ships celebrating America's growing commercial empire abroad bringing "fresh teas, wines, spirits, coffee, Havana sugars" to discerning consumers at home.[11]

Changing consumer habits also helped open new commercial markets for American merchants in the nineteenth century. Before the constitutional convention Tench Coxe had envisioned that, with "strict oeconomy" and less regulation, American merchants could "pay Europe with some of the *produce* of India, for a part of the goods with which they supply us."[12] Further, he hoped the United States could secure commercial privileges from European nations, especially if they were embroiled in conflict among themselves. A neutral America could step in to carry freight for all, thus expanding markets for American produce. As Coxe predicted, American entrepreneurs eventually turned the tables on European commercial supremacy. By the late 1790s, as warfare between Britain and France escalated once more, American merchants became neutral trade partners in several commercial ports, and reexported the growing supply of tea brought to the United States. In 1797, Thomas Handasyd Perkins noted that since "Dutch trade to China is at an end, we think teas may answer in Holland, if permitted." He expected to ship more than 1,200 chests of Bohea, Hyson, and Souchong, along with other East India goods, to Amsterdam that season.[13] Similarly, Philadelphia traders participated in tea reexportation at the turn of the nineteenth century. Stephen Girard, a wealthy merchant and banker who rose to power following the American Revolution, sent his supercargo, George Washington Biddle, to Canton to purchase teas for resale on the Antwerp market.[14] Willings & Francis assured Amsterdam purchasers in 1806, "We are confident that no better cargoes have been received from China this year . . . these Teas are all fresh of the last crop."[15] Continued war between France and Britain, as well as increased parliamentary oversight of the EIC, hurt British tea exports, but smaller American ships operated by private traders could easily supply European consumer demand. By the early nineteenth century, about 27 percent of the tea imported from China by American merchants was transshipped to Europe for resale.[16]

Still, Americans continued to have trouble with tea. Notwithstanding the rise of commercial success in Asia, cycles of scarcity and oversupply plagued the European markets as much as the United States. In 1806, Willings & Francis warned its China agent William Reid that Europeans were not purchasing tea—"Holland is Shut. Antwerp is overstocked"—and they feared that other ports in Germany "will not more than realize cost, Freights & Charges."[17] And American merchants bristled at commercial regulation and taxation when it failed to align with their interests. Like individual agents of the EIC and interlopers in the early eighteenth century, many American merchants used the reexport markets to avoid paying customs and port duties on goods that they could not sell in the United States.[18] By the 1820s the American tax on teas had risen to 100 percent or more of the average cost. For instance, a pound of Hyson Skin that cost 20 cents in Canton was taxed at 28 cents per pound, and Imperial tea that cost 51 cents per pound carried an additional 50 cents per pound in taxes. A consortium of Philadelphia merchants petitioned Congress in 1828, demanding a reduction "from the high rate of duty on Tea" imported directly; they hoped to "promote so important a branch of commerce as that to China." Paradoxically, American merchants who complained about high tax duties also protested "the *smuggling of teas*" across the border from Canada as a source of economic concern. The Philadelphia consortium accused the British government of "sending teas [to Canada] direct from Canton, not only sufficient for the supply of said provinces, but greatly *beyond the consumption of the country*," thus encouraging the illegal trade in tea with America. Merchants begged Congress to reduce the high duties and allow Americans to sell their teas at competitive prices, even while some American traders benefited from smuggling their own goods across the Canadian border.[19] Excess teas, which did not get sold in the United States or reexported to European markets, just as often were shipped north into British Canada, much to the annoyance of the EIC. In 1820, the company sent an agent to Canada to investigate smuggling and found that American merchants could sell teas "at half the price a regular dealer can procure them from in England."[20] The report estimated that up to three-quarters of tea that Canadians drank came illegally from the United States and censured British colonial tea merchants for colluding with American smugglers. Oddly enough, cross-border suspicions and blame could not counteract the intractable interdependence of British and American economies.

Still, tea's appeal—its social value, its addictiveness, its mobility and marketability, its political and economic usefulness—drove the engines of American commerce during the eighteenth and early nineteenth centuries. Rather than being simply the starting point of revolution in America, tea opened a window onto the politics of consumption. Tea served merchant self-interest; it was a commodity that created new markets, opened distant commercial ports, was easily smuggled, purchased, sold for cash, or exchanged for needed labor and goods. Tea shaped consumer behaviors; although supply preceded demand in the early eighteenth century, Americans eventually became habituated to drinking tea. Indeed, consumer habits proved useful to American political activists, who vilified tea as a symbol of empire and corporate malfeasance to inspire participation in the nonimportation movements of the 1760s and 1770s. But tea and consumer desires also remained malleable and resilient. After the American Revolution, consumer demand for tea provided a platform to build an American commercial presence in the West Indies, Europe, and Asia. Taking advantage of a global marketplace, American merchants used tea to extract commercial policies that assured them not just trade free from mercantilist restraints but also domestic markets free from foreign competition. In turn, state and national governments tapped tea imports for tax revenue. Americans and their tea had come full circle from a revolution in consumption, through a tempest in a teapot, to an independent political economy shaped by consumer desires and global aspirations.

Abbreviations

AAS	American Antiquarian Society, Worcester, MA
APS	American Philosophical Society Library, Philadelphia, PA
Customs 3	Great Britain, Board of Customs & Excise, Ledgers of Imports and Exports, 1696–1780, in the Public Records Office, London, reels 3–49
EAIE	Early American Imprints, Series I: Evans, 1639–1800
EAS	*Early American Studies: An Interdisciplinary Journal*
EIC Factory Records	*East India Company Factory Records, Sources from the British Library, London, Part 1: China and Japan* (Adam Matthew Publications, 2005)
HSP	Historical Society of Pennsylvania, Philadelphia, PA
JCC	*Journals of the Continental Congress, 1774–1789*, ed. Worthington C. Ford et al. (Washington, DC: Government Printing Office, 1904–1937)
JKL	John Kidd Letterbook, 1749–1763, HSP
LCP	The Library Company of Philadelphia, Philadelphia, PA
MHS	Massachusetts Historical Society, Boston, MA
PMHB	*Pennsylvania Magazine of History and Biography*
PTPC	Philadelphia Tea Party Correspondence, 1773–1778, James & Drinker Correspondence transcribed by Francis R. Taylor, 1910, HSP
WMQ	*William and Mary Quarterly*, 3rd series

Introduction · Consumer Revolutions

1. *The Tea-Tax Tempest, or, the Anglo-American Revolution*, 1778, attributed to Carl Guttenberg of Nuremberg, Library of Congress. The snake-emblazoned flag may be in reference to the First Navy Jack flag used by the US Navy in 1776 or other snake motif flags with "Don't Tread on Me" from the Revolutionary War period. The two medallions at the bottom of the engraving depict the Spanish Inquisition and the persecution of Protestant heretics under the auto-da-fé in Holland during 1560 and the William Tell–inspired uprising in Switzerland against Austrian rulers dated 1296. Al-

ternative versions of this engraving are in the collections of the HSP and Library of Congress.

2. T. H. Breen, *The Marketplace of Revolution: How Consumer Politics Shaped American Independence* (New York: Oxford University Press, 2004), xv–xvi. For the most recent history of the Boston Tea Party, see Benjamin L. Carp, *Defiance of the Patriots: The Boston Tea Party and the Making of America* (New Haven, CT: Yale University Press, 2010).

3. Mark M. Smith, "Culture, Commerce, and Calendar Reform in Colonial America," *WMQ* 55, no. 4 (October 1998): 557–84. Adam Anderson, an eighteenth-century political economist, noted that merchants "and other Persons corresponding with other Nations and Countries" praised the shift from the Julian to Gregorian calendar, approved by the British Parliament in 1751, knowing it would "tend to prevent Mistakes and Disputes concerning the Dates of letters and Accounts, if the like Correction be received and established in his Majesty's Dominions" (Adam Anderson, *An Historical and Chronological Deduction of the Origin of Commerce, from the Earliest Account to the Present Time* [London, 1764], 2:398). See also John J. McCusker and Russell R. Menard, *The Economy of British America, 1607–1789* (1985; rev. ed., Chapel Hill: University of North Carolina Press, 1991).

4. Kenneth Pomeranz, *The Great Divergence: China, Europe, and the Making of the Modern World Economy* (Princeton, NJ: Princeton University Press, 2000), 112–13; David Hancock, "Atlantic Trade and Commodities, 1402–1815," in *The Oxford Handbook of the Atlantic World, 1450–1850*, ed. Nicholas Canny and Philip Morgan (New York: Oxford University Press, 2011), 325–27 and 332–35; Carole Shammas, "America, the Atlantic, and Global Consumer Demand, 1500–1800," *OAH Magazine of History* 19, no. 1 (January 2005): 59–64.

5. David Armitage, "Three Concepts of Atlantic History," in *The British Atlantic World, 1500–1800*, ed. David Armitage and Michael J. Braddick (New York: Palgrave Macmillan, 2002), 17.

6. For silver, see Kent G. Deng, "Miracle or Mirage? Foreign Silver, China's Economy and Globalization from the Sixteenth to the Nineteenth Centuries," *Pacific Economic Review* 13, no. 3 (2008): 320–58; Andre Gunder Frank, *ReOrient: Global Economy in the Asian Age* (Berkeley: University of California Press, 1998), 131–64; and Adam Smith, *An Inquiry into the Nature and Causes of the Wealth of Nations* (Dublin, 1776), 1:306–25. For scholarship that explores beyond Atlantic history, see Philip J. Stern, "British Asia and British Atlantic: Comparisons and Connections," *WMQ* 63, no. 4 (October 2006): 693–712; Nicholas Canny, "Atlantic History and Global History," in *Atlantic History: A Critical Appraisal*, ed. Jack P. Greene and Philip D. Morgan (New York: Oxford University Press, 2009), 317–36; and Peter A. Coclanis, "Beyond Atlantic History," in Greene and Morgan, *Atlantic History*, 337–56.

7. Sudipta Sen, *Empire of Free Trade: The East India Company and the Making of the Colonial Marketplace* (Philadelphia: University of Pennsylvania Press, 1998), 5–6. Sen is critical of dependency and world-systems theorists such as Immanuel Wallerstein and Andre Gunder Frank.

8. Pomeranz, *Great Divergence*, 70. See also Peter Manning, "Asia and Europe in the World Economy," *American Historical Review* 107, no. 2 (2002): 419; Alan Smith,

Creating a World Economy: Merchant Capital, Colonialism, and World Trade, 1400–1825 (Boulder, CO: Westview Press, 1991).

9. Smith, *Wealth of Nations*, 1:285, 307–11.

10. Felicity A. Nussbaum, introduction to *The Global Eighteenth Century*, ed. Felicity A. Nussbaum (Baltimore: Johns Hopkins University Press, 2003), 2, 10; Pomeranz, *Great Divergence*, 19; Kenneth Pomeranz and Steven Topik, *The World That Trade Created: Society, Culture, and the World Economy, 1400 to the Present* (New York: M. E. Sharpe, 2000), xiv; Matthew P. Romaniello, "Through the Filter of Tobacco: The Limits of Global Trade in the Early Modern World," *Comparative Studies in Society and History* 49, no. 4 (October 2007): 914–37.

11. Sidney W. Mintz, *Sweetness and Power: The Place of Sugar in Modern History* (New York: Penguin, 1986), 214. More recently, commodity studies have evolved to include Atlantic world perspectives and the context of consumer culture. See David Hancock, *Oceans of Wine: Madeira and the Emergence of American Trade and Taste* (New Haven, CT: Yale University Press, 2009); James Walvin, *Fruits of Empire: Exotic Produce and British Taste, 1660–1800* (New York: New York University Press, 1997); Mark Kurlansky, *Cod: A Biography of the Fish That Changed the World* (New York: Penguin, 1998); Kurlansky, *Salt: A World History* (New York: Penguin, 2003); Dan Koeppel, *Banana: The Fate of the Fruit That Changed the World* (New York: Penguin, 2008); Jack Turner, *Spice: The History of a Temptation* (New York: Vintage, 2006); Amy Butler Greenfield, *A Perfect Red: Empire, Espionage, and the Quest for the Color of Desire* (New York: HarperCollins, 2005); and Jennifer L. Anderson, *Mahogany: The Costs of Luxury in Early America* (Cambridge, MA: Harvard University Press, 2012); Michelle McDonald, *Caffeine Dependence: Coffee and the Early American Economy* (Philadelphia: University of Pennsylvania Press, forthcoming).

12. Jan de Vries, *The Industrious Revolution: Consumer Behavior and the Household Economy, 1650 to the Present* (New York: Cambridge University Press, 2008), 30–32; Gregory E. O'Malley, *Final Passages: The Intercolonial Slave Trade of British America, 1619–1807* (Chapel Hill: University of North Carolina Press, 2014), 10–11. For slave economies and consumption, see Roderick A. McDonald, *The Economy and Material Culture of Slaves: Goods and Chattels on the Sugar Plantations of Jamaica and Louisiana* (Baton Rouge: Louisiana State University Press, 1994), and Ira Berlin and Philip Morgan, eds., *Cultivation and Culture: Labor and the Shaping of Slave Life in the Americas* (Charlottesville: University Press of Virginia, 1993).

13. Lisa Jardine, *Worldly Goods: A New History of the Renaissance* (New York: Norton, 1996), 9, 15, 30–33.

14. De Vries, *Industrious Revolution*, 10, 37. De Vries mainly engages with economic theorists rather than cultural historians, thus dealing with present-day theories of the psychology of consumption. For instance, he argues that boredom drove consumption.

15. Maxine Berg, "Luxury, the Luxury Trades, and the Roots of Industrial Growth," in *The Oxford Handbook of the History of Consumption*, ed. Frank Trentmann (Oxford: Oxford University Press, 2012), 184.

16. Cary Carson, "The Consumer Revolution in Colonial British America: Why Demand?," in *Of Consuming Interests: The Style of Life in the Eighteenth Century*, ed. Cary Carson, Ronald Hoffman, and Peter J. Albert (Charlottesville: University Press

of Virginia, 1994), 486. Lorna Weatherill, "The Meaning of Consumer Behavior in Late Seventeenth- and Early Eighteenth-Century England," in *Consumption and the World of Goods*, ed. John Brewer and Roy Porter (London: Routledge, 1993), 216, and K. N. Chaudhuri, *The Trading World of Asia and the English East India Company, 1660–1760* (Cambridge: Cambridge University Press, 1978), 388, also argue that consumer demand precipitated supply.

17. Maxine Berg, *Luxury and Pleasure in Eighteenth-Century Britain* (Oxford: Oxford University Press, 2005), 5.

18. Woodruff Smith, *Consumption and the Making of Respectability, 1600–1800* (New York: Routledge, 2002), 3; Maxine Berg, "In Pursuit of Luxury: Global History and British Consumer Goods in the Eighteenth Century," *Past & Present* 182 (February 2004): 92; Ann Smart Martin, *Buying into the World of Goods: Early Consumers in Backcountry Virginia* (Baltimore: Johns Hopkins University Press, 2008), 9–10; Carl Robert Keyes, "Early American Advertising: Marketing and Consumer Culture in Eighteenth-Century Philadelphia" (PhD diss., Johns Hopkins University, 2007).

19. Richard Bushman, *The Refinement of America: Persons, Houses, Cities* (New York: Knopf, 1992), xii; de Vries, *Industrious Revolution*, 52, 55–56; Colin Campbell, "Understanding Traditional and Modern Patterns of Consumption in Eighteenth-Century England: A Character-Action Approach," in Brewer and Porter, *Consumption and the World of Goods*, 40–41; Anne E.C. McCants, "Exotic Goods, Popular Consumption, and the Standard of Living: Thinking about Globalization in the Early Modern World," *Journal of World History* 18, no. 4 (December 2007): 449; Paul G. E. Clemens, "The Consumer Culture of the Middle Atlantic, 1760–1820," *WMQ* 62, no. 4 (October 2005), 577; Martin, *Buying into the World of Goods*, 9–10. Weatherill, "Meaning of Consumer Behaviour," 206–7, cautions against trying to pinpoint exactly how early modern consumers defined a "luxury" or "necessity." She defines luxuries as goods that had not been owned by an earlier generation, marked rank and status, and were "desirable but not indispensable." See also Maxine Berg and Elizabeth Eger, "The Rise and Fall of the Luxury Debates," in *Luxury in the Eighteenth Century: Debates, Desires, and Delectable Goods*, ed. Berg and Eger (New York: Palgrave Macmillan, 2003), 13, and John E. Crowley, *The Invention of Comfort: Sensibilities and Design in Early Modern Britain and Early America* (Baltimore: Johns Hopkins University Press, 2001).

20. Carole Shammas, "Standard of Living, Consumption, and Political Economy over the Past 500 Years," in *The Oxford Handbook of the History of Consumption*, ed. Frank Trentmann (Oxford: Oxford University Press, 2012), 213.

21. Quoted in de Vries, *Industrious Revolution*, 69. See also Berg and Eger, "Rise and Fall of the Luxury Debates," 7, 11–12.

22. Walvin, *Fruits of Empire*, ix–xiii; Nancy F. Koehn, *The Power of Commerce: Economy and Governance in the First British Empire* (Ithaca, NY: Cornell University Press, 1994), 61–85, 180; John E. Crowley, *This Sheba, Self: The Conceptualization of Economic Life in Eighteenth-Century America* (Baltimore: Johns Hopkins University Press, 1974), 6–12. Anna Neill, *British Discovery Literature and the Rise of Global Commerce* (New York: Palgrave Macmillan, 2002), 29, argues that "the expansion of a world economy depended upon disciplining passions in the peripheral parts of the globe, even while commercial expansion required that appetites be stimulated in the metro-

politan regions." For the intersection of economies and ethics, see Christopher Clark, "A Wealth of Notions: Interpreting Economy and Morality in Early America," *EAS* 8, no. 3 (Fall 2010): 672–83.

23. Thomas Doerflinger, "Philadelphia Merchants and the Logic of Moderation, 1760–1775," *WMQ* 40, no. 2 (April 1983): 214; John E. Crowley, *The Privileges of Independence: Neomercantilism and the American Revolution* (Baltimore: Johns Hopkins University Press, 1993), 25.

24. Margaret Ellen Newell, *From Dependency to Independence: Economic Revolution in Colonial New England* (Ithaca, NY: Cornell University Press, 1998), 238–39.

25. David Hancock, "The Triumphs of Mercury: Connection and Control in the Emerging Atlantic Economy," in *Soundings in Atlantic History: Latent Structures and Intellectual Currents, 1500–1830*, ed. Bernard Bailyn and Patricia L. Denault (Cambridge, MA: Harvard University Press, 2009), 115–21.

26. William J. Ashworth, *Customs and Excise: Trade, Production, and Consumption in England, 1640–1845* (Oxford: Oxford University Press, 2003), 9.

27. Breen, *Marketplace of Revolution*, x–xvi.

28. Kate Haulman, *The Politics of Fashion in Eighteenth-Century America* (Chapel Hill: University of North Carolina Press, 2011), 5.

29. Elizabeth Kowaleski-Wallace, *Consuming Subjects: Women, Shopping, and Business in the Eighteenth Century* (New York: Columbia University Press, 1997), 25.

30. Recent scholarship that links American colonies with Britain's Asian empire includes Koehn, *Power of Commerce;* P. J. Marshall, *The Making and Unmaking of Empires: Britain, India, and America c. 1750–1783* (New York: Oxford University Press, 2005); Elizabeth Mancke, "Negotiating an Empire: Britain and Its Overseas Peripheries, c. 1550–1780," in *Negotiated Empires: Centers and Peripheries in the Americas, 1500–1820*, ed. Christine Daniels and Michael Kennedy (New York: Routledge, 2002); Stern, "British Asia and British Atlantic"; Philip J. Stern, *The Company-State: Corporate Sovereignty and the Early Modern Foundations of the British Empire in India* (Oxford: Oxford University Press, 2011); and Nussbaum, *Global Eighteenth Century.*

31. Staughton Lynd and David Waldstreicher, "Free Trade, Sovereignty, and Slavery: Toward an Economic Interpretation of American Independence," *WMQ* 68, no. 4 (October 2011): 600, revives Charles Beard's contention that revolutionary leadership acted on mostly economic motives. E. P. Thompson, "The Moral Economy of the English Crowd in the Eighteenth Century," *Past & Present* 50 (February 1971): 76–136, introduced the term "moral economy" as a category for historical analysis, which has mostly been the domain of those studying early modern Europe and the emergence of class consciousness among laborers. See also Thompson "The Moral Economy Reviewed," in *Customs in Common: Studies in Traditional Popular Culture* (New York: New Press, 1993), 259–351; Ruth Bogin, "Petitioning and the New Moral Economy of Post-Revolutionary America," *WMQ* 45, no. 3 (July 1988): 391–425; Barbara Clark Smith, "Food Rioters and the American Revolution," *WMQ* 51, no. 1 (January 1994): 3–38; and Michael Zuckerman, "A Different Thermidor: The Revolution beyond the American Revolution," in *The Transformation of Early American History: Society, Authority, and Ideology*, ed. James A. Henretta, Michael Kammen, and Stanley N. Katz (New York: Knopf, 1991), 180–81. Charlotte Sussman, *Consuming Anxieties: Consumer Protest, Gender, and British Slavery, 1713–1833* (Stanford, CA: Stanford University

Press, 2000), 2, also emphasizes a moralist component in the politics of consumption, describing the many "consumerist critiques of colonialism" during the eighteenth century.

32. Crowley, *Privileges of Independence*, xii, 25, 158–59; Shammas, "America, the Atlantic, and Global Consumer Demand," 62; Hancock, "Atlantic Trade and Commodities," 339; Eliga H. Gould, *Among the Powers of the Earth: The American Revolution and the Making of a New World Empire* (Cambridge, MA: Harvard University Press, 2012); Paul A. Gilje, *Free Trade and Sailors' Rights in the War of 1812* (Cambridge: Cambridge University Press, 2013).

Chapter 1 · The English Commercial Empire Expands

1. Richard Hakluyt, "Discourse of Western Planting (1584)," in *The Original Writings and Correspondence of the Two Richard Hakluyts*, ed. E. G. R. Taylor (London: Hakluyt Society, 1935), 2:211, 238.

2. Adam Smith, *An Inquiry into the Nature and Causes of the Wealth of Nations* (Dublin, 1776), 2:483. By its second edition, Smith had revised *Wealth of Nations* so the passage read: "It is, however, a project altogether unfit for a nation of shopkeepers; *but extremely fit for a nation whose government is influenced by shopkeepers*" (Adam Smith, *An Inquiry into the Nature and Causes of the Wealth of Nations* [London, 1805], 2:484, emphasis added).

3. John J. McCusker and Russell R. Menard, *The Economy of British America, 1607–1789* (1985; rev. ed., Chapel Hill: University of North Carolina Press, 1991), 35–38, provide a good definition of mercantilism. See also Cathy Matson, *Merchants and Empire: Trading in Colonial New York* (Baltimore: Johns Hopkins University Press, 1998), 6–7; David Hancock, "Atlantic Trade and Commodities, 1402–1815," in *The Oxford Handbook of the Atlantic World, 1450–1850*, ed. Nicholas Canny and Philip Morgan (Oxford: Oxford University Press, 2013), 326; and Jonathan Barth, "Reconstructing Mercantilism: Consensus and Conflict in British Imperial Economy in the Seventeenth and Eighteenth Centuries," *WMQ* 73, no. 2 (April 2016): 257–90. Steve Pincus, "Rethinking Mercantilism: Political Economy, the British Empire, and the Atlantic World in the Seventeenth and Eighteenth Centuries," *WMQ* 69, no. 1 (January 2012): 4, notes that modern-day historians and economists have perhaps mistakenly embraced Adam Smith's "notion that there was an early modern period of mercantilist consensus."

4. Quoted in John E. Crowley, *This Sheba, Self: The Conceptualization of Economic Life in Eighteenth-Century America* (Baltimore: Johns Hopkins University Press, 1974), 39; Mark Valeri, "William Petty in Boston: Political Economy, Religion, and Money in Provincial New England," *EAS* 8, no. 3 (Fall 2010): 553.

5. Crowley, *This Sheba, Self*, 15; David S. Shields, *Oracles of Empire: Poetry, Politics, and Commerce in British America, 1690–1750* (Chicago: University of Chicago Press, 1990), 17; Peter S. Onuf and Cathy D. Matson, *A Union of Interests: Political and Economic Thought in Revolutionary America* (Lawrence: University Press of Kansas, 1990), 16–20.

6. Adam Anderson, *An Historical and Chronological Deduction of the Origin of Commerce, from the earliest Accounts to the present Time* (London, 1764), i. See also Lisa Jardine, *Worldly Goods: A New History of the Renaissance* (New York: Norton, 1996), 37–90.

7. James Steuart, *An Inquiry into the Principles of Political Oeconomy: being an Essay on the Science of Domestic Policy in Free Nations* (London, 1767), 1:207.

8. Elizabeth Mancke, "Negotiating an Empire: Britain and Its Overseas Peripheries, c. 1550–1780," in *Negotiated Empires: Centers and Peripheries in the Americas, 1500–1820*, ed. Christine Daniels and Michael Kennedy (New York: Routledge, 2002), 235–36. See also Philip J. Stern, "British Asia and British Atlantic: Comparisons and Connections," *WMQ* 63, no. 4 (October 2006): 700–701.

9. Mancke, "Negotiating an Empire," 242–44.

10. Patrick O'Brien, "Inseparable Connections: Trade, Economy, Fiscal State, and the Expansion of Empire, 1688–1815," in *The Oxford History of the British Empire, Vol. II: The Eighteenth Century*, ed. P. J. Marshall (Oxford: Oxford University Press, 1998), 73–74; J. H. Parry, *Trade and Dominion: The European Oversea Empires in the Eighteenth Century* (London: Phoenix Press, 1971), 74–79.

11. Anderson, *Origin of Commerce*, v. See Shields, *Oracles of Empire*, 4, and Nancy F. Koehn, *The Power of Commerce: Economy and Governance in the First British Empire* (Ithaca, NY: Cornell University Press, 1994), 3–12.

12. Shields, *Oracles of Empire*, 4.

13. Abbé (Guillaume-Thomas-Francois) Raynal, *A Philosophical and Political History of the Settlements and Trade of the Europeans in the East and West Indies* (London, 1777), 1:1; Smith, *Wealth of Nations*, 2:500.

14. Kenneth Pomeranz and Steven Topik, *The World That Trade Created: Society, Culture, and the World Economy, 1400 to the Present* (New York: M. E. Sharpe, 2000), 7.

15. Raynal, *Philosophical and Political History*, 2:90; John E. Wills Jr. "European Consumption and Asian Production in the Seventeenth and Eighteenth Centuries," in *Consumption and the World of Goods*, ed. John Brewer and Roy Porter (London: Routledge, 1993), 134. For non-European agency and control of early modern global trade, see Scott Levi, "India, Russia and the Eighteenth-Century Transformation of the Central Asian Caravan Trade," *Journal of the Economic and Social History of the Orient* 42, no. 4 (1999): 519–48; Scott Levi, "The Indian Merchant Diaspora in Early Modern Central Asia and Iran," *Iranian Studies* 32, no. 4 (Autumn 1999): 483–512; and Matthew P. Romaniello, "Through the Filter of Tobacco: The Limits of Global Trade in the Early Modern World," *Comparative Studies in Society and History* 49, no. 4 (October 2007): 914–37.

16. William Mildmay, *The Laws and Policy of England Relating to Trade* (London, 1765), 53. See O'Brien, "Inseparable Connections," 53–54.

17. Mildmay, *Laws and Policy of England Relating to Trade*, 100.

18. Ibid., 7, 38; Elizabeth Mancke, "Chartered Enterprises and the Evolution of the British Atlantic World," in *The Creation of the British Atlantic World*, ed. Elizabeth Mancke and Carole Shammas (Baltimore: Johns Hopkins University Press, 2005), 238–40; John E. Crowley, *The Privileges of Independence: Neomercantilism and the American Revolution* (Baltimore: Johns Hopkins University Press, 1993), 4–5; Matson, *Merchants and Empire*, 6–8; James Walvin, *Fruits of Empire: Exotic Produce and British Taste, 1660–1800* (New York: New York University Press, 1997), x, 12.

19. Edward Knipe to the Court of Directors, 19 January 1643/44, Supplement to China Materials, Book II, China, 1606–1699, p. 99, IOR/G/12/10, reel 4, *EIC Factory Records*; Nuala Zahedieh, "Overseas Expansion and Trade in the Seventeenth Century,"

in *The Oxford History of the British Empire, Vol. I: The Origins of Empire: British Overseas Enterprise to the Close of the Seventeenth Century*, ed. Nicholas Canny (Oxford: Oxford University Press, 1998), 400–401.

20. John Bruce, *Annals of the Honorable East-India Company* (London, 1810), 2:674; *A New Universal History of Voyages and Travels: collected from the most authentic authors in all languages* (London, 1754), 2:108; John Shaw, *Charters Relating to the East India Company, from 1600 to 1761* (Madras, 1887), vi, 32–46; Stern, "British Asia and British Atlantic," 703.

21. K. N. Chaudhuri, *The Trading World of Asia and the English East India Company, 1660–1760* (Cambridge: Cambridge University Press, 1978), 387–88. See also K. N. Chaudhuri, *The English East India Company: The Study of an Early Joint-Stock Company, 1600–1640* (New York: Routledge, 1965); John Keay, *The Honourable Company: A History of the English East India Company* (New York: HarperCollins, 2010), 130–35; Kenneth Andrews, *Trade, Plunder, and Settlement: Maritime Enterprise and the Genesis of the British Empire, 1480–1630* (Cambridge: Cambridge University Press, 1984), 278ff; and P. J. Marshall, "The English in Asia to 1700," in Canny, *Oxford History of the British Empire: British Overseas Enterprise*, 281–83.

22. *Some Thoughts Relating to Trade in General, and to the East India Trade in Particular* (London, 1754), 30.

23. Anderson, *Origin of Commerce*, 2:285–89, warned that the EIC could become another South Sea Company, which went bankrupt in the 1720s after it promised to assume the national debt in exchange for bonds. South Sea Company stock rose as rumors circulated that it would merge with the EIC and the Bank of England. When the South Sea Company announced a 10% dividend based on nothing more than speculation, the stock bubble burst, taking the bond value down as well.

24. H. V. Bowen, *The Business of Empire: The East India Company and Imperial Britain, 1756–1833* (Cambridge: Cambridge University Press, 2008), 30; K. N. Chaudhuri, "The English East India Company in the 17th and 18th centuries: A Pre-modern Multinational Organization," in *The Organization of Interoceanic Trade in European Expansion, 1450–1800*, ed. Pieter Emmer and Femme Gaastra (Brookfield, VT: Ashgate, 1996), 190–91.

25. Bowen, *Business of Empire*, 30; Mancke, "Negotiating an Empire," 244. Pilar Nogués Marco and Camila Vam Malle-Sabouret, "East India Bonds, 1718–1763: Early Exotic Derivatives and London Market Efficiency," *European Review of Economic History* 11, no. 3 (December 2007): 368, 373, note that the government loans were secured with debentures issued by the EIC that yielded 3%. The short-term bonds often continued to circulate after maturity, which had a "hedging" effect against market declines, effectively making them long-term bonds.

26. *A New Universal History of Voyages and Travels: collected from the most authentic authors in all languages* (London, 1754), 2:108; Keay, *Honourable Company*, 130–31; Marshall, "English in Asia to 1700," 281–82.

27. Edmund Waller, "Of Tea, Commended by her Majesty," *Works in Verse and Prose* (London, 1729), 221; Elizabeth Kowaleski-Wallace, *Consuming Subjects: Women, Shopping, and Business in the Eighteenth Century* (New York: Columbia University Press, 1997), 22.

28. Anderson, *Origin of Commerce*, 2:111, 182.

29. Ibid., 2:328. See also Hosea Ballou Morse, *The Chronicles of the East India Company, Trading to China, 1635–1834* (Taipei: Ch'eng-wen, 1966), 1:1–3, 9, 72–73; Bruce, *Annals of the Honorable East-India Company,* 1:11–13.

30. Great Britain, *An Act for Laying Additional Duties on Hides and Skins, Vellom and Parchment, and New Duties on Starch, Coffee, Tea, Drugs, Gilt and Silver Wire* ([London?], [1712?]), 365, 545, Eighteenth-Century Collections Online (N052397); Chaudhuri, *The Trading World of Asia,* 20, 43; Paul Langford, *A Polite and Commercial People: England, 1727–1783* (Oxford: Clarendon Press, 1989), 179.

31. Great Britain, *Act for Laying Additional Duties on Hides and Skins,* 367.

32. Meeting between the EIC Committee on Duties and Commissioners of the Customs, 22 April 1718, Misc. China Papers, 19 December 1712–24 December 1725, p. 1355–56, IOR/G/12/8, Reel 2, *EIC Factory Records.* The Commissioners of Customs pressed for 8 shillings 3 pence per pound in duty, which the EIC insisted would raise the price of tea to 17 shillings 10 pence per pound, far too much for an average consumer.

33. Great Britain, *An Act for Repealing Certain Duties therein mentioned, payable upon coffee, tea, cocoa nuts, chocolate, and cocoa paste imported* ([London?], [1724?]), 220, 222, Eighteenth Century Collections Online (N050499). To further problematize importation figures, Hoh-Cheung Mui and Lorna H. Mui, "'Trends in Eighteenth-Century Smuggling' Reconsidered," *Economic History Review* 28, no. 1 (February 1975), 37, warn that the most complete source for tea sales (and most often used), William Milburn, *Oriental Commerce: Containing a Geographical Description of the Principle Places in the East Indies, China, and Japan* (London, 1813), is "grossly inaccurate" for certain years, underestimating the amount of tea sold, though not the value.

34. "Sir Robert Walpole's defence of his Excise Bill, 1733," in *English Historical Documents, 1714–1783,* ed. D. B. Horn and Mary Ransome (New York: Oxford University Press, 1957), 310, 337. The national debt peaked in 1724 at £53,323,570 but declined to £46,497,500 in 1738 before rising again (O'Brien, "Inseparable Connections," 65–67).

35. R. F. F. Dominick Fernandez Navarette, *An Account of the Empire of China, Historical, Political, Moral and Religious,* in *A Collection of Voyages and Travels, Some now first Printed from Original Manuscripts* (London, 1704), 1:60; Timothy Brook, *The Confusions of Pleasure: Commerce and Culture in Ming China* (Berkeley: University of California Press, 1998), 119–24; Caroline Frank, *Objectifying China, Imagining America: Chinese Commodities in Early America* (Chicago: University of Chicago Press, 2011), 38–39; Andre Gunder Frank, *ReOrient: Global Economy in the Asian Age* (Berkeley: University of California Press, 1998), 197–98.

36. T'ung Yang-chia Requests the Opening of Canton to Macaonese, 5 June 1647, in *A Documentary Chronicle of Sino-Western Relations (1644–1820),* comp. and trans. Lo-Shu Fu (Tucson: University of Arizona Press, 1966), 1:7; Pin-tsun Chang, "The Evolution of Chinese Thought on Maritime Foreign Trade from the Sixteenth to the Eighteenth Century," *International Journal of Maritime History* 1, no. 1 (June 1989): 56.

37. George Shelvocke, *A Voyage Round the World by the Way of the Great South Sea* (London, 1726), 458.

38. *The Chinese Traveller: Containing a geographical, commercial, and political history of China* (London, 1775), 1:200.

39. Charles Lockyer, *An Account of the Trade in India* (London, 1711), 106; Chaudhuri, *Trading World of Asia*, 399. For a detailed explanation of the Chinese duties on tea, see F. Hirth, "The Hoppo-Book of 1753," *Journal of the North-China Branch of the Royal Asiatic Society* 17 (1882): 221–35.

40. Lockyer, *Account of the Trade in India*, 5–6.

41. Journal of the *Carnaroon*, 14 July 1718, Misc. China Papers, 19 December 1712–24 December 1725, p. 1349, IOR/G/12/8, reel 2, *EIC Factory Records*.

42. Alexander Hamilton, *A New Account of the East Indies, Giving an exact and copious description of the situation, product, manufactures, laws, customs, religion, trade, &c* (London, 1744), 2:227–29.

43. Maxine Berg, *Luxury and Pleasure in Eighteenth-Century Britain* (Oxford: Oxford University Press, 2005), 74–75. Although manuals and guidance for an emerging Chinese merchant class were infused with Confucian moralism, commercial practices also bowed to the realities of politics in a highly stratified society. Like their English counterparts, Chinese merchants learned to manipulate the markets, to time the market, and to hoard certain commodities until prices rose to make a profit. See Richard John Lufrano, *Honorable Merchants: Commerce and Self-Cultivation in late Imperial China* (Honolulu: University of Hawaii Press, 1997), 137.

44. Diary of the *Carnaroon*, 16 August 1720, Misc. China Papers, 19 December 1712–24 Dec. 1725, p. 1372, IOR/G/12/8, reel 2, *EIC Factory Records*.

45. Dr. John Francis Gemelli Careri, *A Voyage Round the World* (1695), in *Collection of Voyages and Travels*, 4:384; Hamilton, *New Account of the East Indies*, 2:288; Albert Feuerwerker, *State and Society in Eighteenth-Century China: The Ch'ing Empire in Its Glory* (Ann Arbor: Center for Chinese Studies, University of Michigan, 1976), 80; Robert Gardella, *Harvesting Mountains: Fujian and the China Tea Trade, 1757–1937* (Berkeley: University of California Press, 1994), 29.

46. *Chinese Traveller*, 1:236–237.

47. Lockyer, *Account of the Trade in India*, 116–17.

48. *The East-India Sale, September the First, 1719* (London, 1719), 110–76.

49. At Consultation, 29 September 1731, China Diary and Consultations, 1730–1732, p. 126, IOR/G/12/31, reel 10, *EIC Factory Records*; Pehr Osbeck, *A Voyage to China and the East Indies* (London, 1771), 1:251–52.

50. Macclesfield China Diary 1724, Instructions, China Diary and Consultations, 1722–1724, IOR/G/12/24, reel 10, *EIC Factory Records*.

51. Chaudhuri, *Trading World of Asia*, 406–7.

52. China Diary and Consultations, 1721–1723, 8 October 1722, IOR/G/12/21, and Instructions to Capt. Robert Hudson, 8 October 1728, China Diary and Consultations, 1726–28, p. 77, IOR/G/12/26, reel 10, *EIC Factory Records*.

53. Hoh-Cheung Mui and Lorna H. Mui, "Smuggling and the British Tea Trade before 1784," *American Historical Review* 74, no. 1 (October 1968): 45–46, 50.

54. "London September 7," *Boston News-Letter*, January 30–February 6, 1735; William J. Ashworth, *Customs and Excise: Trade, Production, and Consumption in England, 1640–1845* (Oxford: Oxford University Press, 2003), 177.

55. *A Proposal to Prevent the Smuggling of Tea* (London, [1745?]), 1; Mui and Mui, "'Trends in Eighteenth-Century Smuggling' Reconsidered," 29.

56. Instructions, December 1720, Misc. China Papers, 19 December 1712–24 December 1725, p. 1382, IOR/G/12/8, reel 2, and China Diary and Consultations, 1720–1722, 28 August 1721, IOR/G/12/23, reel 10, *EIC Factory Records*; Tan Chung, "The Britain-China-India Trade Triangle (1771–1840)," *Indian Economic Social History Review* 11 (1974): 411–12. Chaudhuri, *Trading World of Asia*, 390–91, implies that the EIC decided to corner the market at the end of the 1720s as a result of Ostender activities and Dutch resumption of direct trade to China. However, the EIC instructions to engross the tea market started much earlier. See also Parry, *Trade and Dominion*, 84–85.

57. Diary and Consultation, 27 June 1729, China Diary and Consultations, 1728–30, p. 16, IOR/G/12/28, reel 10, *EIC Factory Records.*

58. In 1740 the EIC sent four ships with instructions to coordinate cornering the market in Hyson tea, but the agents failed to negotiate the contracts (Morse, *Chronicles of the East India Company*, 1:272).

59. Parry, *Trade and Dominion*, 74–78.

60. Customs 3, reels 4–19. Germany was second to Holland in the quantity of tea purchased from the EIC: 26,643.25 pounds (1700–1710) and 35,897 pounds (1711–20). Holland, Germany, and Flanders stopped purchasing EIC teas altogether in the mid-1750s.

61. Chaudhuri, "English East India Company," 193.

62. Diary and Consultation, 4 November 1729, China Diary and Consultations, 1728–30, p. 42, IOR/G/12/28, reel 10, *EIC Factory Records.*

63. Letter to the Directors, 10 December 1730, China Diary and Consultations, 1729–31, IOR/G/12/30, reel 10, *EIC Factory Records.*

64. Customs 3, reels 25–29. See P. J. Marshall, "The British in Asia: Trade to Dominion, 1700–1765," in Marshall, *Oxford History of the British Empire, Vol. II*, 490–491, for comparative success of European trade companies from the 1720s to the 1740s. Jacob M. Price, "The Imperial Economy, 1700–1776," in Marshall, *Oxford History of British Empire, Vol. II*, 79. *A Proposal to Prevent the Smuggling of Tea* (London, [1745?]), 1–2, estimated that smuggled teas from France, for which French merchants paid 2 shillings per pound, sold for 4–5 shillings in England. In the early 1730s, comparable teas sold at the EIC auction for 3–7 shillings per pound, which did not include the inland duty of 1 shilling or the ad valorem (value-added) duty of 14%.

65. Letter to the Directors, 9 April 1728, from Cape of Good Hope, China Diary and Consultations, 1726–28, pp. 40–41, IOR/G/12/26, reel 10, *EIC Factory Records.* Between 1719 and 1833, 70–90% of all cargo leaving Canton was tea (Gardella, *Harvesting Mountains*, 33). Tea production in China increased sixfold between 1719 and 1762 because of European demand (Susan Naquin and Evelyn S. Rawski, *Chinese Society in the Eighteenth Century* [New Haven, CT: Yale University Press, 1987], 170).

66. Morse, *Chronicles of the East India Company*, 1:194; Diary and Consultation, 13 November 1729, China Diary and Consultations, 1728–30, p. 54, IOR/G/12/28, reel 10, *EIC Factory Records.*

67. Diary and Consultations, 26 July 1730, 1729–1731, IOR/G/12/30, reel 10, *EIC Factory Records.*

68. Diary and Consultation, 13 November 1729, China Diary and Consultations, 1728–30, p. 54, IOR/G/12/28, reel 10, *EIC Factory Records*. See Weng Eang Cheong, *The Hong Merchants of Canton: Chinese Merchants in Sino-Western Trade* (Surrey, UK: Curzon Press, 1997), 37.

69. To the Directors, from Batavia, 20 June 1730, China Diary and Consultations, 1729–31, IOR/G/12/30, reel 10, *EIC Factory Records*. See, for instance, Diary of James Naish at Canton, 13 January–24 June, 1731, IOR/G/12/32, reel 10, *EIC Factory Records*.

70. Dissenting opinion of Andrew Reid, 20 October 1736, Diary and Consultation in China, 1736–1737, p. 33–34, IOR/G/12/41, reel 11, *EIC Factory Records*.

71. Journal from the Ship *Normanton*, 3 December 1736, ibid., p. 42.

72. Journal from the Ship *Normanton*, 27 December 1736, ibid., p. 48.

73. Diary and Consultation in China, 25 December 1734, 1734–1735, p. 130, IOR/G/12/37, reel 11, *EIC Factory Records*.

74. James MacPherson, *The History and Management of the East-India Company from Its Origin in 1600 to the Present Times* (London, 1779), 1:10. See K. N. Chaudhuri, "Treasure and Trade Balances: The East India Company's Export Trade, 1660–1720," *Economic History Review* 21, no. 3 (December 1968): 480–502.

75. G. N. Clark, *Guide to English Commercial Statistics, 1696–1782* (London: Offices of the Royal Historical Society, 1938), 77.

76. Marshall, "British in Asia," 488, gives the 80% figure; Dennis O. Flynn and Arturo Giraldez, "Cycles of Silver: Global Economic Unity through the Mid-Eighteenth Century," *Journal of World History* 13, no. 2 (Fall 2002): 411–12, claim it was 90%.

77. Quoted in Pincus, "Rethinking Mercantilism," 21.

78. Chaudhuri, *Trading World of Asia*, 165–69, 173. According to Caroline Frank, *Objectifying China, Imagining America*, 7, China provided four-fifths of the world's commodities prior to the nineteenth century and, in exchange, ended up with 75% of the world's silver.

79. Brook, *Confusions of Pleasure*, 204–10; Kent G. Deng, "Miracle or Mirage? Foreign Silver, China's Economy and Globalization from the Sixteenth to the Nineteenth Centuries," *Pacific Economic Review* 13, no. 3 (2008): 320–21; Flynn and Giraldez, "Cycles of Silver," 395.

80. Naquin and Rawski, *Chinese Society in the Eighteenth Century*, 104.

81. Diary and Consultation in China, 13 August 1734, 1733–1735, p. 51–52, IOR/G/12/36, reel 11, *EIC Factory Records*.

82. Chaudhuri, *Trading World of Asia*, 97. According to Earl H. Pritchard, *Anglo-Chinese Relations during the Seventeenth and Eighteenth Centuries* (New York: Octagon Books, 1970), appendix XIX: "East India Company's Tea Trade," n.p., tea as a portion of total EIC sales was 27–28% in 1723, 25% of all goods in 1731, 24% in 1745, and still roughly 25% in 1750. By 1770, tea made up nearly 45% of all goods sold at auction. Maxine Berg, *Luxury and Pleasure in Eighteenth Century Britain*, 57, by contrast, asserts that "tea imports from China reached 19.2 per cent of total import values in 1722, and declined after that until 1747 when they rose again to 20 per cent, and 31 per cent in 1748, and as high as 39.5 per cent of import values in 1760."

83. Consultation on board the *Compton*, 22 June 1732, Diary and Consultations at Canton, 1731–1733, IOR/G/12/33, reel 10, *EIC Factory Records*.

Chapter 2 · The Rise of a "Tea-fac'd Generation"

1. Margaret Ellen Newell, *From Dependency to Independence: Economic Revolution in Colonial New England* (Ithaca, NY: Cornell University Press, 1998), 97ff; Carole Shammas, *The Pre-Industrial Consumer in England and America* (New York: Oxford University Press, 1990), 3–5, 83–86; Lorena S. Walsh, "Urban Amenities and Rural Sufficiency: Living Standards and Consumer Behavior in the Colonial Chesapeake, 1643–1777," *Journal of Economic History* 43 (March 1983): 109–17; Gloria L. Main and Jackson T. Main, "Economic Growth and the Standard of Living in Southern New England, 1640–1774," *Journal of Economic History* 48 (March 1988): 27–46; Lois Green Carr and Lorena S. Walsh, "Changing Lifestyles and Consumer Behavior in the Colonial Chesapeake," in *Of Consuming Interests: The Style of Life in the Eighteenth Century*, ed. Cary Carson, Ronald Hoffman, and Peter J. Albert (Charlottesville: University Press of Virginia, 1994), 67, 80; K. N. Chaudhuri, *The Trading World of Asia and the English East India Company, 1660–1760* (Cambridge: Cambridge University Press, 1978), 387–88.

2. Shammas, *Pre-Industrial Consumer*, 6, 292. See also Lorna Weatherill, *Consumer Behaviour and Material Culture in Britain, 1660–1760* (London: Routledge, 1988), 25–31, 86.

3. Peter Baynton to Francis Richardson, 30 May 1724, Peter Baynton Ledger and Letterbook, 1721–1726, HSP. For ship ownership information, see Port of Philadelphia Ship Registers, 8 May 1736, 1722–1770, HSP.

4. James Bonsall Account Book, 1722–1729, Collection of Business Accounts, HSP, and Baynton Ledger and Letterbook.

5. Wilbur C. Plummer, "Consumer Credit in Colonial Philadelphia," *PMHB* 66, no. 4 (1942): 385–90; Gary B. Nash, *The Urban Crucible: The Northern Seaports and the Origins of the American Revolution*, abridged ed. (Cambridge, MA: Harvard University Press, 1986), 110.

6. Walsh, "Urban Amenities and Rural Sufficiency," 112; Newell, *From Dependency to Independence*, 96; Neil McKendrick, John Brewer, and J. H. Plumb, *The Birth of a Consumer Society: The Commercialization of Eighteenth-Century England* (Bloomington: Indiana University Press, 1982), 2. Marc Egnal, "The Economic Development of the Thirteen Continental Colonies, 1720 to 1775," *WMQ* 32, no. 2 (April 1975): 203–4, notes little growth of agriculture and the rural standard of living in Great Britain, as compared to a relatively robust American colonial economy, where commodity prices were on the rise. Maxine Berg, "In Pursuit of Luxury: Global History and British Consumer Goods in the Eighteenth Century," *Past & Present* 182 (February 2004): 92, sees "an upscaling of consumer aspirations" throughout the eighteenth century. Caroline Frank, *Objectifying China, Imagining America: Chinese Commodities in Early America* (Chicago: University of Chicago Press, 2011), chapters 1 and 2, argues that American colonists may have incorporated exotic Asian goods into their household inventories far earlier than thought. In the 1690s, American seafarers participated in early privateering adventures to the East Indies.

7. Main and Main, "Economic Growth and the Standard of Living," 29.

8. Ibid., 43, table 5.

9. Newell, *From Dependency to Independence*, 96.

10. Entry for 11 October 1728, William Becket, Letter and Commonplace Book, 1727–1742, HSP. See also T. H. Breen, "The Meanings of Things: Interpreting the Consumer Economy in the Eighteenth Century," in *Consumption and the World of Goods*, ed. John Brewer and Roy Porter (London: Routledge, 1993), 253.

11. Carr and Walsh, "Changing Lifestyles and Consumer Behavior," 80.

12. Walsh, "Urban Amenities and Rural Sufficiency," 111.

13. Robert Pringle to Richard Thompson, Hull, 2 September 1738; Robert Pringle to William Cookson & William Welfitt, Hull, 25 September 1742, in *The Letterbook of Robert Pringle*, ed. Walter B. Edgar (Columbia: University of South Carolina Press, 1972), 1:31, 424.

14. In the early eighteenth century, Ireland's population remained steady at 2–3 million people. America's population grew more dramatically, from about 265,000 in 1700 to 445,000 in 1720, and passed 1 million by midcentury. Jacob M. Price, "The Imperial Economy, 1700–1776," in *The Oxford History of the British Empire, Vol. II: The Eighteenth Century*, ed. P. J. Marshall (Oxford: Oxford University Press, 1998), 100; Richard R. Johnson, "Growth and Mastery: British North America, 1690–1748," in Marshall, *Oxford History of the British Empire, Vol. II*, 279.

15. Chaudhuri, *Trading World of Asia*, 131.

16. Quoted in ibid., 390.

17. Hosea Ballou Morse, *The Chronicles of the East India Company, Trading to China, 1635–1834* (Taipei: Ch'eng-wen, 1966), 1:149.

18. Quoted in Chaudhuri, *Trading World of Asia*, 390.

19. Quoted in ibid., 391–92.

20. *American Weekly Mercury*, March 17, 1720.

21. *American Weekly Mercury*, September 14, 1727.

22. *American Weekly Mercury*, June 8, 1738, and *Pennsylvania Gazette*, June 22, 1738. In the late 1730s, when asked by London suppliers for his opinion, Samuel Powel speculated that smaller, convenient packaging like canisters worked best for an American consumer (Samuel Powel to Benjamin and William Bell, 26 July 1739, Samuel Powel Letterbook, 1727–1739, vol. 1, HSP).

23. *Boston News-Letter*, June 11–June 18, 1730, 2.

24. *Boston Gazette*, August 13–August 20, 1733, 4.

25. John Merrett began selling goods in Boston but ended up retailing tea in New York, *New-England Weekly Journal*, May 9, 1738; Jacob and John Wendell, *New-England Weekly Journal*, March 7, 1738.

26. Carl Robert Keyes, "Early American Advertising: Marketing and Consumer Culture in Eighteenth-Century Philadelphia" (PhD diss., Johns Hopkins University, 2007), 20–21, 43–45, 53–54, examines the growth and development of advertising in Philadelphia over the eighteenth century.

27. John Kidd to Rawlinson & Davison, 27 August 1752, John Kidd Letterbook, 1749–1763, HSP; James & Drinker to Neate, Pigou & Booth, 6 November 1764, James & Drinker Letterbook, 1764–1766, Henry Drinker Business Papers, 1756–1869, HSP.

28. Thomas Lawrence to Samuel Storke, 12 October 1721, Thomas Lawrence Letterbook, 1718–1725, HSP.

29. Samuel Powel to Benjamin Bell, 12 July 1736, Powel Letterbook vol. 1. John J. McCusker and Russell R. Menard, *The Economy of British America, 1607–1789* (1985;

rev. ed., Chapel Hill: University of North Carolina Press, 1991), 205–6, assert that Philadelphia merchants relied especially on the West Indian provisions trade to sell colonial products and importation of foreign goods only came after Americans found markets to sell their commodities.

30. John Reynell [for Jane Fenn], to John Hayward, 25 November 1737, John Reynell Letterbook, 1734–1774, Coates and Reynell Papers, 1702–1843, HSP. Jane Fenn, a Quaker minister who traveled around North Carolina, Virginia, Maryland, Pennsylvania, and New England during the 1720s, married Joseph Hoskins, a prosperous merchant, in 1738. Her autobiography, *The Life and Spiritual Sufferings of that Faithful Servant of Christ Jane Hoskens, a Public Preacher Among the People Called Quakers*, was published posthumously in 1771.

31. See Samuel Coates Daybook, 1729–1737, Coates and Reynell Collection, 140A, HSP. Reynell married Samuel's sister Mary Coates and became guardian of Samuel's children when he died in 1748 (HSP abstract and finding aid for Coates and Reynell Family Papers at http://hsp.org/sites/default/files/legacy_files/migrated/findingaid 0140coatesreynell.pdf).

32. In the 1740s, Powel purchased tea at 2 to 3 shillings a pound and sold it for 6 shillings or more per pound (Samuel Powel to Benjamin and William Bell, 2 February 1742/43, and Samuel Powel to Benjamin and William Bell, 31 October 1744, Samuel Powel Letterbook, 1739–1746, vol. 2, HSP).

33. Boylston Family Papers, Thomas Boylston Wastebook (Boston), 1735–1738, vol. 56; [Thomas Boylston] Ledger, 1735–1767, vol. 57; and [Thomas Boylston] Wastebook (Boston), 1738–1767, vol. 60, MHS. See also Benjamin Greene Account Books, 1734–1756, MHS. Between 1738 and 1751 he sold 453.5 pounds of tea for just over £757.

34. Samuel Powel to Nicholas Witchell, 4 October 1728, Powel Letterbook vol. 1.

35. Samuel Powel to Thomas Hyam, 12 November 1731, ibid. See also Samuel Powel to David Barclay, 22 December 1730, and Samuel Powel to Benjamin Bell, 6 November 1733, ibid.

36. Samuel Powel to David Barclay, 6 November 1733, ibid.; Anne Bezanson, Robert D. Gray, and Miriam Hussey, *Prices in Colonial Pennsylvania* (Philadelphia: University of Pennsylvania Press, 1935), 254.

37. Samuel Powel to Benjamin Bell, 4 [March] 1734/35, Powel Letterbook vol. 1.

38. Samuel Powel to Benjamin Bell, 21 April 1735, ibid.

39. John Reynell [for Jane Fenn] to John Hayward, 24 July 1738, Reynell Letterbook. In 1744, Reynell ordered tea again for Jane Fenn Hoskins, perhaps with better results (John Reynell to Elias Bland, 21 December 1744, ibid.).

40. Reynell [for Jane Fenn] to Hayward, 24 July 1738, ibid.

41. Samuel Powel to Benjamin Bell, 9 September 1735, Powel Letterbook vol. 1.

42. Samuel Powel to Bell & Son, 2 April 1739, ibid.

43. Abigail Franks to Naphtali Franks, 12 December 1735, in *The Lee Max Friedman Collection of American Jewish Colonial Correspondence: Letters of the Franks Family (1733–1748)*, ed. Leo Hershkowitz and Isidore S. Meyer (Waltham, MA: American Jewish Historical Society, 1968), 50. Abigail's brother Nathan Levy partnered with his brother Isaac Levy in Philadelphia during the 1730s before going into business with nephew David Frank (Abigail's son) in 1742.

44. Samuel Powel to Benjamin Bell, 6 November 1733, Powel Letterbook, vol. 1.

45. Samuel Powel to Benjamin Bell, 28 May 1734, ibid.

46. Samuel Powel to Benjamin Bell, 22 August 1737, ibid.; Bezanson, Gray, and Hussey, *Prices in Colonial Pennsylvania*, 253–54. The price of tea dropped below 10 shillings in the late 1730s, and by the early 1740s it averaged about 6 shillings 6 pence per pound. The price drop reflected retail competition but also a respective drop in the average sale price at the EIC annual auction (Earl H. Pritchard, *Anglo-Chinese Relations during the Seventeenth and Eighteenth Centuries* [New York: Octagon Books, 1970], appendix XIX: "East India Company's Tea Trade," n.p.).

47. Samuel Powel to Benjamin and William Bell, 16 March 1740/41, Powel Letterbook vol. 2. Patriarch Jacob Franks (1688–1769), a wealthy New York merchant, coordinated efforts with his brother Aaron, who lived in London. After sending his son Naphtali to apprentice under Aaron's guidance, Jacob encouraged Naphtali "to Continue the Tea Trade" with other New York and Boston merchants (Jacob Franks to Naphtali Franks, 22 November 1743, in *The Letters of Abigaill Levy Franks, 1733–1748*, ed. Edith B. Gelles [New Haven, CT: Yale University Press, 2004], 133, 137). Meanwhile, two other sons, David and Moses, became merchandisers in Philadelphia.

48. Samuel Powel to Benjamin Bell, 23 November 1737, Powel Letterbook vol. 1. For competition and commercial connections between New York and Philadelphia in the early eighteenth century, see Cathy Matson, *Merchants and Empire: Trading in Colonial New York* (Baltimore: Johns Hopkins University Press, 1998), 128, 190, 200–201, and Thomas M. Doerflinger, *A Vigorous Spirit of Enterprise: Merchants and Economic Development in Revolutionary Philadelphia* (Chapel Hill: University of North Carolina Press, 1986), 59.

49. Powel to Benjamin and William Bell, 26 July 1739.

50. Samuel Powel to Benjamin Bell, 1 December 1737; and Powel to Bell & Son, 2 April 1739, Powel Letterbook vol. 1.

51. Cary Carson, "The Consumer Revolution in Colonial British America: Why Demand?" in Carson, Hoffman, and Albert, *Of Consuming Interests*, 486. Lorna Weatherill, "The Meaning of Consumer Behavior in Late Seventeenth- and Early Eighteenth-century England," in Brewer and Porter, *Consumption and the World of Goods*, 216, and Chaudhuri, *Trading World of Asia*, 388, argue that supply followed demand.

52. Kevin M. Sweeney, "High-Style Vernacular: Lifestyles of the Colonial Elite," in Carson, Hoffman, and Albert, *Of Consuming Interest*, 8–9. By the 1770s, even among the poor in Massachusetts, "nearly 50% had tea equipment and glassware, 39.6% had knives and forks, while 24.2% had ceramic dishes of some sort" (Shammas, *Pre-Industrial Consumer*, 183).

53. Entries for 10 August 1743 and 1737, [Thomas Boylston II] Ledger, 1735–1767, vol. 57, Boylston Family Papers, MHS.

54. Entries for 1738 and 1739, ibid.

55. Benjamin Greene Account Books.

56. David Evins, debtor, 1738; John Davis, debtor, 1738–1740; Moses Purce [brazier], debtor, 1740–1741; and Samuel Henshaw [distiller], debtor, 1739–1740, ibid.

57. Shammas, *Pre-Industrial Consumer*, 142–43, table 5.8: "Poorhouse diets: 1589–1795." Anne E. C. McCants, "Exotic Goods, Popular Consumption, and the Standard of Living: Thinking about Globalization in the Early Modern World," *Journal of World*

History 18, no. 4 (December 2007): 448, notes that a similar diffusion of tea among poorer classes occurred in the Dutch Republic as more and cheaper Bohea tea came to Amsterdam in the early 1730s.

58. Sidney W. Mintz, *Sweetness and Power: The Place of Sugar in Modern History* (New York: Penguin, 1986), 67; Richard Dunn, *Sugar and Slaves: The Rise of the Planter Class in the English West Indies, 1624–1713* (New York: Norton, 1972), 205, notes that the price of English muscovado sugar dropped from £4 per hundredweight in the 1640s to 16 shillings per hundredweight in 1686–87. By the 1730s, French sugar was more plentiful and affordable. See Woodruff D. Smith, "Complications of the Commonplace: Tea, Sugar, and Imperialism," *Journal of Interdisciplinary History* 23, no. 2 (1992): 263.

59. McCusker and Menard, *Economy of British America*, 49, 157–58.

60. Shammas, *Pre-Industrial Consumer*, 84. See also Chaudhuri, *Trading World of Asia*, 385. W. A. Cole, "Trends in Eighteenth-Century Smuggling," in *The Growth of English Overseas Trade in the Seventeenth and Eighteenth Centuries*, ed. W. E. Minchinton (London: Methuen, 1969), 128, table I, estimates that between 1726 and 1730, the average annual consumption of legal tea in England was 0.10 pounds, which rose to only 0.11 pounds from 1731 to 1735; 0.17 pounds between 1736 and 1740; and 0.13 pounds from 1741 to 1745. He sees a significant rise in consumption to over 0.50 pounds only in the late 1740s and 1750s, as the relative price of tea began to decline.

61. Samuel Wharton, "Observations upon the Consumption of Teas in North America, 1773," Notes and Queries, *PMHB* 25, no. 1 (1901): 139–40. Carole Shammas, *Pre-Industrial Consumer*, 84, indicates that colonists drank 0.5 to 0.8 pounds of tea annually, while Billy Smith, "The Material Lives of Laboring Philadelphians, 1750–1800," *WMQ* 38, no. 2 (April 1981): 170, estimates that a laborer in the 1760s consumed only 0.2 pounds. Both estimates do not take smuggled tea into account, just direct importation.

62. John E. Crowley, *This Sheba, Self: The Conceptualization of Economic Life in Eighteenth-Century America* (Baltimore: Johns Hopkins University Press, 1974), 42. See also Maxine Berg and Elizabeth Eger, "The Rise and Fall of the Luxury Debates," in *Luxury in the Eighteenth Century: Debates, Desires, and Delectable Goods*, ed. Berg and Eger (New York: Palgrave Macmillan, 2003). During the sixteenth century, China also participated in "luxury debates" that mirrored those of the English-speaking world in the seventeenth and eighteenth centuries. Confucian scholars lamented the corrupting influence of urban markets and merchants on rural peasants and their "simple" habits. Gentry blamed the rising merchant class, even as they benefitted from a new Chinese prosperity (Timothy Brook, *The Confusions of Pleasure: Commerce and Culture in Ming China* [Berkeley: University of California Press, 1998], 124–52).

63. Mark Valeri, "Religious Discipline and the Market: Puritans and the Issue of Usury," *WMQ* 54 (1997): 747–68; Valeri, "William Petty in Boston: Political Economy, Religion, and Money in Provincial New England," *EAS* 8, no. 3 (Fall 2010): 549–80.

64. Thomas Mun, *England's Treasure by Forraign Trade or the Balance of Our Forraign Trade in the Rule of our Treasure* (London, 1664), 180–81, quoted in Jan de Vries, *The Industrious Revolution: Consumer Behavior and the Household Economy, 1650 to the Present* (New York: Cambridge University Press, 2008), 44.

65. Cotton Mather, *Advice from Taberah: a Sermon Preached after the Terrible Fire* (Boston, 1711), 25, quoted in Crowley, *This Sheba, Self,* 62.

66. Crowley, *This Sheba, Self,* 78.

67. *New England Weekly Journal,* January 24, 1732; *Boston Gazette,* May 15, 1727, and November 20, 1732. For the need to regulate markets, see *Boston Gazette,* February 26, 1733.

68. Quoted in McKendrick, Brewer, and Plumb, *Birth of a Consumer Society,* 18. See also Crowley, *This Sheba, Self,* 15.

69. James Steuart, *An Inquiry into the Principles of Political Oeconomy: being an Essay on the Science of Domestic Policy in Free Nations* (London, 1767), 1:307–8, 310.

70. Ibid., 1:325, 326. David Hume, readily available to American readers, saw the consumption of foreign commodities as a means to stimulate production, even to create a system of upward mobility (John E. Crowley, *The Privileges of Independence: Neomercantilism and the American Revolution* [Baltimore: Johns Hopkins University Press, 1993], 7; de Vries, *Industrious Revolution,* 45; David Hume, "Of Refinement in the Arts," part II, in *Essays, Moral, Political and Literary* [1752; London, 1989], 270; Emma Rothschild, "The Atlantic Worlds of David Hume," in *Soundings in Atlantic History: Latent Structures and Intellectual Currents, 1500–1830,* ed. Bernard Bailyn and Patricia L. Denault [Cambridge, MA: Harvard University Press, 2009], 408, 414–15).

71. Daniel Defoe, *The Complete English Tradesman* (1726; 5th ed., London, 1745) 2:318, 325.

72. Frank, *Objectifying China, Imagining America,* 19; Maxine Berg, "Asian Luxuries and the Making of the European Consumer Revolution," in Berg and Eger, *Luxury in the Eighteenth Century,* 238–39; Jonathan Spence, *The Chan's Great Continent: China in Western Minds* (New York: Norton, 1998), 62ff (on chinoiserie and Defoe's change of mind). *The Orphan of China: A Tragedy,* trans. from French of Voltaire by Thomas Francklin (1755), was performed in London and Philadelphia in the mid-eighteenth century.

73. Dr. John Francis Gemelli Careri, *A Voyage Round the World* (1695), in *A Collection of Voyages and Travels, Some now first Printed from Original Manuscripts* (London, 1704), 4:384.

74. Pierre Pomet, *A Compleat History of Druggs,* 3rd ed. (London, 1737), 85; *The Chinese Traveller: Containing a geographical, commercial, and political history of China* (London, 1775), 238.

75. Thomas Short, *Discourses on Tea, Sugar, Milk, Made-wines, Spirits, Punch, Tobacco, &c: With Plain and Useful Rules for Gouty People* (London, 1750), 40–41, 59.

76. John Coakley Lettsom, *The Natural History of the Tea-tree, with Observations on the Medical Qualities of Tea, and Effects of Tea-Drinking* (London, 1772), 45, 40–41 (frog experiment).

77. Jonas Hanway, *Letters on the Importance of the Rising Generation of the Laboring Part of our Fellow-Subjects* (London, 1767), 2:179, 180–81.

78. Duncan Forbes, *Some Considerations on the Present State of Scotland* (Edinburgh, 1744), 7.

79. John Wesley, *A Letter to a Friend Concerning Tea,* 2nd ed. (Bristol, 1749), 5; Lettsom, *Natural History of the Tea-tree,* 62.

80. Short, *Discourses on Tea,* 59.

81. Shammas, *Pre-Industrial Consumer*, 297.

82. In the mid-eighteenth century, male laborers were generally paid about 2 shillings a day, making a pound of tea worth as much as a week's pay. See James T. Lemon, *The Best Poor Man's Country: A Geographical Study of Early Southeastern Pennsylvania* (Baltimore: Johns Hopkins University Press, 1972), 179, and Mary M. Schweitzer, *Custom and Contract: Household, Government, and the Economy in Colonial Pennsylvania* (New York: Columbia University Press, 1987), 51–52.

83. Shammas, *Pre-Industrial Consumer*, 298–99.

84. Defoe, *Complete English Tradesman*, 1:197.

85. Nicholas Amhurst, "To a Friend in LONDON, upon my returning to College," *Poems on Several Occasions* (1723), 51; Christopher Pitt, "The Fable of the Young Man and his Cat," in *Poems and Translations* (London, 1727), 170; and William Shenstone, "The Tea-Table," in *Poems upon Various Occasions* (Oxford, 1737), 46, all in Chadwyck-Healey English Poetry Database, University of Virginia Library, http://search.lib.vir ginia.edu/?f[digital_collection_facet][]=Chadwyck-Healey+English+Poetry (accessed July 19, 2013).

86. "On Seeing the Archers &c. The Answer," in *Poems by Allan Ramsay* (Edinburgh, 1729), 2:43; "Content. A Poem," in *The Works of Allan Ramsay*, ed. Burns Martin and John W. Oliver (Edinburgh and London: Scottish Text Society, 1944–1973), 1:102; Allan Ramsay, "Song LXIX," in *The Tea-Table Miscellany: or, a collection of choice songs, Scots and English* (London, 1763), 286–87. Ramsay's work was reprinted for decades, even after his death, in 1758. See David Shields, *Civil Tongues and Polite Letters in British America* (Chapel Hill: University of North Carolina Press, 1997).

87. *New-England Courant*, March 15–March 22, 1725.

88. Letter to "Mr. Gazatteer" from "Alice Addertongue," *Pennsylvania Gazette*, September 12, 1732.

89. [Benjamin Franklin], *Poor Richard's Almanack, 1738*, AMDOCS, http://www .vlib.us/amdocs/texts/prichard38.html (accessed July 19, 2013). Franklin's public condemnation of tea belied his own relationship to and consumption of the beverage.

90. See for example *Pennsylvania Gazette*, February 1, 1733. One pseudonymed "honest Tradesman's only Daughter" [Patience Teacraft] reminded readers that she weaned her husband's addiction "to Drinking & Gaming" by use of tea, making him do "more Work, gets more Money, and is in good Credit with his Neighbours" (*Pennsylvania Gazette*, May 31, 1733).

91. Keyes, "Early American Advertising," 227.

92. *Pennsylvania Gazette*, March 15, 1733. Elizabeth Kowaleski-Wallace, *Consuming Subjects: Women, Shopping, and Business in the Eighteenth Century* (New York: Columbia University Press, 1997), 5.

93. Patricia Cleary, *Elizabeth Murray: A Woman's Pursuit of Independence in Eighteenth-Century America* (Amherst: University of Massachusetts Press, 2000); Ann Smart Martin, *Buying into the World of Goods: Early Consumers in Backcountry Virginia* (Baltimore: Johns Hopkins University Press, 2008), 158–59; Ellen Hartigan-O'Connor, *The Ties That Buy: Women and Commerce in Revolutionary America* (Philadelphia: University of Pennsylvania Press, 2009), 4–5.

94. John Reynell Day Book, 1731–1732, APS; John Reynell Account book, 1738–1767, Coates and Reynell Papers, HSP.

95. Samuel Coates Daybook.

96. Benjamin Greene Account Book.

97. Karin Wulf, *Not All Wives: Women in Colonial Philadelphia* (Ithaca, NY: Cornell University Press, 2000), 142.

98. Quoted in Peter J. Law, "Samuel Johnson on Consumer Demand, Status, and Positional Goods," *European Journal of the History of Economic Thought* 11, no. 2 (June 2004): 191.

99. Quoted in Carson, "Consumer Revolution in Colonial British America," 684.

100. "The Itinerarium of Dr. Alexander Hamilton," in *Colonial American Travel Narratives*, ed. Wendy Martin (New York: Penguin, 1994), 186–87; Breen, "Meanings of Things," 249–50.

101. *New-York Weekly Journal*, April 22, 1734.

102. Forbes, *Present State of Scotland*, 9.

103. *New-York Gazette*, December 21, 1747, and reprinted in many newspapers, including *Maryland Gazette*, March 9, 1748, and *Boston Gazette*, January 19, 1748.

104. *Boston Evening Post*, August 18, 1746. A remedy for profligate consumer behavior came from John Locke. In 1748 the *Evening Post* reprinted an excerpt from Locke's *Discourse on Money and Trade*, which reiterated the need to "regulate our Expences" in order to succeed in business. He advised that nations consume only what their commodities could purchase, maintaining a balance of trade and regulation of bullion (*Boston Evening Post*, March 28, 1748).

Chapter 3 · Politicizing American Consumption

1. Verse for the month of May, in Nathaniel Ames, *An Astronomical Diary; or, Almanack for the Year of our Lord Christ, 1762* (Boston, 1761), LCP.

2. Bruce C. Daniels, *The Fragmentation of New England: Comparative Perspectives on Economic, Political, and Social Divisions in the Eighteenth Century* (New York: Greenwood Press, 1988), 142.

3. Phyllis Whitman Hunter, *Purchasing Identity in the Atlantic World: Massachusetts Merchants, 1670–1780* (Ithaca, NY: Cornell University Press, 2001), 144.

4. Margaret Ellen Newell, *From Dependency to Independence: Economic Revolution in Colonial New England* (Ithaca, NY: Cornell University Press, 1998), 205–7; David Hancock, "The Triumphs of Mercury: Connection and Control in the Emerging Atlantic Economy," in *Soundings in Atlantic History: Latent Structures and Intellectual Currents, 1500–1830*, ed. Bernard Bailyn and Patricia L. Denault (Cambridge, MA: Harvard University Press, 2009), 115–21; Marc Egnal, "The Economic Development of the Thirteen Continental Colonies, 1720 to 1775," *WMQ* 32, no. 2 (April 1975): 208.

5. Egnal, "Economic Development of the Thirteen Colonies," 218; John J. McCusker and Russell R. Menard, *The Economy of British America, 1607–1789* (1985; rev. ed., Chapel Hill: University of North Carolina Press, 1991), 79.

6. Wilbur C. Plummer, "Consumer Credit in Colonial Philadelphia," *PMHB* 66, no. 4 (1942): 388. Customs 3 indicates that in 1750 Pennsylvania imported £217,713 worth of British goods but exported only £28,191 worth of provincial commodities. Since the customs office used notoriously outdated values for computations, Franklin's £500,000 figure may be closer to the truth. Certainly his ratio between exports and imports is on target.

7. John Hunt to Israel Pemberton, 28 February 1748/49, John Hunt Letterbook, 1747–1749, HSP.

8. Hancock, "Triumphs of Mercury," 115–21; Nathan Perl-Rosenthal and Evan Haefeli, "Introduction: Transnational Connections," *EAS* 10, no. 2 (Spring 2012): 227–38.

9. T. H. Breen, "'Baubles of Britain': The American and Consumer Revolutions of the Eighteenth Century," in *Of Consuming Interests: The Style of Life in the Eighteenth Century*, ed. Cary Carson, Ronald Hoffman, and Peter J. Albert (Charlottesville: University Press of Virginia, 1994), 476–77; Cary Carson, "The Consumer Revolution in Colonial British America: Why Demand?" in ibid., 513–22; John E. Crowley, *The Privileges of Independence: Neomercantilism and the American Revolution* (Baltimore: Johns Hopkins University Press, 1993), xii.

10. Samuel Wharton, "Observations upon the Consumption of Teas in North America, 1773," Notes and Queries, *PMHB* 25, no. 1 (1901): 140; Paul A. Gilje, *Free Trade and Sailors' Rights in the War of 1812* (Cambridge: Cambridge University Press, 2013), 20–21.

11. Great Britain, *An Act for permitting Tea to be exported to Ireland, and His Majesty's Plantations in America, without paying the Inland duties* (London, 1748), 607, Eighteenth Century Collections Online (N052685); K. N. Chaudhuri, *The Trading World of Asia and the English East India Company, 1660–1760* (Cambridge: Cambridge University Press, 1978), 394; Anne Bezanson, Robert D. Gray, and Miriam Hussey, *Prices in Colonial Pennsylvania* (Philadelphia: University of Pennsylvania Press, 1935), 256–57; Benjamin Woods Labaree, *The Boston Tea Party* (New York: Oxford University Press, 1961), 8.

12. John Hunt to Samuel Sansom, 29 June 1748, Hunt Letterbook; Great Britain, *Act for permitting Tea to be exported to Ireland*, 604–7.

13. Diary and Consultation in China, 23 May 1734, 1734–1735, IOR/G/12/37, reel 11, *EIC Factory Records*.

14. Peter D. G. Thomas, *The Townshend Duties Crisis: The Second Phase of the American Revolution, 1767–1773* (Oxford: Oxford University Press, 1987), 18; Hoh-Cheung Mui and Lorna H. Mui, "Smuggling and the British Tea Trade before 1784," *American Historical Review*, 74 (October 1968): 48, 53–54; Francis S. Drake, ed., *Tea Leaves: Being a Collection of Letters and Documents Relating to the Shipment of Tea to the American Colonies in the Year 1773, by the East India Company* (Boston, 1884), 198.

15. *Boston Post Boy*, October 28, 1745; *Boston Evening Post*, October 28, 1745. The total figure for Dutch imports in 1745 (2,083,958 pounds, as reported in the *Boston Post Boy*) raises questions about the accuracy of Dermigny's figures for non-English tea importations. Dermigny indicates that between 1741 and 1748 the Dutch supposedly imported a total of 2,017,683 pounds of tea directly from China (Louis Dermigny, *La Chine et l'Occident: Le commerce à Canton au XVIIIᵉ siècle, 1719–1833* [Paris: École pratique des hautes études, 1964], 2:539). Perhaps Dermigny does not include tea sold through private merchants, only the Dutch East India Company (Vereenigde Oost-Indische Compagnie [VOC]).

16. Wim Klooster, "Inter-Imperial Smuggling in the Americas, 1600–1800," in Bailyn and Denault, *Soundings in Atlantic History*, 170, 174–75; Michael Jarvis, *In the Eye of All Trade: Bermuda, Bermudians, and the Maritime Atlantic World, 1680–1783*

(Chapel Hill: University of North Carolina Press, 2010), 165; Victor Enhoven, "'That Abominable Nest of Pirates': St. Eustatius and the North Americans, 1680–1780," *EAS* 10, no. 2 (Spring 2012): 239–301; Joshua M. Smith, *Borderland Smuggling: Patriots, Loyalists, and Illicit Trade in the Northeast, 1783–1820* (Gainsville: University Press of Florida, 2006), 10; Arthur Maier Schlesinger, *The Colonial Merchants and the American Revolution, 1763–1776* (1918; repr., New York: Beard Books, 1939), 41. For examples of smuggling via St. Eustatius, see Gerard G. Beekman to John Bennit (Ship Captain), 28 January 1756; Gerard G. Beekman to Henry Lloyd, Boston, 22 March and 19 April 1756, in *The Beekman Mercantile Papers, 1746–1799*, ed. Philip L. White (New York: New-York Historical Society, 1956), 1:272, 276, 279.

17. Quoted in Klooster, "Inter-Imperial Smuggling in the Americas," 142.

18. Samuel Powel to BW Bell, 21 May 1746, Samuel Powel Letterbook, 1739–1746, vol. 2, HSP; "William Shirley and William Bollan: Report on Illegal Trade in the Colonies (26 February 1743)," in *American Colonial Documents to 1776*, English Historical Documents no. 9, ed. Merrill Jensen (London: Eyre & Spottiswoode, 1964), 373.

19. Alex Barclay to John Swift, Esqr, Collector of his Majesty's Customs, 13 March 1764, Custom House Papers, November 1761–October 1764, HSP.

20. John Kidd to Messrs Farmer, Narbel & Montiagut, in Lisbon, 21 May 1752, JKL.

21. Daniel Clark to John & Andrew French, 31 May 1762, Daniel Clark Letter and Invoice Book, 1759–1763, HSP.

22. Orr, Dunlap, and Glenholme to Messrs William Beath & Co., 16 October 1767, Orr, Dunlap, and Glenholme Letterbook, 1767–1769, HSP.

23. Thomas Hancock to Mr Martin Dubois Godet, at St. Eustasia, 7 March 1746, and Thomas Hancock to Messrs Thomas & Adrian Hope, 20 February 1745/46, Thomas Hancock Letterbook, 1745–1750, Hancock Family Papers, microfilm, P277, reel 1, MHS; John W. Tyler, *Smugglers and Patriots: Boston Merchants and the Advent of the American Revolution* (Boston: Northeastern University Press, 1986), 30.

24. Thomas Hancock to Thomas and Adrian Hope, 31 August 1747, and Thomas Hancock to Thomas and Adrian Hope, 20 November 1747, Hancock Letterbook.

25. Thomas Hancock to Kilby & Bernard, 12 November 1748, Hancock Letterbook. See also Schlesinger, *Colonial Merchants and the American Revolution*, 58 n1, and Thomas C. Barrow, *Trade and Empire: The British Customs Service in Colonial America, 1660–1775* (Cambridge, MA: Harvard University Press, 1967), 151.

26. John Kidd to Rawlinson & Davison, 4 April 1750 and 5 May 1750, JKL.

27. John Kidd to Rawlinson & Davison, 19 April 1753, JKL.

28. John Reynell to Cousin Thomas Sanders, 19 December 1754, John Reynell Letterbook, 1734–1774, Coates and Reynell Papers, 1702–1843, HSP; William Gough to John Kidd in London, 21 October 1754, JKL.

29. William Gough to Rawlinson and Davison, 5 April 1755, JKL. Many American merchants followed news of the EIC and events in India to better track the fluctuations in the supply and cost of East India goods at London. See, for example, Thomas Willing to cousin Thomas Willing, 26 August 1755, Charles Willing Letterbook, 1754–1761, HSP.

30. Thomas Willing to Messrs Connell & Morony, 14 April 1755, Willing Letterbook. Most of the correspondence in this letterbook is from Charles's son Thomas, who

took over the family business by November 1754, along with the help of their young clerk, Robert Morris.

31. Thomas Willing to Messrs Mayne Burn & Mayne, 18 August 1755, and Willing to cousin Willing, 26 August 1755, Willing Letterbook.

32. Thomas Willing to Uncle Thomas, 1 September 1757, ibid.

33. Thomas Willing to Messrs Mayne Burn & Mayne, 17 October 1757, ibid.

34. Joseph S. Tiedemann, "Interconnected Communities: The Middle Colonies on the Eve of the American Revolution," *Pennsylvania History: A Journal of Mid-Atlantic Studies* 76, no. 1 (Winter 2009): 4–9.

35. Thomas Wharton to Joseph Borden Jr., 7 February 1756, Thomas Wharton Letterbook, 1752–1759, HSP; Tiedemann, "Interconnected Communities," 21.

36. Waddell Cunningham to Martin Kuyckvan Mierop, London, 27 October 1756, *Letterbook of Greg & Cunningham, 1756–57, Merchants of New York and Belfast*, ed. Thomas M. Truxes (Oxford: Oxford University Press, 2001), 228.

37. Virginia D. Harrington, *The New York Merchant on the Eve of the Revolution* (Gloucester, MA: P. Smith, 1964), 255; Barrow, *Trade and Empire*, 148.

38. Waddell Cunningham to Isaac & Zachary Hope, Rotterdam, 14 June 1756, in Truxes, *Letterbook of Greg & Cunningham*, 138.

39. Waddell Cunningham to Thomas Greg, Belfast, 12 November 1756, in Truxes, *Letterbook of Greg & Cunningham*, 238.

40. John Kidd to Rawlinson and Davison, 24 February 1752; William Gough to John Kidd, 3 October 1754; John Kidd to Rawlinson & Davison, 1 October 1755; John Kidd to Rawlinson & Davison, 23 November 1755, all in JKL. On tea from Ireland, see Thomas M. Doerflinger, *A Vigorous Spirit of Enterprise: Merchants and Economic Development in Revolutionary Philadelphia* (Chapel Hill: University of North Carolina Press, 1986), 56. For "Imported in the Palantine Ships," see also John Kidd to Rawlinson & Davison, 24 September 1750, JKL.

41. John Kidd to Rawlinson & Davison, 25 June 1755, JKL.

42. Thomas Willing to Mayne Burn & Mayne, 6 May 1757, Willing Letterbook.

43. Thomas Willing to Mayne Burn & Mayne, 28 June 1758, ibid.; entry for 27 June 1758, Thomas Richee (Riché) Records, 1757–1761, vol. 1, HSP.

44. Entries for 19 October and 21 December 1759, Richee (Riché) Records.

45. James & Drinker to Nehemiah Champion, 20 December 1756, James & Drinker Letterbook, 1756–1759, Drinker Papers, HSP.

46. James & Drinker to Samuel Green, 19 July 1757, ibid.

47. James & Drinker to John Clitherall, 13 October 1757, and James & Drinker to David Barclay & Sons, 23 November 1758, ibid.

48. James & Drinker to Hillary & Scott, 14 November 1760, and James & Drinker to William Neate, 15 November 1760, ibid.

49. Waddell Cunningham to Capt John Nealson, Master of the snow *Prince of Wales*, 29 May 1756, in Truxes, *Letterbook of Greg & Cunningham*, 130. Goods were to be sent to John Lloyd in Stamford, Connecticut, to be "lodged where you think they will be safest" (Waddell Cunningham to John Lloyd, 29 May 1756, in ibid., 130).

50. Thomas M. Truxes, *Defying Empire: Trading with the Enemy in Colonial New York* (New Haven, CT: Yale University Press, 2008), 46.

51. Thomas Richee to Jacob VanZandt, 19 August 1756, Thomas Richee (Riché) Letterbook, 1750–1763, HSP.

52. Daniel Clark to Thomas Dromgoole, 22 June 1761, Clark Letter and Invoice Book.

53. Correspondence of John Swift, Port of Philadelphia Custom House Records, 1766–1768, collection 157, HSP; Great Britain, *An Act for permitting Tea to be exported to Ireland*, 607. American merchants had to produce certificates within eighteen months from the date of sale attesting to the legality of their imported tea.

54. Nancy F. Koehn, *The Power of Commerce: Economy and Governance in the First British Empire* (Ithaca, NY: Cornell University Press, 1994), 6–7.

55. Crowley, *Privileges of Independence*, 13. Koehn, *Power of Commerce*, 50, asserts that the American mainland and Caribbean colonies absorbed 44 percent of all "British exportable goods."

56. Commissioners of Customs in London to the Surveyor General in American Colonies, 3 November 1763, Port of Philadelphia Custom House Records, November 1761 to October 1764, HSP.

57. Alfred S. Martin, "The King's Customs: Philadelphia, 1763–1774," *WMQ* 5, no. 2 (April 1948): 204–5.

58. [Stephen Hopkins], *The Rights of Colonies Examined* (Providence, RI, 1765), 12–14.

59. Quoted in Elija H. Gould, *The Persistence of Empire: British Political Culture in the Age of the American Revolution* (Chapel Hill: University of North Carolina Press, 2000), 117.

60. Steve Pincus, "The Stamp Act Crisis in Global and Imperial Perspective" (unpublished paper, 2015), 8, 26, 35–36.

61. [John Dickinson], *The Late Regulations Respecting the British Colonies on the continent of America Considered* (London, 1766), 6.

62. Ibid., 33.

63. Pincus, "Stamp Act Crisis in Global and Imperial Perspective," 37.

64. "Non-importation agreement of New York merchants (31 October 1765)," in Jensen, *American Colonial Documents to 1776*, 671.

65. Quoted in Robert F. Oaks, "Philadelphia Merchants and the Origins of American Independence," *Proceedings of the American Philosophical Society* 121 (December 1977): 409.

66. "Testimony of British merchants on colonial trade and the effects of the Stamp Act (1766)," in Jensen, *American Colonial Documents to 1776*, 687. See also Gould, *Persistence of Empire*, 122, and Pincus, "Stamp Act Crisis in Global and Imperial Perspective," 38–47.

67. George Spencer to members of Parliament, 8 January 1766, quoted in Truxes, *Defying Empire*, 199, 273 n48.

68. The Townshend Act, 20 November 1767, The Avalon Project, Documents in Law, History, and Diplomacy, http://avalon.law.yale.edu/18th_century/townsend_act_1767.asp (accessed August 24, 2011).

69. "Act creating the American Board of Customs Commissioners (29 June 1767)," in Jensen, *American Colonial Documents to 1776*, 703; Martin, "King's Customs," 206.

70. Schlesinger, *Colonial Merchants and the American Revolution*, 52, 65, 94.

71. Thomas Cushing to [?], 9 May 1767, Miscellaneous Bound Letters, 1766–1769, MHS.

72. John Dickinson, Letter XII, in *The Political Writings of the Late John Dickinson, Esq.* (Wilmington, DE, 1814), 1:278.

73. Entry for 1 March 1768, in *Letters and Diary of John Rowe, Boston Merchant, 1759–1762, 1764–1779*, ed. Anne Rowe Cunningham (1903; repr., New York: Arno, 1969), 153; Oaks, "Philadelphia Merchants and the Origins of American Independence," 412.

74. [Dickinson], *Late Regulations Respecting the British Colonies*, 18–19.

75. "Boston, November 16," *Pennsylvania Gazette*, November 26, 1767.

76. Nonimportation subscription list, 28 October 1767, Boston, Houghton Library, http://blogs.law.harvard.edu/houghton/2013/07/11/a-revolutionary-discovery-in -the-stacks/ (accessed July 15, 2013). Interestingly, this recently found subscriber list with 650 names (including many women, merchants, and Paul Revere) did not include a prohibition on tea but listed textiles, glass, silversmith work, and paper.

77. Margaret E. Newell, "A Revolution in Economic Thought: Currency and Development in Eighteenth-Century Massachusetts," in *Entrepreneurs: The Boston Business Community, 1700–1850*, ed. Conrad Edick Wright and Katheryn P. Viens (Boston: Massachusetts Historical Society, 1997), 20. Tyler, *Smugglers and Patriots*, 20, notes that in Boston, at least, both smugglers and dry goods merchants used the boycotts for their own purposes, to maintain the flow of profitable West Indies trade goods as well as to cut out the weaker competition.

78. Egnal, "Economic Development of the Thirteen Colonies," 214–15.

79. Entry for 4 March 1768, in Cunningham, *Letters and Diary of John Rowe*, 153–54.

80. "Boston non-importation agreement (1 August 1768)," in Jensen, *American Colonial Documents to 1776*, 724–25.

81. [John Dickinson], *To the Merchants, and Traders, of the City of Philadelphia, Gentlemen, the worthy and patriotic writer of the Farmer's Letters* (Philadelphia, 1768), LCP.

82. Customs 3, reel 42; Tiedemann, "Interconnected Communities," 19. See McCusker and Menard, *Economy of British America*, 73–76, for discussion of trade deficit inaccuracies. Customs figures represent trade only to and from England and Wales and do not include "invisibles," such as unrecorded balance of payments, commercial services, insurance, sales of ships and freighting charges. In addition, the valuation of the pound sterling used by customs did not reflect the shifting value of colonial currency. Still, existing customs figures show an obvious imbalance of trade.

83. *Pennsylvania Gazette*, February 2, 1769; Oaks, "Philadelphia Merchants and the Origins of American Independence," 414.

84. R. L. Brunhouse, "The Effect of the Townshend Act in Pennsylvania," *PMHB* 54 (1930): 365; *Pennsylvania Gazette*, February 2, February 16, and April 13, 1769.

85. Thomas Doerflinger, "Philadelphia Merchants and the Logic of Moderation, 1760–1775," *WMQ* 40, no. 2 (April 1983): 219; R. A. Ryerson, "Political Mobilization and the American Revolution: The Resistance Movement in Philadelphia, 1765 to 1776," *WMQ* 31 (October 1974): 577.

86. Thomas Clifford to Walter Franklin, 11 March 1769, Thomas and John Clifford Letterbook, 1767–1773, Clifford Family Papers, 1722–1832, HSP.

87. "Letter from a Committee of Merchants in Philadelphia to the Committee of Merchants in London, 1769," *PMHB* 27 (1903): 85.

88. Richard Waln to Harford & Powell, 18 April 1769, Richard Waln Letterbook, 1766–1794, box 1, Richard Waln Papers, HSP; William Strahan to David Hall, 11 January 1770, William Strahan Letters, 1751–1776, HSP.

89. "Annapolis (in Maryland) June 22, 1769. We, the Subscribers, his Majesty's loyal and dutiful subjects, the Merchants, Traders, Freeholders, Mechanics," broadside, p. 1, EAIE 11158.

90. Virginia Assembly, House of Burgesses, Williamsburg, Thursday the 18th May, 1769, At a farther Meeting, according to Adjournment, the Committee appointed Yesterday made this Report, p. 1, EAIE 11513.

91. Woody Holton, *Forced Founders: Indians, Debtors, Slaves, and the Making of the American Revolution in Virginia* (Chapel Hill: University of North Carolina Press, 1999), 90–91.

92. Nonimportation subscription list, 28 October 1767.

93. John E. Crowley, *This Sheba, Self: The Conceptualization of Economic Life in Eighteenth-Century America* (Baltimore: Johns Hopkins University Press, 1974), 126; T. H. Breen, *The Marketplace of Revolution: How Consumer Politics Shaped American Independence* (New York: Oxford University Press, 2004), xv–xvi.

94. *Pennsylvania Journal and Weekly Advertiser*, December 10, 1767.

95. *Pennsylvania Journal and Weekly Advertiser*, December 3, 1767. Also published *Boston Post-Boy*, November 16, 1767 and *New York Gazette*, November 26, 1767.

96. "Providence, December 19," *Pennsylvania Gazette*, January 14, 1768.

97. "At a Town Meeting of the freeholders & other Inhabitants of the town of Watertown Regularly Assembled January ye 18 1768," Misc. correspondence, U.S. Revolution Collection, 1754–1928, box 1, folder 3, 1754–1773, AAS.

98. *The Female Patriot, No. I, Addressed to the Tea-Drinking Ladies of New-York* (New York, May 10, 1770), LCP.

99. Catherine La Courreye Blecki and Karin A. Wulf, eds., *Milcah Martha Moore's Book: A Commonplace Book from Revolutionary America* (University Park: Penn State University Press, 1997), 172–73.

100. Francis S. Drake, ed., *Tea Leaves: Being a Collection of Letters and Documents Relating to the Shipment of Tea to the American Colonies in the Year 1773, by the East India Company* (Boston, 1884), ix.

101. Customs 3, reels 31–42; Oaks, "Philadelphia Merchants and the Origins of American Independence," 418; Labaree, *Boston Tea Party*, 32.

102. See, for instance, "The Dying Speech of the Effigy of a wretched Importer, which was exalted upon a Gibbet, and afterwards committed to the Flames, at New-York, May 10, 1770," pamphlet, LCP.

103. Samuel Coates, Ciphering and Invoice Books, 1724–1758, inside cover; Thomas Wharton Ledger, 1752–1756; Mifflin and Massey Ledger, vol. 1, 1760–1763, and vol. 2, 1763–1766, Business Accounts; John Chevalier Daybook, 1760–1766; Charles Wharton Cashbook, 1765–1771, Wharton Family Papers; William Clarkson and George Morrison Ledger, 1767–1779, Commercial Records, Simon Gratz Collection, all at HSP.

104. Smith, "Material Lives of Laboring Philadelphians," 188; Shammas, *Preindustrial Consumer*, 65, 183, 184.

105. John Tudor Account Book, 1762–1771, vol. 1, John Tudor Papers, 1732–1793, MHS.

106. Stephen to Samuel Salisbury, 15 February 1768 and 4 March 1768, box 1, folder 3, business letters for 1767 and 1768, Salisbury Family Papers, AAS.

107. "Invoice of Sundries received from Boston, Oct. 1767," Samuel and Stephen Salisbury, Invoice Book, 1767–1781, Folio vol. 5, Salisbury Family Papers.

108. Samuel to Stephen Salisbury, 4 August 1769, box 2, folder 1, 1769, Salisbury Family Papers.

109. Samuel to Stephen Salisbury, 30 October 1769, ibid.

110. Michelle L. Craig (McDonald), "Grounds for Debate? The Place of the Caribbean Provisions Trade in Philadelphia's Prerevolutionary Economy," *PMHB* 128, no. 2 (April 2004): 150–53, notes the continued importance of the provisions trade between Philadelphia and the British West Indies, and the emergence of a coffee trade in the Caribbean, which helped Pennsylvania merchants adhere to boycotts of London commercial goods prior to 1774.

111. Samuel Coates, Merchants Journal, 1760–1776, Business Accounts, Am.986, HSP. See William Clarkson and George Morrison Ledger, 1767–1779, Commercial Papers, Simon Gratz Collection, HSP, for a similar pattern of sales.

112. William West Wastebook, 1769–1771, Q-39, West Family Business Records, 1769–1804, HSP.

113. "Tea Dr Account," Folio 3, 68, and 199, Levi Hollingsworth Account Book, 1768–1775, vol. 535, Hollingsworth Family Papers, HSP. Between October 1, 1768, and March 29, 1769, for example, Hollingsworth received over 6,300 pounds of tea from various sources. Again in late 1769 Hollingsworth had 6,332.5 pounds of tea on hand worth a few shillings over £1,461. In the fall of 1770, he had 6,854 pounds of tea on hand worth £1,566.

114. John Kidd to Rawlinson & Davison, 28 January 1757, JKL. Using M. P. George Spencer's conservative estimate of 300 pounds per chest, at least 12,000 pounds of tea was smuggled into Pennsylvania per year in the early 1750s. Thomas, *Townshend Duties Crisis*, 28; Klooster, "Inter-Imperial Smuggling in the Americas," 170, 174–75. McCusker and Menard, *Economy of British America*, 77, argue that smuggling may not have been as widespread as even eighteenth-century contemporaries thought.

115. Thomas Hutchinson to Thomas Palmer & Co., 27 August 1767, Thomas Hutchinson Letterbooks, transcription, vol. 25, 156, MHS; Shammas, *Pre-Industrial Consumer*, 83; James Walvin, *Fruits of Empire: Exotic Produce and British Taste, 1660–1800* (New York: New York University Press, 1997), 18; Mui and Mui, "Smuggling and the British Tea Trade before 1784," 44–73; W. A. Cole, "Trends in Eighteenth-Century Smuggling," in *The Growth of English Overseas Trade in the Seventeenth and Eighteenth Centuries*, ed. W. E. Minchinton (London: Methuen, 1969), 121–43.

116. Charles Wharton Cashbook, 1765–1771, Wharton Family Papers, 1679–1834, HSP; Charles Wharton to Benjamin and Amos Underhill, New York, 8 September, 16 December and 28 December 1768, Charles Wharton Letterbook, 1766–1771, box 2, Sarah Smith Collection, HSP; entry for 5 September 1770, Levi Hollingsworth Account Book, 1768–1775, vol. 535, Hollingsworth Family Papers, HSP; Charles Wharton Cashbook, 1765–1771, and Charles Wharton Cashbook, 1771–1780, Wharton Family Papers, 1679–1834, HSP.

117. Charles Wharton to Cornelius Sebring, New York, 11 May 1771, Charles Wharton Letterbook, 1766–1771, box 2, Sarah Smith Collection, HSP.

118. Tyler, *Smugglers and Patriots*, 122–27.

119. Stephen to Samuel Salisbury, 3 January 1770, box 2, folder 2, 1770, Salisbury Family Papers.

120. "An Account of what Tea has been Imported into Boston since the year 1768, distinguishing each year and the vessel & Owners in which it was Imported," Great Britain Customs Papers, Great Britain Commissioner of Customs in America, 1765–1774, MHS.

121. Thomas Hutchinson to Thomas Pownall, 29 January 1769, Hutchinson Letterbooks, vol. 26, 714–15.

122. Thomas Hutchinson to Lord Hillsborough, 25 August 1771, ibid., vol. 27, 361. Hutchinson estimated that the colonies as a whole consumed some 19,200 chests of Bohea tea each year (Thomas Hutchinson to Lord Hillsborough, 10 September 1771, ibid., 375–76). Although his sons Elias and Thomas Jr. maintained the public face of their business ventures, Thomas Sr. controlled the business correspondence even as he tried to downplay his involvement in their tea investments. Hutchinson had many reasons to hide his commercial activities from scrutiny. At the height of nonimportation, in October 1769, he instructed William Palmer, a principal exporter of teas to New England, to keep his orders and their commercial relationship a secret (Thomas Hutchinson to William Palmer, 5 October 1769, ibid., vol. 26, 826).

123. John & Jonathan Amory to Messrs. Bruce, Wheeler, & Higginson, 5 December 1769, John & Jonathan Amory Letters, vols. 141–44, Amory Family Papers, MHS.

124. Entry for 1769, [John Boylston] Ledger, 1735–1795, vol. 58, Boylston Family Papers, MHS.

125. "NEW YORK, May 21," *Pennsylvania Gazette*, May 24, 1770.

126. Richard Waln to Elijah Brown, 26 May 1770, Waln Letterbook. In November 1770, once American merchants had given up on nonimportation, Waln explicitly asked that his order be shipped during the limbo between repeal of the tea tax and official enactment of new duties, perhaps to forego scrutiny from local patriots who called for a continued boycott of tea (Richard Waln to Harford & Powell, 14 November 1770, Waln Letterbook).

127. Circular letter from New York Merchants . . . to Committee of Merchants in New Haven, 12 July 1769, Miscellaneous Bound Letters, 1766–1769, MHS.

128. Advertisement, New York, June 12, 1770; *Whereas an act was passed last session of Parliament, for repealing the act imposing a duty on paper, paint and glass*, pamphlet, LCP.

129. James & Drinker to unknown, 26 May 1770, in "Effects of the 'Non-Importation Agreement' in Philadelphia, 1769–1770," *PMHB* 14, no. 1 (1890): 44–45.

130. *To the Freeholders, Merchants, Tradesmen, and Farmers, of the City and County of Philadelphia* (Philadelphia, 26 September 1770), pamphlet, LCP.

131. Philadelphus, *To the Public* (Philadelphia, 3 October 1770), pamphlet, LCP.

132. "Philadelphia, July 19," *Pennsylvania Gazette*, July 19, 1770.

133. Pennsylvanian, *To the Inhabitants of the City and County of Philadelphia, July 14, 1770*, pamphlet, LCP.

134. Clement Biddle to David Crawford, 7 August 1770, Clement Biddle Letter-book, 1769–1770, vol. 1, HSP.

135. Samuel Coates [Jr.], to Will Logan, 26 September 1770, Samuel Coates Letter-book, 1763–1781, Coates and Reynell Collection, HSP. Reynell was married to Samuel Sr.'s sister Mary Coates and became guardian of his children when Samuel died in 1748. See HSP abstract and finding aid for Coates and Reynell Family Papers, http://hsp.org/sites/default/files/legacy_files/migrated/findingaid0140coatesreynell.pdf. By late 1769, in the wake of a September Friends Meeting that warned against getting involved in the politics of business, John Reynell and several other Quakers withdrew from the merchants' association, although they did not resign. See Oaks, "Philadelphia Merchants and the Origins of Independence," 418, and Doerflinger, *Vigorous Spirit of Enterprise*, 191–92, esp. n87.

136. *Pennsylvania Gazette*, September 20 and September 27, 1770; *Philadelphia, July 12, 1770. The Inhabitants of the City of New-York* (Philadelphia, 1770), pamphlet, LCP; Oaks, "Philadelphia Merchants and the Origins of American Independence," 421; Doerflinger, "Philadelphia Merchants and the Logic of Moderation," 220–22.

137. "Oct. 17, 1769, Merchants agreement, Boston, Nov. 20," *Pennsylvania Gazette*, December 7, 1769; Schlesinger, *Colonial Merchants and the American Revolution*, 122.

138. "Oct. 17, 1769, Merchants agreement, Boston, Nov. 20." See also John & Jonathan Amory to Samuel Eliot, 21 October 1769, Amory Letters, vols. 141–44.

139. "At a Meeting of the Merchants & Traders, at Faneuil-Hall, on the 23d January 1770," broadside, Boston, AAS.

140. Tyler, *Smugglers and Patriots*, 140, 163–69; Labaree, *Boston Tea Party*, 49.

141. Thomas Pownall, March 5th, 1770, "Mr. S_____r. I did endeavour to move this house, to come to . . . taking off duties, payable in America," [Boston?, 1770?], p. 3, EAIE 42157.

142. Thomas Hutchinson to Thomas Whately, 3 October 1770, Hutchinson Letterbooks, vol. 27, 18–19; Thomas Hutchinson to Francis Bernard, 18 February 1770, ibid., 965. After repeal, the importation and sale of enumerated EIC tea rose again in Boston. In 1770, 48,070 pounds were imported and 86,946 pounds in 1771.

Chapter 4 · The Global Dimensions of the American Tea Crisis

1. H. V. Bowen, "Perceptions from the Periphery: Colonial American Views of Britain's Asiatic Empire, 1756–1783," in *Negotiated Empires: Centers and Peripheries in the Americas, 1500–1820*, ed. Christine Daniels and Michael Kennedy (New York: Routledge, 2002), 295–96; Emma Rothschild, "Global Commerce and the Question of Sovereignty in the Eighteenth-Century Provinces," *Modern Intellectual History* 1, no. 1 (2004): 4–5.

2. Arthur Schlesinger, "The Uprising against the East India Company," *Political Science Quarterly* 32 (1917): 71–75; Bowen, "Perceptions from the Periphery," 292–94; Philip J. Stern, *The Company-State: Corporate Sovereignty and the Early Modern Foundations of the British Empire in India* (Oxford: Oxford University Press, 2011), 12–15.

3. Edmund Burke, "Speech on American Taxation, April 19, 1774," in *The Works of the Right Honourable Edmund Burke* (London, 1792), 1:519.

4. John Bruce, *Annals of the Honorable East-India Company* (London, 1810), 2:674;

An Enquiry into the rights of the East-India Company of Making War and Peace (London, 1772), 4–5.

5. Sudipta Sen, *Empire of Free Trade: The East India Company and the Making of the Colonial Marketplace* (Philadelphia: University of Pennsylvania Press, 1998), 62–63, 75–88; John Keay, *The Honourable Company: A History of the English East India Company* (New York: HarperCollins, 2010), 222–37.

6. *The Conduct of the East-India Company, with Respect to their Wars, &c.* (London, 1767), 35.

7. Keay, *Honourable Company*, 310–19.

8. *Conduct of the East-India Company*, 27, 46–47; Paul Langford, *A Polite and Commercial People: England, 1727–1783* (Oxford: Clarendon Press, 1989), 353–54; K. N. Chaudhuri, *The Trading World of Asia and the English East India Company, 1660–1760* (Cambridge: Cambridge University Press, 1978), 20; Stern, *Company-State*, 185–86; P. J. Marshall, *The Making and Unmaking of Empires: Britain, India, and America, c. 1750–1783* (New York: Oxford University Press, 2005), 122.

9. Marshall, *Making and Unmaking of Empires*, 129.

10. Earl H. Pritchard, *Anglo-Chinese Relations during the Seventeenth and Eighteenth Centuries* (New York: Octagon Books, 1970), appendix XIX: "East India Company's Tea Trade," n.p.

11. Tan Chung, "The Britain-China-India Trade Triangle (1771–1840)," *Indian Economic Social History Review* 11 (1974): 413; H. V. Bowen, *The Business of Empire: The East India Company and Imperial Britain, 1756–1833* (Cambridge: Cambridge University Press, 2008), 223–24. According to William Strahan, the EIC collected revenue with the help of its army: "Add to this, the Difficulty of investing these Revenues (for they cannot be remitted in Specie) and of converting their Commodities into Money, when the European Marketts are so glutted" (William Strahan to David Hall, 13 February 1768, William Strahan Letters, 1751–1776, HSP).

12. Chung, "Britain-China-India Trade Triangle," 417; Bowen, *Business of Empire*, 223–25.

13. H. B. Morse, *The Chronicles of the East India Company Trading to China, 1635–1834, Volume V* (1929), reprinted in *Britain and the China Trade, 1635–1842*, ed. Patrick Tuck (London: Routledge, 2000), 5:100, 134. A Chinese tale (tael) was a measurement of weight of pure silver, but the EIC treated it as currency equivalent to 6 shillings 8 pence in their account books (Chaudhuri, *Trading World of Asia*, 176).

14. Morse, *Chronicles of the East India Company Trading to China*, 5:86, 93, 100–101.

15. Ibid., 5:80, 109.

16. Ibid., 5:89–90.

17. Ibid., 5:116. In 1771 the Co-Hong dissolved, which opened up competition in the Canton market. The EIC used this shake-up to its advantage, forcing Chinese merchants to discount the price of teas, thus further exacerbating their indebtedness (Weng Eang Cheong, *The Hong Merchants of Canton: Chinese Merchants in Sino-Western Trade* [Surrey, UK: Curzon Press, 1997], 109–11).

18. Morse, *Chronicles of the East India Company Trading to China*, 5:136.

19. Ibid., 5:144. See also Bowen, *Business of Empire*, 226.

20. Morse, *Chronicles of the East India Company Trading to China*, 5:144–45.

21. Ibid., 5:146.

22. Nancy F. Koehn, *The Power of Commerce: Economy and Governance in the First British Empire* (Ithaca, NY: Cornell University Press, 1994), 104.

23. Proceedings in the House of Commons, May 1767, in *English Historical Documents, 1714–1783*, ed. D. B. Horn and Mary Ransome (New York: Oxford University Press, 1957), 804–5; Peter D. G. Thomas, *The Townshend Duties Crisis: The Second Phase of the American Revolution, 1767–1773* (Oxford: Oxford University Press, 1987), 26–28; Koehn, *Power of Commerce*, 98, 143.

24. Proceedings in the House of Lords upon the Dividend Bill, 26 June 1767, in Horn and Ransome, *English Historical Documents, 1714–1783*, 806–7.

25. Langford, *Polite and Commercial People*, 372–73; Arthur Maier Schlesinger, *The Colonial Merchants and the American Revolution, 1763–1776* (1918; repr., New York: Beard Books, 1939), 94; Elija H. Gould, *The Persistence of Empire: British Political Culture in the Age of the American Revolution* (Chapel Hill: University of North Carolina Press, 2000), 141–42.

26. Bowen, *Business of Empire*, 35.

27. H. V. Bowen, "The 'Little Parliament': The General Court of the East India Company, 1750–1784," *Historical Journal* 34, no. 4 (December 1991): 865.

28. Quoted in Emma Rothschild, "Global Commerce and the Question of Sovereignty in the Eighteenth-Century Provinces," *Modern Intellectual History* 1, no. 1 (2004): 8; Langford, *Polite and Commercial People*, 534; Benjamin L. Carp, *Defiance of the Patriots: The Boston Tea Party and the Making of America* (New Haven, CT: Yale University Press, 2010), 14.

29. Bowen, "Little Parliament," 861.

30. P. J. Marshall, *Problems of Empire: Britain and India, 1757–1813* (London: Allen & Unwin, 1968), 145–46.

31. Quoted in Philip Lawson and Jim Phillips, "'Our Execrable Banditti': Perceptions of Nabobs in Mid-Eighteenth Century Britain," *Albion* 16, no. 3 (1984): 238.

32. *An Infallible remedy for the high prices of provisions. Together with a scheme for laying open the trade to the East-Indies* (London, 1768), 24, 26. See also *Enquiry into the Rights of the East-India Company*, v.

33. William Bolts, *Considerations on Indian Affairs; Particularly Respecting the Present State of Bengal* (London, 1772), iv–v. Many other pamphlets of the late 1760s and early 1770s argued for the elimination of the EIC's trade monopoly and extension of free trade to all British subjects. See *An Attempt to Pay off the National Debt, by Abolishing the East-India company of Merchants; and all other Monopolies. With other Interesting Measures* (London, 1767), viii–ix, 19, 26–27; and Emma Rothschild, "The Atlantic Worlds of David Hume," in *Soundings in Atlantic History: Latent Structures and Intellectual Currents, 1500–1830*, ed. Bernard Bailyn and Patricia L. Denault (Cambridge, MA: Harvard University Press, 2009), 408, 414–15, 419.

34. *Town and Country Magazine*, 1771, quoted in Tillman W. Nechtman, "Nabobs Revisited: A Cultural History of Imperialism and the Indian Question in Late-Eighteenth-Century Britain," *History Compass* 4, no. 4 (2006): 646. See Tillman W. Nechtman, *Nabobs: Empire and Identity in Eighteenth-Century Britain* (Cambridge:

Cambridge University Press, 2010), for a deeper discussion of the Nabob figure as political metaphor and as mnemonic device for empire and the ways that global entanglements changed Britain.

35. Marshall, *Problems of Empire*, 147–48; Langford, *Polite and Commercial People*, 533–34; Lawson and Phillips, "Our Execrable Banditti," 225, 230.

36. William Strahan to David Hall, 13 February 1768, Strahan Letters; *A Letter to the Right Honourable Lord North, on the Present Proceedings Concerning the East-India Company* (London, 1773), 12.

37. *The Minutes of the Select Committee Appointed by the Honourable House of Commons, to enquire into the nature, state, and condition of the East India Company* (London, 1772), 10, 18.

38. Ibid., 6–7; Marshall, *Making and Unmaking of Empires*, 131.

39. "Speech by Lord Clive in the House of Commons in defence of his conduct and that of the Company's servants in Bengal, 30 March 1772," in Horn and Ransome, *English Historical Documents, 1714–1783*, 809, 811.

40. East India Company, *The Present State of the English East-India Company's Affairs* (London, [1772]), 1–29.

41. *Report from the Committee of Proprietors, Appointed on the 1st of December, 1772, by the General Court of the United East-India Company, to enquire into the present State and Condition of the Company's Affairs* (London, 1773), 5, 9, 14, 17; Koehn, *Power of Commerce*, 136.

42. Carp, *Defiance of the Patriots*, 13; Bowen, *Business of Empire*, 58–66.

43. East India Company, *Present State of the English East-India Company's Affairs*, 34–36; *Report from the Committee of Proprietors*, 18–23; Marshall, *Making and Unmaking of Empires*, 214–16.

44. Benjamin Franklin to Thomas Cushing, 5 January 1773, Papers of Benjamin Franklin, sponsored by the American Philosophical Society and Yale University, digital edition, http://franklinpapers.org/franklin (accessed October 3, 2014).

45. Lord North's Regulating Act, 1773, in Horn and Ransome, *English Historical Documents, 1714–1783*, 812.

46. Langford, *Polite and Commercial People*, 532–33; Bowen, *Business of Empire*, 70–72; Carp, *Defiance of the Patriots*, 15; W. M. Elofson, "The Rockingham Whigs in Transition: The East India Company Issue, 1772–1773," *English Historical Review* 104, no. 413 (October 1989): 953; H. V. Bowen, *Elites, Enterprise, and the Making of the British Overseas Empire* (London: Macmillan, 1996), 184; Koehn, *Power of Commerce*, 215; Marshall, *Problems of Empire*, 111–16.

47. East India Company, *Present State of the English East-India Company's Affairs*, 46–47.

48. William Palmer of London to the Directors of the East India Company, 19 May 1773, in *Tea Leaves: Being a Collection of Letters and Documents Relating to the Shipment of Tea to the American Colonies in the Year 1773, by the East India Tea Company*, ed. Francis S. Drake (Boston, 1884), 189; Schlesinger, *Colonial Merchants and the American Revolution*, 262.

49. East India Company, *Present State of the English East-India Company's Affairs*, 49.

50. Morse, *Chronicles of the East India Company Trading to China*, 5:177–78; Ben-

jamin Woods Labaree, *The Boston Tea Party* (New York: Oxford University Press, 1961), 75.

51. Great Britain, *An Act to allow a Drawback of the Duties of Customs on the Exportation of Tea to any of His Majesty's Colonies or Plantations in America; to increase the Deposit on Bohea Tea to be sold at the India Company's sales; and to impower the Commissioners of the Treasury to grant Licences to the East India Company* (London, 1773), 897, 900, rare books, LCP; *Attempt to Pay off the National Debt*, 20–29; *Infallible Remedy for the High Prices of Provisions*, 18–27.

52. Great Britain, *Act to allow a Drawback of the Duties of Customs on the Exportation of Tea*, 902.

53. Schlesinger, *Colonial Merchants and the American Revolution*, 263.

54. Barrow, *Trade and Empire*, 249; Labaree, *Boston Tea Party*, 73.

55. William Palmer of London to Directors of EIC, 19 May 1773, in Drake, *Tea Leaves*, 190–91; Labaree, *Boston Tea Party*, 73–74.

56. Gilbert Barclay, Philadelphia Merchant, to Court of Directors, EIC, 26 May 1773, in Drake, *Tea Leaves*, 200.

57. Labaree, *Boston Tea Party*, 74.

58. Samuel Wharton, "Observations upon the Consumption of Teas in North America, 1773," Notes and Queries, *PMHB* 25, no. 1 (1901): 140–41.

59. Benjamin Franklin to Thomas Cushing, 12 September 1773, Papers of Benjamin Franklin.

60. Drake, *Tea Leaves*, 206.

61. Memorial of Gilbert Barclay, merchant in Philadelphia for 16 years, to the Court of Directors of the East India Company, 26 May 1773, in Drake, *Tea Leaves*, 200.

62. Wharton, "Observations upon the Consumption of Teas," 140–41.

63. James & Drinker to William Henry, 17 July 1773, James & Drinker Letterbook, 1772–1786, Henry Drinker Business Papers, 1756–1869, HSP.

64. James & Drinker to Pigou & Booth, London, 27 August 1773, ibid.

65. The Philadelphia tea ship *Polly*, with Captain Samuel Ayres in command, carried 568 chests and 130 quarter-chests (Drake, *Tea Leaves*, 256). The usual commission for selling another merchant's tea was 2.5 percent.

66. Drake, *Tea Leaves*, 250–52; EIC Instructions, 1 October 1773, Philadelphia Tea Shipment Papers, 1769–1773, HSP; Labaree, *Boston Tea Party*, 75–79.

67. Drake, *Tea Leaves*, 218–19; 273; Elofson, "Rockingham Whigs in Transition," 963; Langford, *Polite and Commercial People*, 372; Pigou & Booth to James & Drinker, 8 October 1773, PTPC.

68. *Massachusetts Spy*, October 14, 1773, quoted in Schlesinger, "Uprising against the East India Company," 69.

69. Pennsylvania, *To the Tradesmen, Mechanics, &c. of the Province of Pennsylvania, Dec. 4, 1773*, pamphlet, HSP.

70. HAMPDEN, *The Alarm. Number III* (New York, 1773), EAIE 12801. American activists and their English supporters drew on the reign of the early Stuarts (James I and Charles I) and "the evil of prerogative powers" in their critique of parliamentary claims to tax America. See Eric Nelson, "Patriot Royalism: The Stuart Monarchy in American Political Thought, 1769–75," *WMQ* 68, no. 4 (October 2011): 542–43; Carp, *Defiance of the Patriots*, 21.

71. Labaree, *Boston Tea Party*, 90.

72. Ibid., 78.

73. Pigou & Booth to James & Drinker, 10 November 1773, PTPC.

74. Mechanic, *To the Tradesmen, Mechanics, etc.* (Philadelphia, 1773), broadside, HSP. Also printed as Pennsylvania, *To the Tradesmen, Mechanics, &c. of the Province of Pennsylvania, Dec. 4, 1773.*

75. Frank M. Etting, *The Philadelphia Tea Party of 1773: A chapter from the history of the old state house* (Philadelphia, 187?), 6, 4–5.

76. *To the Inhabitants of Pennsylvania,* 13 October 1773, broadside, LCP.

77. James & Drinker to Pigou & Booth, 26 October 1773, PTPC.

78. Notes from the Committee appointed to wait on the gentlemen commissioners, 17 October 1773 and 19 October 1772, Manuscripts and documents, 1765–1775, relating to Pennsylvania's Provincial Nonimportation resolutions, APS.

79. James & Drinker reply, 22 October 1773, Manuscripts and documents, 1765–1775, relating to Pennsylvania's Provincial Nonimportation resolutions, APS.

80. Benjamin Booth to James & Drinker, 4 October 1773, PTPC.

81. Thomas to Samuel Wharton, n.d., in "Selections from the Letter-Books of Thomas Wharton, of Philadelphia, 1773–1783," *PMHB* 33, no. 3 (1909), 319; Cathy Matson, *Merchants and Empire: Trading in Colonial New York* (Baltimore: Johns Hopkins University Press, 1998), 305–6.

82. Pigou & Booth to James & Drinker, 13 October 1773, PTPC.

83. Benjamin Booth to James & Drinker, 4 October 1773, PTPC.

84. Pigou & Booth to James & Drinker, 18 October 1773, PTPC.

85. Pigou & Booth to James & Drinker, 25 October 1773, PTPC.

86. Pigou & Booth to James & Drinker, 24 November 1773, PTPC.

87. Philadelphia, "A Card," 2 December 1773, Manuscripts and documents, 1765–1775, relating to Pennsylvania's Provincial Nonimportation Resolutions, APS.

88. Thomas to Samuel Wharton, 30 November 1773, in "Selections from the Letter-books of Thomas Wharton," 320.

89. Thomas Wharton to Thomas Walpole, 24 December 1773, in "Selections from the Letter-books of Thomas Wharton," 321–22.

90. Thomas Wharton to Thomas Walpole, 27 December 1773, "Notes and Queries, Account of the Arrival and Departure of the Tea-Ship at Philadelphia in 1773," *PMHB* 14 (1890): 79.

91. Samuel Ayres testament, 27 December 1773, Philadelphia Tea Shipment Papers, 1769–1773, HSP; Drake, *Tea Leaves,* 256.

92. James & Drinker to Thomas and Elisha Hutchinson et al., 17 December 1773, PTPC.

93. Sons of Liberty of New York, *The Association of the Sons of Liberty of New-York,* 29 November 1773, broadside, New-York Historical Society.

94. Pigou & Booth to James & Drinker, 31 December 1773, PTPC.

95. Benjamin Booth to James & Drinker, 11 March 1774, PTPC.

96. Thomas H. Peck to Messrs Lane Son & Fraser, 14 October and 26 October 1773, Thomas H. Peck Letterbook, 1763–1776, MHS.

97. Entries for 2 November and 3 November 1773, in *Letters and Diary of John Rowe, Boston Merchant, 1759–1762, 1764–1779,* ed. Anne Rowe Cunningham (1903;

repr., New York: Arno, 1969), 252–53; entry for 3 November 1773, in "Diary for 1773 to the End of 1774 of Mr. Thomas Newell," in *Proceedings of the Massachusetts Historical Society, 1876–1877*, vol. XV (Boston, 1878), 343.

98. *The Votes and Proceedings of the Freeholders and other Inhabitants of the Town of Boston, in Town meeting Assembled, According to Law, the 5th and 18th days of November, 1773* (Boston, 1773), p. 3, EAIE 12692.

99. Ibid., 5.

100. Ibid., 6–7.

101. Thomas Hutchinson to Lord Dartmouth, Secretary of State for the Colonies, 15 November 1773, Thomas Hutchinson Letterbooks, vol. 27, transcription, 1073–74, MHS.

102. Entry for 18 November 1773, in Cunningham, *Letters and Diary of John Rowe*, 254. For Benjamin Clark's gunplay, see Samuel Cooper to Benjamin Franklin, 17 December 1773, Papers of Benjamin Franklin.

103. *Votes and Proceedings of the Freeholders*, 15; entry for 18 November 1773, in "Diary for 1773 to the End of 1774 of Mr. Thomas Newell," 344.

104. Entry for 29 November 1773, in "Diary for 1773 to the End of 1774 of Mr. Thomas Newell," 345; Cunningham, *Letters and Diary of John Rowe*, 256; Boston Tea Party Meeting Minutes, 29 November 1773, MHS; L. F. S. Upton, "Proceedings of Ye Body Respecting the Tea," *WMQ* 22, no. 2 (April 1965): 288.

105. Boston Tea Party Meeting Minutes, 30 November 1773, MHS.

106. Upton, "Proceedings of Ye Body Respecting the Tea," 290.

107. Thomas Hutchinson to William Tryon, 1 December 1773, Hutchinson Letterbooks, vol. 27, 1085–86.

108. Entry for 8 December 1773, in Cunningham, *Letters and Diary of John Rowe*, 257.

109. Quoted in Upton, "Proceedings of Ye Body Respecting the Tea," 294.

110. Ibid., 296.

111. Thomas Hutchinson to Lord Dartmouth, 20 December 1773, Hutchinson Letterbooks, vol. 27, 1132; Boston Tea Party Meeting Minutes, 16 December 1773, MHS.

112. Entry for 16 December 1773, in Cunningham, *Letters and Diary of John Rowe*, 257–58; entry for 16 December 1773, "Diary for 1773 to the End of 1774 of Mr. Thomas Newell," 346.

113. Entry for 19 December 1773, Diary, 1732–1793 (photocopy), John Tudor Papers, 1732–1793, MHS; Thomas Hutchinson to Lord Dartmouth, 17 December 1773, Hutchinson Letterbooks, vol. 27, 1119.

114. Samuel to Stephen Salisbury, 17 December 1773, box 2, folder 5, 1773, Salisbury Family Papers, AAS.

115. Quoted in Phyllis Whitman Hunter, *Purchasing Identity in the Atlantic World: Massachusetts Merchants, 1670–1780* (Ithaca, NY: Cornell University Press, 2001), 147, and Labaree, *Boston Tea Party*, 145.

116. Labaree, *Boston Tea Party*, 143; Carp, *Defiance of the Patriots*, 122–24, 295–96, has a nice bibliographic explanation of "Race, Slavery, and Indian Disguises," which especially picks apart white America's penchant for "playing Indian."

117. *Massachusetts Gazette*, December 23, 1773, in Drake, *Tea Leaves*, lxviii; *Connecticut Courant*, December 28, 1773.

118. *Boston Evening-Post*, December 20, 1773; Caroline Frank, *Objectifying China, Imagining America: Chinese Commodities in Early America* (Chicago: University of Chicago Press, 2011), 24.

119. B. B. (Benjamin Bussey) Thatcher, *Traits of the Tea Party: being a memoir of George R. T. Hewes, one of the last survivors; with a history of that transaction; reminiscences of the massacre, and the siege, and other stories of old times* (New York, 1835), 180; Alfred F. Young, "George Robert Twelves Hewes (1742–1840): A Boston Shoemaker and the Memory of the American Revolution," *WMQ* 38, no. 4 (October 1981): 590–92; and Carp, *Defiance of the Patriots*, chapter 7: "Resolute Men (Dressed as Mohawks)."

120. Thatcher, *Traits of the Tea Party*, 181.

121. Michael H. Fisher, "Asians in Britain: Negotiations of Identity through Self-Representation," in *A New Imperial History: Culture, Identity and Modernity in Britain and the Empire, 1660–1840*, ed. Kathleen Wilson (Cambridge: Cambridge University Press, 2004), 94–95; Rozina Visram, *Asians in Britain: 400 Years of History* (London: Pluto Press, 2002), 15–16.

122. Pennsylvania, *To the Tradesmen, Mechanics, &c*, also published as Mechanic, *To the Tradesmen, Mechanics, etc.*

123. Stern, *Company-State*, 204–6.

124. John Dickinson, *The Political Writings of the Late John Dickinson, Esq.* (Wilmington, DE, 1814), 1:48–50.

125. "Rusticus" [John Dickinson], *A Letter from the Country, to a Gentleman in Philadelphia* ([Philadelphia?], 1773), broadside, LCP.

126. Adam Smith, *The Wealth of Nations*, intro. D. D. Raphael (1910; repr., New York: Knopf, 1991), 573–74.

127. "Rusticus," *Letter from the Country*. See also Thomas Pownall, *The Right, Interest, and Duty, of Government, As concerned in The Affairs of the East Indies* (London, 1773), for the former Massachusetts governor's critique of the EIC. Similar to Citizen's United today, which grants corporations rights as individuals, Pownall argued that the EIC charters "are the like powers of incorporation, with rights of the same nature . . . as have been given to all other colonists and emigrants. Whoever will compare the charters of the one and of the other, clause by clause, word by word, will find this unvarying similarity extend through the whole" (quoted in Philip J. Stern, "British Asia and British Atlantic: Comparisons and Connections," *WMQ* 63, no. 4 (October 2006): 702).

128. "Extract from Edmund Burke's speech on American Taxation, 19 April 1774," in Horn and Ransome, *English Historical Documents, 1714–1783*, 758. See Langford, *Polite and Commercial People*, 537–38.

129. Edmund Burke, "Speech on American Taxation, April 19, 1774," 1:521.

130. Peter S. Onuf and Cathy D. Matson, *A Union of Interests: Political and Economic Thought in Revolutionary America* (Lawrence: University of Kansas Press, 1990), 24.

Chapter 5 · Repatriating Tea in Revolutionary America

1. Thomas Short, *Discourses on Tea, Sugar, Milk, Made-wines, spirits, punch, Tobacco, &c: With plain and useful rules for gouty people* (London, 1750), 59; S. A. D. Tissot, *Three Essays: First, on the disorders of people of fashion* (Dublin, 1772), 68, 58–59,

83. Earlier editions of *Three Essays* came out in 1769 and 1771, both published in Philadelphia.

2. *Boston Evening-Post*, October 25, 1773.

3. "Postscript to the *Pennsylvania Gazette*, No. 2375," *Pennsylvania Gazette*, June 29, 1774.

4. Lexington Resolves, 13 December 1773, Lexington (Mass.) Local Records, 1765–1784, folio vol. 1, 28–33, AAS; *Portsmouth Resolves Respecting Tea*, 16 December 1773, Portsmouth, New Hampshire, broadside, Boston Public Library.

5. Draft Report, 13 December 1773, Lexington (Mass.) Local Records, 1765–1784, folio vol. 1, 31, 32–33, AAS. See also Lincoln [MA] Resolution, 27 December 1773, U.S. Revolution Collection, 1754–1928, box 1, folder 3, 1754–1773, and Watertown [MA] Resolutions, 3 January 1774, box 1, folder 4, 1774, U.S. Revolution Collection, 1754–1928, AAS.

6. John Russell Bartlett, ed., *Records of the Colony of Rhode Island and Providence Plantations in New England*, vol. VII: *1770–1776* (Providence, RI, 1862), 2:273. The following month, Bristol, Rhode Island, met and with similar language passed a condemnation of tea and the EIC; citing "the public safety" as paramount to their decision, the Rhode Island towns of Richmond, New Shoreham, Cumberland, and Barrington all resolved to boycott tea immediately (ibid., 2:274, 277).

7. "Postscript to the *Pennsylvania Gazette*," 24 December 1773, in Frank M. Etting, *The Philadelphia Tea Party of 1773: A chapter from the history of the old state house* (Philadelphia, 187?), n.p.

8. Entry for 31 December 1773, in *Letters and Diary of John Rowe, Boston Merchant, 1759–1762, 1764–1779*, ed. Anne Rowe Cunningham (1903; repr., New York: Arno, 1969), 259; entry for 1 January 1774, in "Diary for 1773 to the End of 1774 of Mr. Thomas Newell," in *Proceedings of the Massachusetts Historical Society, 1876–1877*, vol. XV (Boston, 1878), 347; B. B. (Benjamin Bussey) Thatcher, *Traits of the Tea Party: being a memoir of George R. T. Hewes, one of the last survivors; with a history of that transaction; reminiscences of the massacre, and the siege, and other stories of old times* (New York, 1835), 189.

9. Joseph M. Beatty, "Letters of the Four Beatty Brothers of the Continental Army, 1774–1794," *PMHB* 44, no. 3 (July 1920): 196.

10. Cyrus Baldwin to the Committee of Correspondence, 25 January 1774, Miscellaneous Bound Letters, 1774–1775, 58, MHS.

11. David Stoddard Greenough to John Greenough, 4 January 1774, John Greenough Papers, 1766–1820, MHS. See Benjamin Woods Labaree, *The Boston Tea Party* (New York: Oxford University Press, 1961), 150–51.

12. John Greenough to Thomas Greenough, 1 March 1774; Naaman Holbrook to John Greenough, 16 April 1774, both in John Greenough Papers, 1766–1820, MHS.

13. John Greenough to Messrs Richard Clarke & Sons, 26 March 1774, in ibid.

14. John Greenough to Thomas Greenough, 22 March 1774; Eastham town meeting March 1774, both in ibid. Refusing to face the committee, Greenough managed to retrieve the tea in June 1774 "& sold it there in Spight of all their Malice but not without some considerable Opposition from a number of factious Persons" (John Greenough to Richard Clarke Esq & Sons, 2 June 1774, Miscellaneous Bound Letters, 1774–1775, MHS).

15. T. H. Breen, *American Insurgents, American Patriots: The Revolution of the People* (New York: Hill & Wang, 2010), 76ff.

16. *New-York Journal,* April 28, 1773.

17. Benjamin Booth to James & Drinker, 25 April 1774, PTPC; entry for 2 May 1774, in "Diary for 1773 to the End of 1774 of Mr. Thomas Newell," 351; entry for 30 April 1774, in Cunningham, *Letters and Diary of John Rowe,* 269.

18. *At a Meeting of the Committees,* Annapolis, 22 June 1774, broadside, HSP; "Annapolis, October 20," *Pennsylvania Gazette,* October 26, 1774; *Boston Evening Post,* July 25, 1774; *The Brig Peggy Stewart,* Annapolis, 20 October 1774, pamphlet, LCP; *The Brig Peggy Stewart,* Annapolis, 18 October 1774, pamphlet, LCP. An Annapolis crowd threatened to tar and feather the shipowner, Anthony Stewart, who, despite the advice of friends, had paid the tea duty in order to land and store the shipment. The Annapolis Committee of Association, which had unanimously voted to bar the tea from port, agreed that "if the tea was destroyed by the voluntary act of the owners, and proper concessions made, that nothing further ought to be required" (*Pennsylvania Gazette,* October 26, 1774; John Galloway to Thomas Ringgold, 20 October and 25 October 1774, "Account of the Destruction of the Brig 'Peggy Stewart,' at Annapolis, 1774," *PMHB* 15, no. 25 [1901]: 250–51, 253–54).

19. John Adams, 6 October 1774, Notes of Debates, in *Letters of Members of the Continental Congress,* ed. Edmund Cody Burnett (Washington, DC: Carnegie Institution of Washington, 1921), 1:64.

20. "The Association of the First Continental Congress (20 October 1774)," in *American Colonial Documents to 1776,* English Historical Documents no. 9, ed. Merrill Jensen (London: Eyre & Spottiswoode, 1964), 813, 814; Staughton Lynd and David Waldstreicher, "Free Trade, Sovereignty, and Slavery: Toward an Economic Interpretation of American Independence," *WMQ* 68, no. 4 (October 2011): 620–21.

21. "The Association of the First Continental Congress (20 October 1774)," in Jensen, *American Colonial Documents to 1776,* 815.

22. Thursday, 20 October 1774, the Association, passed 5 September 1774, *JCC,* 1:79.

23. Entry for 21 October 1774, *The Journals of each Provincial Congress of Massachusetts in 1774 and 1775, and the Committee of Safety, with an Appendix* (Boston, 1838), 25; Jonathan Amory to Harrison & Ausley, 17 December 1774, John and Jonathan Amory Letters, vols. 141–44, Amory Family Papers, MHS.

24. Entry for 21 October 1774, *Journals of each Provincial Congress of Massachusetts,* 26.

25. Nathan Baldwin to Stephen Salisbury, 5 November 1774, box 3, folder 2, 1774, August through December, and Samuel to Stephen Salisbury, 13 May 1774, box 3, folder 1, 1774, January through July, Salisbury Family Papers, AAS.

26. Jonathan Amory to Harrison and Ausley, 17 December 1774, John and Jonathan Amory Letters, vols. 141–44, Amory Family Papers, MHS.

27. Samuel to Stephen Salisbury, 28 September 1774, box 3, folder 2, 1774, August through December, and Samuel to Stephen Salisbury, 13 June 1774, box 3, folder 1, 1774, January through July, Salisbury Family Papers, AAS.

28. William Barrell to Messrs Hayley & Hopkins, 30 June 1774, William Barrell Letterbook, 1771–1776, MHS; John W. Tyler, *Smugglers and Patriots: Boston Mer-*

chants and the Advent of the American Revolution (Boston: Northeastern University Press, 1986), 212–13; William Barrell to Messrs Hayley and Hopkins, 5 December 1774, William Barrell Letterbook, 1771–1776, MHS.

29. Annual Summary of Imports and Exports, Customs 3, reels 45, 46, and 47.

30. Entry for 15 February 1775, *Journals of each Provincial Congress of Massachusetts*, 101–2.

31. Annual Summary of Imports and Exports, Customs 3, reels 47 and 48. Robert F. Oaks, "Philadelphia Merchants and the Origins of American Independence," *Proceedings of the American Philosophical Society* 121 (December 1977): 431, notes that overall American exports declined "from £2,457,062 in 1775, to £185,816 in 1776." See also Thomas M. Doerflinger, *A Vigorous Spirit of Enterprise: Merchants and Economic Development in Revolutionary Philadelphia* (Chapel Hill: University of North Carolina Press, 1986), 195; Michelle L. Craig (McDonald), "Grounds for Debate? The Place of the Caribbean Provisions Trade in Philadelphia's Prerevolutionary Economy," *PMHB* 128, no. 2 (April 2004): 172–77; Cathy Matson, *Merchants and Empire: Trading in Colonial New York* (Baltimore: Johns Hopkins University Press, 1998), 308.

32. Samuel Wharton, "Observations upon the Consumption of Teas in North America, 1773," Notes and Queries, *PMHB* 25, no. 1 (1901): 139–40. Importation figures bear out his guesstimates. In the years following the Seven Years' War, tea importation from England increased dramatically, with 1768 a high point (see table 5.1).

33. Entries for 1771 and 1772, Great Britain Customs Papers, Great Britain Commissioner of Customs in America, 1765–1774, MHS; Customs 3, reels 44–47.

34. Charles Wharton Cashbook, 1765–1771, and Charles Wharton Cash Book, 1771–1780, Wharton Family Papers, 1679–1834, HSP. See Matson, *Merchants and Empire*, 306–11, for discussion of internal debates among New York merchants over nonimportation and nonexportation, which pitted smugglers against nonsmugglers.

35. Charles Wharton to Messrs TenEyck & Seaman 2 May 1771, and Charles Wharton to Cornelius Sebring, 11 May 1771, Charles Wharton Letterbook, 1766–1771, Sarah Smith Collection, box 2, HSP.

36. Sales of Tea on Account of John Vanderbilt Dr to Sundry Accounts, 12 May 1774; Sales of Tea on account of Cornelius and John Sebring Dr to Sundry Accounts, 13 May 1774; and Sales of Tea on Account of TenEyck & Seaman Dr to Sundry Accounts, 14 May 1774, Charles Wharton Cash Book, 1771–1780, Wharton Family Papers, 1679–1834, HSP.

37. William Smith to Mercer & Ramsay, 18 December 1773, William Smith Letterbook, 1771–1775, HSP. See also William Smith to Mercer & Ramsay, 14 December and 16 December 1773, ibid.

38. William Smith to Joseph and Robert Totten, Samuel Burling, 15 January 1774, William Smith Letterbook, 1771–1775, HSP.

39. Matson, *Merchants and Empire*, 306–7.

40. Quoted in Lynd and Waldstreicher, "Free Trade, Sovereignty, and Slavery," 621.

41. Quoted in ibid., 626. See also Jack Rakove, "Got Nexus?" *WMQ* 68, no. 4 (October 2011): 638.

42. Friday 13 October 1775, *JCC*, 3:294; "Memorial to the Pennsylvania Assembly by freeholders of Northumberland and Northampton Cos.," in *Pennsylvania Archives*,

1st ser., ed. Samuel Hazard (Philadelphia, 1853), 4:669–78, 660, 661; Richard Smith diary, 13 December 1775, in Burnett, *Letters of Members of the Continental Congress*, 1:275.

43. Tuesday, 13 February 1776, *JCC*, 4:133.

44. Saturday, 6 April 1776, *JCC*, 4:258. See Lynd and Waldstreicher, "Free Trade, Sovereignty, and Slavery," 610, 628–29; Drew R. McCoy, *The Elusive Republic: Political Economy in Jeffersonian America* (Chapel Hill: University of North Carolina Press, 1980), 90. John Tyler, *Smugglers and Patriots*, 23, implies that, because Parliament closed British ports to American trade in 1776, "Congress had no choice but to open America's commerce to the world . . . Free trade had come at last, not so much as the result of a conscious plan, but almost as something the merchants had stumbled into. Without George Grenville's revival of orthodox mercantilism in the early 1760s, Boston merchants might never have realized how many of their true interests lay outside the empire." Rather than "stumbling into" free trade, I would argue that American merchants were well aware of their interests "outside the empire" as they took advantage of free trade in the form of smuggling from the 1740s on.

45. Saturday, 6 April 1776, *JCC*, 4:259.

46. Saturday, 13 April 1776, *JCC*, 4:277–78.

47. Oliver Wolcott to Mrs. Wolcott, 10 April 1776, in Burnett, *Letters of Members of the Continental Congress*, 1:418.

48. Lynd and Waldstreicher, "Free Trade, Sovereignty, and Slavery," 622.

49. Tuesday, 30 April 1776, *JCC*, 4:320.

50. "Draft letter to the Delegates of this Colony at the Continental Congress on the subject of tea," 28 July 1775, in *Journals of the Provincial Congress, Provincial Convention, Committee of Safety and Council of Safety of the State of New-York: 1775–1776–1777* (Albany, NY, 1842), 1:92; "A letter from the Delegates of this Colony at Continental Congress to the Committee of Safety," 20 September 1775, in ibid., 1:155; Paul A. Gilje, *Free Trade and Sailors' Rights in the War of 1812* (Cambridge: Cambridge University Press, 2013), 32–33.

51. Entry for 14 June 1776, in *Journal of the Provincial Congress of New-York*, 1:494.

52. Entry for 2 August 1776, in ibid., 1:553.

53. Resolution, Committee of Safety, 17 October 1776, in ibid., 1:682.

54. Isaac Sears to His Excellency George Washington, 2 May 1776, in ibid., 2:144–45.

55. Entry for 4 June 1776, in ibid., 1:473, 475.

56. *A Sermon on Tea* (Lancaster, PA, 1774), p. 4, EAIE 13606.

57. Ibid., 6–7; see T. H. Breen, *The Marketplace of Revolution: How Consumer Politics Shaped American Independence* (New York: Oxford University Press, 2004), 306ff.

58. Minutes of the Provincial Congress of North Carolina, 27 August 1774, in *The Colonial and State Records of North Carolina*, ed. William Saunders (Raleigh, NC, 1886), 9:1046, http://docsouth.unc.edu/csr/index.html/document/csr09-0303 (accessed September 28, 2011); Erin Michaela Sweeney, "The Patriotic Ladies of Edenton, North Carolina: The Layers of Gray in a Black-and-White Print," *Journal of the American Historical Print Collectors Society* 23, no. 2 (Autumn 1998): 21.

59. Eliza Farmer to "Jackey," 17 February 1775, Eliza Farmer Letterbook, 1774–1776, HSP.

60. Catherine La Courreye Blecki and Karin A. Wulf, eds., *Milcah Martha Moore's Book: A Commonplace Book from Revolutionary America* (University Park: Penn State University Press, 1997), 246, 247–50, 299.

61. Barbara Clark Smith, "Food Rioters and the American Revolution," *WMQ* 51, no. 1 (January 1994): 7–8. See also Bernard Mason, "Entrepreneurial Activity in New York during the American Revolution," *Business History Review* 40, no. 2 (Summer 1966): 197–98, and *Constitutional Gazette*, August 24, 1776.

62. Entry for 26 August 1776, in *Journal of the Provincial Congress of New-York*, 1:590.

63. Smith, "Food Rioters and the American Revolution," 24.

64. James H. Kip, New-Windsor, 14 July 1777, and Jacob Culyer to John Jay, 17 July 1777, in *Journals of the Provincial Congress of New-York*, 2:506, 508.

65. Entry for 22 July 1777, in ibid., 1:1010.

66. Smith, "Food Rioters and the American Revolution," 35–36. See also E. P. Thompson, "The Moral Economy of the English Crowd in the Eighteenth Century," *Past & Present*, 50 (February 1971): 76–136; Ruth Bogin, "Petitioning and the New Moral Economy of Post-Revolutionary America," *WMQ* 45, no. 3 (July 1988): 391–425; John Bohstedt, "The Moral Economy and the Discipline of Historical Context," *Journal of Social History* 26, no. 2 (Winter 1992): 265–84; and Margaret Ellen Newell, *From Dependency to Independence: Economic Revolution in Colonial New England* (Ithaca, NY: Cornell University Press, 1998), 238–39.

67. *Massachusetts Spy*, July 5, 1776.

68. Entry for 19 November 1776, in *The Public Records of the State of Connecticut . . . with the Journal of the Council of Safety*, comp. Charles J. Hoadly (Hartford, CT, 1894), 63.

69. *Providence Gazette*, June 22, 1776.

70. *Pennsylvania Evening Post*, June 22, 1776.

71. Gary Nash, *The Unknown American Revolution: The Unruly Birth of Democracy and the Struggle to Create America* (New York: Penguin, 2005), 232–38.

72. Jonathan R. Dull, *A Diplomatic History of the American Revolution* (New Haven, CT: Yale University Press, 1987), 55, 80, 94; Robert G. Parkinson, "War and the Imperative of Union," *WMQ* 68, no. 4 (October 2011): 633–34.

73. Enclosure, The Secret Committee to Silas Deane, 1 March 1776, in Burnett, *Letters of Members of the Continental Congress*, 1:373, 372 n2.

74. Estienne de Cathalan to Willing and Morris, from Marseilles, 24 January 1776, Robert Morris Papers, 1756–1782, HSP. Saint-Domingue was also referred to as French Santo Domingo.

75. Gerard W. Beekman to William Beekman, Morris County, 8 July 1778, and Gerard W. Beekman to William Beekman, Morris County, 10 November 1778, in *The Beekman Mercantile Papers, 1746–1799*, ed. Philip L. White (New York: New-York Historical Society, 1956), 3:1304, 1316.

76. Gerard W. Beekman to William Beekman, Morris County, 18 March 1779, in ibid., 3:1322.

77. Gerard W. Beekman to William Beekman, Morris County, 19 October 1779, and Gerard W. Beekman to William Beekman, 22 December 1779, in ibid., 3:1344, 1349. See also Gerard W. Beekman to William Beekman, Morris County, 22 November 1779, in ibid., 3:1345.

78. Gerard W. Beekman to William Beekman, Morris County, 24 July 1780, in ibid., 3:1368.

79. Jonathan Williams Jr., Nantes, to Benjamin Franklin, 9 March 1779, Papers of Benjamin Franklin, sponsored by the American Philosophical Society and Yale University, digital edition, http://franklinpapers.org/franklin (accessed October 3, 2014).

80. Benjamin Franklin to Jonathan Williams Jr., 16 March 1779, ibid.; US State Dept., *The Revolutionary Diplomatic Correspondence of the United States*, ed. Francis Wharton (Washington, DC, 1889), 3:84.

81. Benjamin Franklin to Josiah Quincy Sr., 22 April 1779, Papers of Benjamin Franklin.

82. McCoy, *Elusive Republic*, 49, 59. Franklin was always slippery on the subject of taxes and tea. See Benjamin Franklin to Richard Jackson, 11 February 1764, and Franklin to Samuel Cooper, 30 December 1770, Papers of Benjamin Franklin.

83. Benjamin Franklin to Duchesse de Deux-Ponts (Mme. De Forbach), 26 June 1779, Papers of Benjamin Franklin; Passy, Benjamin Franklin to William Carmichael, 17 June 1780, in US State Dept., *Revolutionary Diplomatic Correspondence*, 3:799.

84. Benjamin Franklin to Samuel Cooper, 27 October 1779, in US State Department, *Revolutionary Diplomatic Correspondence*, 3:395. See also Franklin to John Jay, 4 October 1779, in ibid., 3:362, 363, 365.

85. John Adams to Comte de Vergennes, 22 June 1780, in ibid., 3:813–14.

86. Entries for 10 July 1780 and 8 July 1780, in *Minutes of the Supreme Executive Council of Pennsylvania* (Harrisburg, PA, 1853), 12:415–16.

87. "Rum, tea, and sugar" were items frequently requisitioned for the Pennsylvania troops. See *Minutes of the Supreme Executive Council of Pennsylvania*, vols. 10–12.

88. David Ramsay, *An Oration on the Advantages of American Independence* (Charleston, SC, 1778), 2.

89. Ibid., 8. See also Breen, *Marketplace of Revolution*, 330–31; Gilje, *Free Trade and Sailors' Rights*, 36–37; Cathy D. Matson and Peter S. Onuf, *A Union of Interests: Political and Economic Thought in Revolutionary America* (Lawrence: University of Kansas Press, 1990), 31.

90. Entry for 18 December 1780, *JCC*, 18:1162–63.

Chapter 6 · Chinese Tea and American Commercial Independence

1. James Campbell, *An Oration in Commemoration of the Independence of the United States of North-America* (Philadelphia, 1787), 14; Drew R. McCoy, *The Elusive Republic: Political Economy in Jeffersonian America* (Chapel Hill: University of North Carolina Press, 1980), 86–87; Paul A. Gilje, *Free Trade and Sailors' Rights in the War of 1812* (Cambridge: Cambridge University Press, 2013), chapter 1.

2. Campbell, *Oration in Commemoration of Independence*, 15.

3. [Tench Coxe], *An Enquiring into the Principles on which a Commercial System for the United States of America Should be Founded* ([Philadelphia], 1787), 44.

4. Gilje, *Free Trade and Sailors' Rights*, 11, 16, 36; Thomas M. Doerflinger, *A Vig-*

orous Spirit of Enterprise: Merchants and Economic Development in Revolutionary Philadelphia (Chapel Hill: University of North Carolina Press, 1986), 283–86. See Eliga A. Gould, *Among the Powers of the Earth: The American Revolution and the Making of a New World Empire* (Cambridge, MA: Harvard University Press, 2012).

5. [Coxe], *Commercial System for the United States*, 17, 45–46.

6. Cathy D. Matson and Peter S. Onuf, *A Union of Interests: Political and Economic Thought in Revolutionary America* (Lawrence: University of Kansas Press, 1990), 28.

7. Gilje, *Free Trade and Sailors' Rights*, 19–31; John E. Crowley, *The Privileges of Independence: Neomercantilism and the American Revolution* (Baltimore: Johns Hopkins University Press, 1993), chapters 4 and 5; McCoy, *Elusive Republic*, chapter 3.

8. Doerflinger, *Vigorous Spirit of Enterprise*, 243, 246, 262.

9. Terry Bouton, *Taming Democracy: "The People," the Founders, and the Troubled Ending of the American Revolution* (New York: Oxford University Press, 2007), 67ff. See Woody Holton, *Unruly Americans and the Origins of the Constitution* (New York: Hill & Wang, 2008), chapter 1, for similar tales of debt and economic woes in Virginia, South Carolina, and New York prior to 1787.

10. Cathy Matson, "Accounting for War and Revolution: Philadelphia Merchants and Commercial Risk, 1774–1811," in *The Self-Perception of Early Modern Capitalists*, ed. Margaret Jacobs (New York: Palgrave Macmillan, 2008), 184–85; Holton, *Unruly Americans*, 28; Linda K. Salvucci, "Atlantic Intersections: Early American Commerce and the Rise of the Spanish West Indies (Cuba)," *Business History Review* 79, no. 4 (Winter 2005): 784–85.

11. Margaret Ellen Newell, *From Dependency to Independence: Economic Revolution in Colonial New England* (Ithaca, NY: Cornell University Press, 1998), 300–303; Jonathan Chu, *Stumbling towards the Constitution: The Economic Consequences of Freedom in the Atlantic World* (New York: Palgrave Macmillan, 2012), 18; John W. Tyler, "Persistence and Change within the Boston Business Community, 1775–1790," in *Entrepreneurs: The Boston Business Community, 1700–1850*, ed. Conrad Edick Wright and Katheryn P. Viens (Boston: Massachusetts Historical Society, 1997), 101–9.

12. Crowley, *Privileges of Independence*, 74; McCoy, *Elusive Republic*, 91, 93.

13. Extracts from London papers, "London, Aug. 11," *Massachusetts Spy; or, Worcester Gazette*, October 28, 1784. Restrictions on trade with the British West Indies, as well as the "great and unusual Scarcity of Specie in our Country," worried New York merchant James Beekman (James Beekman to John Relph, London, 29 November 1785, in *The Beekman Mercantile Papers, 1746–1799*, ed. Philip L. White [New York: New-York Historical Society, 1956], 3:1000).

14. "London, June 10," *The Pennsylvania Evening Herald and the American Monitor*, August 10, 1785.

15. David & John Barclay to Richard Waln, 9 November 1782, Richard Waln Foreign Correspondence, London, 1763–1784, box 2, Richard Waln Papers, HSP.

16. Harford & Powell to Richard Waln, 15 November 1782, ibid.; Linzy A. Brekke, "The 'Scourge of Fashion': Political Economy and the Politics of Consumption in the Early Republic," *EAS* 3, no. 1 (Spring 2005): 124.

17. James Beekman to George Clifford and Co., Amsterdam, 15 August 1780, in White, *Beekman Mercantile Papers*, 3:986.

18. *South-Carolina Gazette and General Advertiser*, April 6–8, 1784.

19. Salvucci, "Atlantic Intersections," 786–87; Linda K. Salvucci, "Merchants and Diplomats: Philadelphia's Early Trade with Cuba," *Pennsylvania Legacies* 3, no. 2 (November 2003): 8.

20. *Continental Journal*, August 19, 1784; *American Mercury*, November 22, 1784.

21. *Salem Gazette*, March 1, 1785.

22. *Essex Journal*, December 8, 1784; Doerflinger, *Vigorous Spirit of Enterprise*, 217; Chu, *Stumbling towards the Constitution*, 10; *JCC*, 26: 269–70; Crowley, *Privileges of Independence*, 74; McCoy, *Elusive Republic*, 91, 93.

23. Jonathan Amory to John Amory, 1 December 1781 and 16 July 1782, John & Jonathan Amory Letters, vols. 141–44, Amory Family Papers, MHS.

24. Crowley, *Privileges of Independence*, 82; Chu, *Stumbling towards the Constitution*, 9.

25. John Adams to John Jay, 11 November 1785, US Secretary of Foreign Affairs, *Diplomatic Correspondence of the United States of America, from the Signing of the Definitive Treaty of Peace* (Washington, DC, 1837), 2:533–34.

26. *New York Packet and American Advertiser*, February 23, 1784.

27. "Letters of Some Members of the Old Congress," *PMHB* 29, no. 2 (1905): 204; Dael A. Norwood, "Trading in Liberty: The Politics of the American China Trade, c. 1784–1862" (PhD diss., Princeton University, 2012), 34–36.

28. Tyler, "Persistence and Change within the Boston Business Community," 118.

29. *Pennsylvania Evening Post*, November 10, 1783; *Boston Gazette*, December 22, 1783. See also Philip Chadwick Foster Smith, *The Empress of China* (Philadelphia: Philadelphia Maritime Museum, 1984), 24.

30. Robert E. Peabody, *The Log of the Grand Turks* (Boston: Houghton Mifflin, 1926), 10–11, 47, 50.

31. Foster Smith, *Empress of China*, 60–61; Norwood, "Trading in Liberty," 45.

32. *Pennsylvania Evening Herald and the American Monitor*, May 18, 1785.

33. Paul E. Fontenoy, "Ginseng, Otter Skins, and Sandalwood: the Conundrum of the China Trade," *Northern Mariner* 7, no. 1 (1997): 4; Rhys Richards, "Introduction: United States Trade with China, 1784–1814," *American Neptune* 54, suppl. (1994): 9. See also Susan S. Bean, *Yankee India: American Commercial and Cultural Encounters with India in the Age of Sail, 1784–1860* (Salem, MA: Peabody Essex Museum, 2008), 33, and Chu, *Stumbling towards the Constitution*, 31–32.

34. "New-York, December 26," *Connecticut Courant*, January 9, 1786.

35. See, for instance, *Vermont Gazette*, July 10, 1783, and *Massachusetts Gazette*, October 7, 1783. Philadelphia merchant James C. Fisher accepted "tobacco, bees wax, flaxseed, ginseng, and snake root, taken in part or all payment" (*Independent Gazetteer*, October 25, 1783).

36. "Notes and Queries," *PMHB* 9, no. 4 (1885): 485. Otter and seal skins and ginseng drove the American China trade through the 1790s. Contrary to popular belief, opium did not become a common commodity of exchange until the nineteenth century, although both British and American merchants carried opium to trade in the late eighteenth century.

37. "Extract of a letter from a Swedish Supercargo at Canton," *Essex Journal*, February 15, 1786; "European Intelligence. London, November 5," *Cumberland Gazette*, February 12, 1789.

38. Fontenoy, "Ginseng, Otter Skins, and Sandalwood," 5. Chu, *Stumbling towards the Constitution*, 20, implies that American ginseng helped to capitalize "self-sustaining China trade in a troubled economic time." However, it's clear that cash was king in Canton.

39. Mr. Thomas Randall, New York, to Joseph Barrel, 24 August 1787, Ship *Columbia* Papers, 1787–1817, MHS.

40. Robert Gray to Joseph Barrell & Company, 17 December 1789, and Capt. Gray of *The Washington*, at Canton, to Capt. Kendrick, in Macao, 1 November 1789, Ship *Columbia* Papers, 1787–1817, MHS. Although Gray signs himself as captain of the *Washington*, he and Kendrick had switched boats in the Pacific Northwest; thus he arrived with the *Columbia*.

41. Shaw & Randall to Joseph Barrell, from Canton, 18 December 1789, and Richard Howe and Robert Gray, in Canton, to Joseph Barrell, 18 January 1790, ibid.

42. Capt. Kendrick, in Macao, to Gray and Howe in Canton, 27 January 1790, ibid.

43. Robert Gray, in Canton, to John Kendrick, Macao, 29 January 1790, and Shaw & Randall to Joseph Barrell, 7 February 1790, ibid. Other American merchants faced similar circumstances. See, for instance, the experience of Thomas Handasyd Perkins on Elias Hasket Derby's ship, the *Astrea* (William Chalmers, Macao, to Thomas Handasyd Perkins in Canton, 25 September 1789, box 1, folder 2, Thomas Handaysd Perkins Papers, 1789–1892, box 1, Thomas H. Perkins, 1789–1805, P334, reel 1, MHS).

44. "Notes and Queries," *PMHB* 9, no. 4 (1885): 485.

45. Richards, "Introduction: United States Trade with China," 6.

46. Alejandra Irigoin, "The End of a Silver Era: the Consequences of the Breakdown of the Spanish Peso Standard in China and the United States, 1780s–1850s," *Journal of World History* 20, no. 2 (June 2009): 211, 215–16, 225–26; Hosea Ballou Morse, *The Chronicles of the East India Company, Trading to China, 1635–1834* (Taipei: Ch'eng-wen, 1966), 2:125, 154, 166.

47. Invoice "Owners of the Ship *Columbia*, [debtors] to Shaw & Randall, Canton, 7 February 1790, Ship *Columbia* Papers, 1787–1817, MHS.

48. Samuel W. Woodhouse, "The Voyage of the *Empress of China*," *PMHB* 63, no. 1 (January 1939): 25; Samuel Shaw, *The Journals of Major Samuel Shaw: The First American Consul at Canton* (Boston, 1847), 231; James R. Gibson, *Otter Skins, Boston Ships, and China Goods: The Maritime Fur Trade of the Northwest Coast, 1785–1841* (Seattle: University of Washington Press, 1992), 313.

49. Woodhouse, "Voyage of the *Empress of China*," 30. The import figures for *Empress of China* were calculated with a picul equivalent to 133.3 pounds. See Shaw, *Journals of Major Samuel Shaw*, 217–18, for discussion of profit.

50. Peabody, *Log of the Grand Turks*, 91.

51. Instructions from Joseph Barrell, 12 December 1787, Ship *Columbia* Papers, 1787–1817, MHS.

52. James Duncan Phillips, *Salem and the Indies: The Story of the Great Commercial Era of the City* (Boston: Houghton Mifflin, 1947), 56.

53. Richards, "Introduction: United States Trade with China," 7.

54. David S. Greenough Papers, 1631–1859, vols. 20–31, box 36, Ms. N-1335, MHS. The meticulous family expense books, kept until 1826, indicate a steady increase in tea drinking.

55. Samuel Salisbury to Stephen Salisbury, 11 October 1785, box 5, folder 2, 1785, June–December, Salisbury Family Papers, AAS.

56. Joseph Peirce, trade card (Boston, 1789), AAS.

57. Advertisements from Matthias Keely, James Smith, Junr., and Wharton & Lewis, *Pennsylvania Packet and Daily Advertiser,* August 13, 1789.

58. *Salem Gazette,* March 22, 1791.

59. *Baltimore Evening Post,* July 19, 1793; Carl Robert Keyes, "Early American Advertising: Marketing and Consumer Culture in Eighteenth-Century Philadelphia" (PhD diss., Johns Hopkins University, 2007), 143, 157ff.

60. James Hardie, *The Philadelphia Directory and Register* (Philadelphia, 1793), n.p., AAS.

61. William Redwood, Waste Book, 1775–1797, Amb.7256, vol. 3, William Redwood Papers, HSP.

62. For examples, see ibid. By 1791, Bohea had disappeared from Redwood's records. Even Joseph Henszey purchased Souchong rather than Bohea for the Pennsylvania Hospital (entry for 14 July 1791, ibid.).

63. Edmund Hogan, *The Prospect of Philadelphia, and Check on the Next Directory* (Philadelphia, 1795), 27, 32.

64. James Robinson, *Robinson's Philadelphia Register and City Directory, for 1799* (Philadelphia, 1799). The *New Trade Directory for Philadelphia* (Philadelphia, 1799), 190, listed five full-time tea dealers: John Barnes, Hannah Baker, Eaton S. & Co., Thomas Nathaniel, and Elizabeth Whitesides. By the turn of the nineteenth century, a good number of women were involved in the Philadelphia tea trade. They represented at least half of those traders listed in the directories. New York City distinguished the profession of "tea water man" for individuals licensed to sell water from city-owned and -operated pumps, suggesting the importance of providing potable water for tea consumption (William Duncan, *The New-York Directory, and Register, for the year 1791* [New York, 1791] and for subsequent years).

65. Entries for 26 August 1781, 15 November 1781, and 5 December 1781, Samuel Salisbury and Stephen Salisbury, General Merchandise Daybook, Worcester, MA, 1771–1782, Folio vol. 7, Salisbury Family Papers, AAS.

66. John Hinckley to Stephen Salisbury, from Leicester, 18 October 1786, box 5, folder 3, 1786, ibid.

67. *Vermont Gazette,* September 29, 1788.

68. Mr. Briant Morton Dr, 26 December 1783, John Quinby Account Book, 1782–1792, folio vol. 2, AAS. See also Stephen Jones Dr, 17 December 1793, John Quinby Account Book, 1783–1794, folio vol. 3, AAS; Andrew Walker, Account Book, 1782–1785, Kennebunk, Maine, Walker Family Account Books, 1782–1845, Octavo Volume, AAS.

69. On the outskirts of New York, customers of James Beekman ordered new goods in the postwar period; assuming that the distribution of goods had improved, they no longer relied on the peddler trader. For instance, see Peter Roggers, Kingston, to James Beekman, 1 October 1785, in White, *Beekman Mercantile Papers,* 3:1293. Ann Smart Martin, *Buying into the World of Goods: Early Consumers in Backcountry Virginia* (Baltimore: Johns Hopkins University Press, 2008), notes a similar expansion into the rural South as early as the 1770s.

70. "Upon the Use of Tea," *Freeman's Journal; or, the North-American Intelligencer*, February 18, 1784.

71. Quoted in Holton, *Unruly Americans*, 48. Although best known for his extensive and contentious work on American language, Webster also supported the new Constitution in 1787, hoping that a strong national government would temper the corrupted and rash behavior of the general populace (ibid., 233–34). See Tim Cassedy, "'A Dictionary Which We Do Not Want': Defining America against Noah Webster, 1783–1810," *WMQ* 71, no. 2 (April 2014): 229–54; McCoy, *Elusive Republic*, 96–99; Cary Carson, "The Consumer Revolution in Colonial British America: Why Demand?" in *Of Consuming Interests: The Style of Life in the Eighteenth Century*, ed. Carson, Ronald Hoffman, and Peter J. Albert (Charlottesville: University Press of Virginia, 1994), 514–20.

72. Holton, *Unruly Americans*, 46–54. The call for American austerity in the mid-1780s was not welcomed by all; Abigail Adams complained to her husband that frugality could only go so far before one simply looked shabby and unfit for company (McCoy, *Elusive Republic*, 94–104, 124–25).

73. James Beekman to John Relph, London, 29 November 1785, in White, *Beekman Mercantile Papers*, 3:1000.

74. *The Commercial Conduct of the United States of America Considered, and the True Interest thereof, attempted to be shewn by a Citizen of New-York* (New York, 1786), 16.

75. Ibid., 5–6. See also Crowley, *Privileges of Independence*, 106, who makes the connection between the renewed luxury debate and a rising demand for stronger national commercial regulation; as James Madison's faith in state governments waned, he became a proponent of protectionism.

76. Holton, *Unruly Americans*, 65, places the war requisition figure at $3 million but later (81) he notes it in sterling pounds (£3 million).

77. Entry for 16 December 1782, *JCC*, 23:799; Matson and Onuf, *Union of Interests*, 41–42; Holton, *Unruly Americans*, 67–71.

78. Entry for 29 April 1783, *JCC*, 24:286–87.

79. Gilje, *Free Trade and Sailors' Rights*, 41.

80. "An Act, Laying Duties of Impost and Excise, on Certain Goods, Wares and Merchandize therein Described," broadside (Boston, 1783), p. 8, EAIE 44399; "For the Information of Importers, Retailers, and Others. Articles of Impost and Excise Extracted from the Two Laws of the Commonwealth of Massachusetts," broadside (Boston, 1787), EAIE 45102. The Massachusetts tax on tea was in place in 1785 as well; see, for instance, *Independent Chronicle and the Universal Advertiser*, August 4, 1785.

81. Georgia, *An Act to Revise and Amend an Act for Regulating the Trade, Laying Duties upon all Wares, Goods, Liquors, Merchandise, and Negroes imported into this State* (Savannah, GA, 1786), pp. 1–2, EAIE 44897.

82. Entry for 15 September 1789, in *Records of the State of Rhode Island and Providence Plantations in New England*, ed. John Russell Bartlett (Providence, RI, 1865), 10:341.

83. *Commercial Conduct of the United States of America Considered*, 3.

84. John Adams to John Jay, US Secretary of Foreign Affairs, 11 November 1785, *Diplomatic Correspondence of the United States of America*, 2:533–34.

85. "New-York, December 26," *Connecticut Courant*, January 9, 1786.

86. Holton, *Unruly Americans*, 136–37; Max M. Edling, *A Revolution in Favor of Government: Origins of the US Constitution and the Making of the American State* (Oxford: Oxford University Press, 2003), 164ff; Gilje, *Free Trade and Sailors' Rights*, 41–42; Gibson, *Otter Skins*, 37.

87. Joseph Gales, comp., *The Debates and Proceedings in the Congress of the United States* (Washington, DC, 1834), 1:107.

88. Norwood, "Trading in Liberty," 63–64, 66; Edgar S. Maclay, ed., *Journal of William Maclay, United States Senator from Pennsylvania, 1789–1791* (New York, 1890), 60–61; Matson and Onuf, *Union of Interests*, 46.

89. McLay, *Journal of William Maclay*, 44–47.

90. "A Summary View of the Proceedings of Congress," *New-York Weekly Museum*, no. 50, April 25, 1789.

91. "A brief examination of Lord Sheffield's observations on the Commerce of the United States of America," *The City Gazette, or Daily Advertiser*, May 16, 1791. The article, reprinted in numerous American newspapers, also noted that the value of teas "as they were actually entered in our custom-houses, was 2,784,000 dollars for the year preceding the first of October, 1790, which is about a seventh of our imports."

92. Quoted in Norwood, "Trading in Liberty," 74.

93. Alexander Hamilton, "Trade with India and China: Communicated to the House of Representatives, February 10, 1791," *American State Papers, Finance*, vol. 1, 1st Cong., 3rd sess., no. 25.

94. Norwood, "Trading in Liberty," 75–77; Tea Act, 3 March 1791, 1st Congress, 3rd Sess., Statutes at Large, in *The Public Statutes at Large of the United States of America*, ed. Richard Peters (Boston, 1845) 1:219–20.

Conclusion • Consumer Desires

1. John H. Coatsworth, "American Trade with European Colonies in the Caribbean and South America, 1790–1812," *WMQ* 24, no. 2 (April 1967): 248–52; James Fichter, *So Great a Proffit: How the East Indies Trade Transformed Anglo-American Capitalism* (Cambridge, MA: Harvard University Press, 2010), 122–23.

2. Instructions to Magee, 21 June 1798, Thomas Handaysd Perkins Papers, 1789–1892, vol. 36, J. & T. H. Perkins Extracts from Letterbook, 1786–1838, P334, reel 6, MHS.

3. Thomas B. Cary, *Memoir of Thomas Handasyd Perkins; Containing Extracts from his Diaries and Letters* (Boston, 1856), 207–8.

4. Thomas Handaysd Perkins to E. Bumstead & Co. in Canton, 24 February 1804, Perkins Extracts from Letterbook.

5. Frederick William Paine, Descriptions of Penang, Canton, and Isle of France (Mauritius), Trade Records, 1804–1805, box 9, folder 3, Paine Family Papers, 1721–1918, AAS; instructions to Capt. Charles Cabot in Calcutta, January 1804, Perkins Extracts from Letterbook.

6. Jacques Downs, "American Merchants and the China Opium Trade, 1800–1840," *Business History Review* 42, no. 4 (Winter, 1968): 421 n12, 422; William Reid to Willings & Francis, 9 January 1805, box 1, Willings & Francis Records, 1698–1855, HSP.

7. William Reid to Willings & Francis, 9 November 1805, "Quadraplicate" copy,

and William Read to Willings & Francis, 27 November 1805, both in folder 3, box 1, Willings & Francis Records; Downs, "American Merchants," 423; Tan Chung, "The Britain-China-India Trade Triangle (1771–1840)," *Indian Economic and Social History Review* 11, no. 4 (October 1974): 411–31; *China; As it Was and As it Is. With a Glance at the Tea and Opium Trades* (New York, 1846), 54.

8. Thomas H Perkins to Ephraim Bumstead, 10 July 1804, Perkins Extracts from Letterbook.

9. Quoted in Jacques M. Downs, *The Golden Ghetto: The American Commercial Community at Canton and the Shaping of American China Policy, 1784–1844* (Bethlehem, PA: Lehigh University Press, 1997), 98; William Reid to Willings & Francis, Addendum, 27 November 1805, box 1, Willings & Francis Records; Fichter, *So Great a Proffit*, 91.

10. William Read "List of Return Cargo for the Ship Bingham," box 1, series 1, Willings & Francis Records.

11. William B. Bradford Jr. wholesale & retail grocer, trade card (Boston, [between 1810 and 1820]), and Andrew Brimmer, trade card (Boston, [1799]), AAS; Carl Robert Keyes, "A Revolution in Advertising: 'Buy American' Campaigns in the Late Eighteenth Century," in *We Are What We Sell: How Advertising Shapes American Life . . . and Always Has*, vol. 1: *Creating Advertising Culture: Beginnings to the 1930s*, ed. Danielle Coombs and Bob Batchelor (New York: Praeger, 2014), 2.

12. [Tench Coxe], *An Enquiring into the Principles on which a Commercial System for the United States of America Should be Founded* ([Philadelphia], 1787), 44.

13. Thomas Handasyd Perkins to Messrs Rochquette Elsivien & Bieddamaker, Rotterdam, 2 May 1797, Perkins Extracts from Letterbook.

14. Nicholas Webrouck and Franc Prevost, Antwerp, to George Washington Biddle, 18 July 1804, folder 13, box 14, Other Family Members, George Washington Biddle, 1800–1805, Biddle Family Papers, 1683–1954, HSP. Rather than returning with Girard's cargo to Europe, Biddle decided to stay in Canton, with private business advantages in mind. His father, Clement, was horrified that George went against Girard's instructions. Indeed, Girard sued Biddle for breach of contract in 1806, accusing him of making disastrous agreements with merchants in Canton "without any examination" of the teas (George Washington Biddle to Stephen Girard, 26 December 1804, folder 13, and Interrogatories submitted by Stephen Girard, Court of Common Pleas of Philadelphia County, September Term 1806, both in box 14, Biddle Family Papers). See Matson, "Accounting for War and Revolution," 196.

15. Willings & Francis to Messrs. Hope & Co., 10 April 1806, folder 5, box 1, series 1, Willings & Francis Records.

16. Fichter, *So Great a Proffit*, 88ff.

17. Willings & Francis to William Reid, 14 April 1806 and 10 March 1807, folder 5, box 1, series 1, Willings & Francis Records.

18. Willings & Francis to William Reid, 10 March 1807, ibid.

19. *Memorial of the Merchants of the City of Philadelphia, engaged in the China Trade, on the Subject of a Regulation of the Duty on Tea* (Washington, DC, 1828), 6, 3, 5.

20. Quoted in Fichter, *So Great a Proffit*, 91.

Primary Sources

This study began with curious lines on ledgers, which have the potential to tell us much about commercial and consumer activities. Merchant receipts, account books, and correspondence proved invaluable to guiding my work. Since I argue that the supply of tea preceded demand in the early eighteenth century, these sources were particularly important for showing how and when market drivers shifted. The quantity and quality of records from New England, New York, and Philadelphia also guided the primary geographic location of the research. Merchant records, such as Samuel Powel Letterbook, Coates and Reynell Papers, John Kidd Letterbook, Charles Willing Letterbook, Thomas Richee (Riché) Records, Henry Drinker Business Papers, Richard Waln Papers, Wharton Family Papers, and Hollingsworth Family Papers housed at the Historical Society of Pennsylvania; Massachusetts Historical Society collections, including Benjamin Greene Account Books, Boylston Family Papers, Amory Family Papers, Hancock Family Papers, Thomas Hutchinson Letterbooks, Boylston Family Papers, and John Tudor Papers; and the Salisbury Family Papers at the American Antiquarian Society provided a wealth of information about the gradual rise in tea sales, the exchange of tea for labor, as well as the diffusion of tea across class boundaries and beyond port cities. These records also illuminated the relationships between American merchants and their English counterparts.

Another source important to understanding tea production, supply, purchase, and distribution, especially as a function of corporate enterprise, was the *East India Company (EIC) Factory Records*, which the British Library has made available on microfilm. Compared to the heavily edited volumes of Hosea Ballou Morse, *The Chronicles of the East India Company, Trading to China, 1635–1834* (Taipei: Ch'eng-wen, 1966), the *EIC Factory Records* offer a more complete picture of the EIC China Council strategies, negotiations between company supercargoes and Canton merchants, and the subsequent conflicts within and among the EIC agents doing business in China throughout the eighteenth century.

Also on microfilm, the British Public Records Office (PRO) Board of Customs & Excise, Ledgers of Imports and Exports, 1696–1780 (Customs 3), have been the basis of my data for importation, exportation, and distribution of tea throughout the British Empire. Historians use a variety of sources for tea importation, which do not always yield comparable figures; nor do import figures always correspond to retail tea sales, let alone tea consumption. For example, annual importation figures from Customs 3 are often larger than those from the EIC General Ledgers, which K. N. Chaudhuri, *The Trading World of Asia and the English East India Company, 1660–1760* (Cambridge: Cambridge University Press, 1978), has used to good effect. Customs 3 probably includes all legal tea imports by the EIC, as well as by its agents, who were granted a small "private trade" as part of their pay package, or by others who purchased tea through intermediaries. On the other hand, the EIC General Ledgers include previously warehoused tea inventories sold at annual auctions.

To further problematize tea figures, Hoh-Cheung Mui and Lorna H. Mui, "'Trends in Eighteenth-Century Smuggling' Reconsidered," *Economic History Review* 28, no. 1 (February 1975): 37, warn that the most complete source for tea sales (and the most often used), William Milburn's *Oriental Commerce: Containing a Geographical Description of the Principal Places in the East Indies, China, and Japan* (London, 1813), is "grossly inaccurate" for certain years, underestimating the amount of tea sold, though not the value. And although some historians dispute the accuracy of his numbers, Louis Dermigny, *La Chine et L'Occident: Le commerce à Canton au XVIIIe siècle, 1719–1833* (Paris: École pratique des hautes études, 1964), is one of the few sources that provide comparative tea import figures for several nations. Of course, it is nearly impossible to calculate how much tea was smuggled into both Great Britain and the North American colonies over the course of the eighteenth century, further complicating the estimates of retail tea sales and consumption. For a good overview of PRO customs data, see G. N. Clark, *Guide to English Commercial Statistics, 1696–1782* (London: Offices of the Royal Historical Society, 1938), and John J. McCusker and Russell R. Menard, *The Economy of British America, 1607–1789* (1985; repr., Chapel Hill: University of North Carolina Press, 1991).

Secondary Sources

Although this book touches on several themes familiar to those interested in early American economies and consumer culture, the following topics and scholarship were most pertinent. David Armitage, "Three Concepts of Atlantic History," in *The British Atlantic World, 1500–1800*, ed. David Armitage and Michael J. Braddick (New York: Palgrave Macmillan, 2002), is recognized as the godfather of the Atlantic world discipline, a paradigm that is nonetheless limited for a study of the tea trade and consumer behavior. The work of David Hancock makes more practical sense of how commodities, trade, and consumption operated in an Atlantic setting; see, for instance, *Oceans of Wine: Madeira and the Emergence of American Trade and Taste* (New Haven, CT: Yale University Press, 2009). Other sources build better connections between British imperial colonies, Asia, and global markets, such as Andre Gunder Frank, *ReOrient: Global Economy in the Asian Age* (Berkeley: University of California Press, 1998); Anna Neill, *British Discovery Literature and the Rise of Global Commerce* (New York: Palgrave Macmillan, 2002); and Kenneth Pomeranz, *The Great Divergence: China, Europe, and the Making of the Modern World Economy* (Princeton, NJ: Princeton University Press, 2000).

Earlier versions of this manuscript dealt more directly with T. H. Breen, whom I have called the Frederick Jackson Turner of early American consumer culture, for all who follow feel compelled to question, include, or exclude his assertions. While introducing the politics of consumption as a concept in provocative ways, Breen finds far greater consensus among Americans in the 1760s and 1770s than may be justified. His use of prescriptive literature and published materials provides wonderful guidance for other historians; however, Breen makes no systematic analysis of archival sources, such as merchant records, which would better explain the consumer behavior of "ordinary men and women" who "negotiated market expectations with storekeepers eager to make a sale" (*The Marketplace of Revolution: How Consumer Politics Shaped American Independence* [New York: Oxford University Press, 2004], 127). Cary Carson, "The Consumer Revolution in Colonial British America: Why Demand?" in *Of Consuming Interests: The Style of Life in the Eighteenth Century*, ed. Carson, Ronald Hoffman, and Peter J. Albert (Charlottesville: University Press of Virginia, 1994), also helped formulate the initial field of earlier American consumer culture.

More recent studies take early American consumer behavior and the politics of consumption in new directions. Gender and women's complicated role in consumer culture are explored in depth by Elizabeth Kowaleski-Wallace, *Consuming Subjects: Women, Shopping, and Business in the Eighteenth Century* (New York: Columbia University Press, 1997), and Ellen Hartigan-O'Connor, *The Ties That Buy: Women and Commerce in Revolutionary America* (Philadelphia: University of Pennsylvania Press, 2009). Linzy A. Brekke, "The 'Scourge of Fashion': Political Economy and the Politics of Consumption in the Early Republic," *Early American Studies, An Interdisciplinary Journal* 3, no. 1 (Spring 2005), and Kate Haulman, *The Politics of Fashion in Eighteenth-Century America* (Chapel Hill: University of North Carolina Press, 2011), examine the ways that fashionable consumption could be both political and socially transformative. American consumer behavior in the eighteenth century was intimately tied to the availability of new commodities and the debates that arose about the place of consumption in society. Maxine Berg, in *Luxury and Pleasure in Eighteenth-Century Britain* (Oxford: Oxford University Press, 2005) and many related articles, examines the luxury debates as they pertain to global trade in Asian luxury goods. Caroline Frank, *Objectifying China, Imagining America: Chinese Commodities in Early America* (Chicago: University of Chicago Press, 2011), demonstrates how American colonists incorporated exotic Asian goods into their household inventories far earlier than thought, even revealing American seafarers' participation in privateering adventures to the East Indies in the 1690s.

Consumer behavior did not take place in a vacuum; access to emerging global markets made available new commodities that drove local economies. Scholarship that explores the role of the English East India Company within the British Empire is extensive. Classic works by K. N. Chaudhuri, including *The Trading World of Asia and the English East India Company, 1660–1760* (Cambridge: Cambridge University Press, 1978), are a good place to start, and Philip J. Stern, *The Company-State: Corporate Sovereignty and the Early Modern Foundations of the British Empire in India* (Oxford: Oxford University Press, 2011), expands on the institutional history of the EIC to consider its role as a British sovereign power in Asia. However, historians recently have also taken a more comparative approach, especially juxtaposing various colonial regions. See, for instance, P. J. Marshall, *The Making and Unmaking of Empires: Britain, India, and America, c. 1750–1783* (New York: Oxford University Press, 2005);

H. V. Bowen, *The Business of Empire: The East India Company and Imperial Britain, 1756–1833* (Cambridge: Cambridge University Press, 2008); and many articles by Elizabeth Mancke, such as "Negotiating an Empire: Britain and Its Overseas Peripheries, c. 1550–1780," in *Negotiated Empires: Centers and Peripheries in the Americas, 1500–1820*, ed. Christine Daniels and Michael Kennedy (New York: Routledge, 2002). H. V. Bowen, Elizabeth Mancke, and John G. Reid, eds., *Britain's Oceanic Empire: Atlantic and Indian Ocean Worlds, c. 1550–1850* (Cambridge: Cambridge University Press, 2012), bring together scholarship that starts to challenge the predominance of an Atlantic world perspective in early Anglo-American history.

A final body of literature that informed the postrevolutionary expansion of American trade to China in the late eighteenth century should be mentioned. Although classics like Drew R. McCoy, *The Elusive Republic: Political Economy in Jeffersonian America* (Chapel Hill: University of North Carolina Press, 1980); Cathy D. Matson and Peter S. Onuf, *A Union of Interests: Political and Economic Thought in Revolutionary America* (Lawrence: University of Kansas Press, 1990); and John E. Crowley, *The Privileges of Independence: Neomercantilism and the American Revolution* (Baltimore: Johns Hopkins University Press, 1993), remain important to understanding the American political economy in the war's aftermath, more recent scholarship ties the commercial interests of a newly independent United States to Asian trade. See, for instance, James Fichter, *So Great a Proffit: How the East Indies Trade Transformed Anglo-American Capitalism* (Cambridge, MA: Harvard University Press, 2010); Jonathan Chu, *Stumbling towards the Constitution: The Economic Consequences of Freedom in the Atlantic World* (New York: Palgrave Macmillan, 2012); Dael A. Norwood, "Trading in Liberty: the Politics of the American China Trade, c. 1784–1862" (PhD diss., Princeton University, 2012); and Jonathan Eacott, *Selling Empire: India in the Making of Britain and America, 1600–1830* (Chapel Hill: University of North Carolina Press, 2016). Especially helpful to defining free trade and its place in American commercial life at the turn of the nineteenth century is Paul A. Gilje, *Free Trade and Sailors' Rights in the War of 1812* (Cambridge: Cambridge University Press, 2013).

China (*cont.*)
  debates, 169n62; trade restrictions, 4–5,
  19–21, 26–28, 80, 148, 162n43; and US
  trade, 11, 125, 127–28, 131, 133–36, 144–50.
  See also Canton; Co-Hong merchants
chinoiserie, 45, 165n6
Clark, Daniel, 60
Clarke, Jonathan, 107
Clarke, Richard, 95
class, 6–8, 32–33; and consumer behavior,
  40–42, 49, 136–38, 142; corruption of lower,
  43, 45–46, 50; and tea use, 40–43, 49,
  69–71, 171n82
Clifford, Thomas, 66
Clive, Robert, 61, 81, 86–87
Coates, Samuel, Jr., 37, 49, 72, 76
Coercive Acts ("Intolerable Acts") (1774), 103,
  107–8, 109, 117
Co-Hong merchants, 23, 27–29, 83, 135, 147
commercial treaties, 11, 16, 114, 120–21, 125,
  142, 144, 147
Commissioners of Customs (British), 18, 61, 76
committees. *See under* nonimportation
commodity studies, 5–6, 155n11
Congress. *See* Continental Congress;
  Massachusetts Provincial Congress; New
  York Provincial Congress and Committees
  of Safety; Stamp Act Congress; United
  States Congress
Constitution, US, 11–12, 125–26, 127, 142,
  143–44, 149
consumer revolution, 5–7, 31–32, 34, 50, 52,
  97, 123, 151
consumers: aspirational consumption, 7,
  31–32, 42, 49, 142; merchants manipulation
  of, 7, 35–36, 48, 51, 120, 138–39, 149; and
  proliferation of goods, 32–33, 36–39, 45, 57,
  60, 70–71, 136–40; and riots, 104, 119–20;
  shift in demand, 6–7, 40–42, 49–50, 69–70,
  104, 110, 117–19; and tea use, 42–43, 111,
  117–18, 136–38, 169n60. *See also* class;
  marketing; nonconsumption
Continental Army, 115–16, 120, 121
Continental Articles of Association (1774), 10,
  104, 108–9, 110–11, 112, 114, 117, 127
Continental Congress, 11, 102, 104, 108–9,
  110–11, 113–16, 120, 122, 123–24. *See also*
  Continental Articles of Association

Cowell, Elizabeth, 49
Coxe, Tench, 126–27, 149
Cuba, 130, 131
Cunningham, Waddell, 58, 60
Cushing, Thomas, 63, 88
customs collection, 9, 17, 73, 81, 83, 87; in
  Boston, 54–55, 63, 74, 96; by British, 18–19,
  34, 39, 54–55, 58, 60–61, 124; US Customs,
  124, 144–46, 150. *See also* tariffs; tax
  duties

Danish merchants, 24–25, 26, 27
Dartmouth (vessel), 96
Deane, Silas, 120
Defoe, Daniel, 45, 47
Dennie, William, 74, 95
Derby, Elias Hasket, 133, 136, 138, 145–46
De Vries, Jan, 6
Dickinson, John, 62–64, 66, 100
Dividend Bill (1767), 84, 88
diwani, 82, 85, 87
Drinker, Henry, 59, 66, 75–76, 90, 92–94, 128
Dutch trade, 4, 5, 14, 16, 25, 27, 53, 54, 76, 80,
  90, 173n15; with American merchants, 9,
  11, 104, 108, 110–11, 112–14, 121–22, 128,
  130, 133, 149; smuggling, 24, 35, 38, 40, 43,
  54–55, 74–75. *See also* East India Company,
  Dutch; St. Eustatius

East India Company, Dutch, 26, 54
East India Company, English, 3, 5, 14, 16–17,
  80–82; compared to South Sea Company,
  160n23; competition with US merchants in
  China, 126, 128, 133, 141–42, 147–48, 150;
  conquest of Bengal, 61, 79, 80–82, 86–88,
  99–100, 141–42; cornering the tea market,
  5, 24–27, 30, 34–36, 38, 83–84; and credit
  crisis, 79–80, 82–83, 87–89; critique of
  monopoly, 10, 62, 79–80, 85–88, 99–100,
  103, 105; directors of, 17, 21, 25–28, 30, 35,
  44, 85–90, 92; funding occupation of India,
  82–84; interdependence with Great Britain,
  17–18, 79–80, 82, 87–88, 141–42; Parliament's investigation of, 84–88, 126; stock
  and dividend, 16–17, 84–85, 87–88, 160n25;
  surplus in warehouse, 5, 30, 34–35, 84,
  88–89, 101; trade in Canton, 20–26. *See also*
  Bengal; Madras; Sepoys

Stamp Act Congress, 62
standards of living, 7, 33–34, 165n6
Steuart, James, 14, 44–45
St. Eustatius, 55, 75, 121, 123, 130–31
Stiles, Ezra, 62
Strahan, William, 86
sugar, 4, 5–6, 7, 18, 33, 36, 41–43, 46, 51–52, 53, 61, 70, 108, 120, 123, 130, 133, 142, 149
supercargoes: American, 133–35, 136–37; English East India Company agents, 21–23, 24–25, 28, 30, 35, 83
supply and demand, 5–7, 27, 31, 33–34, 37–39, 40–43, 72, 123, 136, 141, 150–51
Suqua (merchant), 27
Swedish merchants, 24–25, 26, 27

tariffs, 12–13, 127–28, 140, 142–46
tax duties, 1–2, 6, 10, 15–16, 19–20, 36, 62–64, 67, 69, 75, 80, 94, 100–101, 105; drawbacks on, 18, 24, 53–54, 60–61, 77–78, 84, 89, 91–92; enacted by US states, 115–16, 123–24. *See also* tariffs
tea: cultivation of, 23–24, 26–28; and importation figures, 18–19, 24, 27, 34, 68–69, 72, 74, 82–83, 111–12, 136–37, 181n142; presumed physical and moral effects of, 9–10, 30, 45–47, 102–4, 117–18, 140–42; re-exportation of, to Europe, 18, 25–26, 30, 34–35, 38–39, 53, 63, 69, 72, 84, 112, 137, 149–50; as symbol of British policy, 67, 100–101, 103–4, 105, 108–9
Tea Act (1773), 10, 80, 89–90, 91–92, 95, 97, 99–100
Tingua (merchant), 29
Townshend Acts (1767), 53, 63–64, 66–68, 73–75, 76–77, 79, 89

trade, intercolonial, 39–40, 52–53, 57–59, 72–73, 75, 111–12. *See also* East India Company, English; economy, Atlantic; merchants, American; provisions trade; smuggling
Treaty of Amity and Commerce (1778), 121
Treaty of Paris (1783), 129–30
Tudor, John, 71, 97

United States Congress, 11, 108–9, 113–16, 119–20, 123–24, 127–28, 132–33, 142–46, 150. *See also* Constitution, US; tariffs

VanZandt, Jacob, 60
Virginia, 33, 39, 41, 66–67, 69, 75, 108, 111–12, 121, 132

Waddell, John, 58
Waller, Edmund (poet), 18
Waln, Richard, 66, 75, 129–30
Walpole, Horace (MP), 85
Walpole, Robert (prime minister), 19
Washington, George, 116
Washington (vessel), 134–35
Webster, Noah, 141
West, William, 66, 72
Wharton, Charles, 73, 111–12
Wharton, Samuel, 53, 90, 111, 137
Wharton, Thomas, 58, 90, 94
Whiteside, William, 138–40
Willard, Hannah, 36
Willing, Thomas, 57–59, 121, 148–50
women: as consumers, 7, 9–11, 48–50, 116–20; as merchants, 138–40; and nonimportation, 67–69. *See also* gender

Young, Thomas, 102, 104, 111